Studies in the Interwar European Economy

Modern Economic and Social History Series

General Editor: Derek H. Aldcroft

Titles in this series include:

Studies in the Interwar European Economy
Derek H. Aldcroft

Whatever Happened to Monetarism? Economic Policy-Making and Social Learning in the United Kingdom since 1979
Michael J. Oliver

Battles for the Standard: Bimetallism and the Spread of the Gold Standard, 1870–1914
Edward R. Wilson

The British Footwear Industry
Peter R. Mounfield

Trade Unions and the Economy
Derek H. Aldcroft and Michael J. Oliver

Raleigh and the British Bicycle Industry: An Economic and Business History since the 1880s
Roger Lloyd-Jones, M. J. Lewis and M. Eason

The British Electronics Industry: Innovation, Markets and Performance, 1930–97
John F. Wilson

The Seaside, Health and the Environment since 1850
John Hassan

Studies in the Interwar European Economy

DEREK H. ALDCROFT

Routledge
Taylor & Francis Group
LONDON AND NEW YORK

First published 1997 by Ashgate Publishing

Reissued 2018 by Routledge
2 Park Square, Milton Park, Abingdon, Oxon, OX14 4RN
711 Third Avenue, New York, NY 10017, USA

Routledge is an imprint of the Taylor & Francis Group, an informa business

A Library of Congress record exists under LC control number: 96040442

Typeset in Sabon by Manton Typesetters, 5-7 Eastfield Road, Louth, Lincolnshire, LN 11 7AJ

ISBN 13: 978-1-138-35966-6 (hbk)
ISBN 13: 978-0-429-43355-9 (ebk)

Contents

For Andrea and Louise

Modern Economic and Social History Series General Editor's Preface

Economic and social history has been a flourishing subject of scholarly study during recent decades. Not only has the volume of literature increased enormously but the range of interest in time, space and subject matter has broadened considerably so that today there are many sub-branches of the subject which have developed considerable status in their own right.

One of the aims of this new series is to encourage the publication of scholarly monographs on any aspect of modern economic and social history. The geographical coverage is world-wide and contributions on non-British themes will be especially welcome. While emphasis will be placed on works embodying original research, it is also intended that the series should provide the opportunity to publish studies of a more general and thematic nature which offer a reappraisal or critical analysis of major issues of debate.

Derek H. Aldcroft

Manchester Metropolitan University

List of Tables

Preface

Most of the chapters in this volume have their origin in papers or lectures presented at various centres of learning in Brussels, Brisbane, Barcelona, Madrid, Milan, Lausanne, Paris, Tenerife and Vienna in recent years. Chapter 7 is a revised version of 'Depression and recovery: the Eastern European experience', which appeared in *Capitalism in Crisis: International Responses to the Great Depression,* edited by W. R. Garside (1993) and published by Pinter of London.

I should like to thank Dr John Hassan and Dr Steven Morewood for reading various chapters and for their helpful comments. Thanks are also due to Alec McAulay for his patience and enthusiasm with a demanding author.

Derek H. Aldcroft
Manchester Metropolitan University

CHAPTER ONE

The Legacy of the Versailles Settlement

Though the First World War caused much loss of life, destruction and devastation which rendered Europe virtually destitute by the latter half of 1918, it can nevertheless be argued that the immediate consequences of more than four years of hostilities were less important than the postwar settlement in determining the longer-term future of Europe. Keynes, in his vitriolic denunciation of the peace treaty with Germany, recognised its defects in regard to the future of Europe (Keynes, 1920, p. 211), but the postwar settlement had far wider connotations than he envisaged at the time of writing. The term Versailles settlement used here therefore embraces not only the formal peace treaties with the enemy powers, but also the varied clearing-up operations which arose such as the question of reparations and war debts, the arrangements for relief and reconstruction, the establishment of the League of Nations, together with the role of the United States in postwar Europe. The position of the United States assumes significance because it emerged from the war as the most powerful nation in the world. While it replaced Europe as the potential leader in world affairs, in practice the United States exercised this role reluctantly, quickly making a political and military retreat from European affairs as isolation took hold, though maintaining an arms-length economic interest until the great depression. Europe, on the other hand, failed to recapture its former pre-eminence partly because the postwar settlement precluded that possibility, even though European leaders played a major role in designing that settlement, and partly because American policy indirectly worked against Europe's revival.

This chapter concentrates on some of the features of the settlement deemed especially relevant in the context of Europe's future: the redrawing of the map of Europe; the treatment of Germany; the machinery for reconstruction; and the equivocal attitude of the United States towards the problems of Europe. The following chapter takes up some additional themes and provides an overall conclusion.

The new Europe

The new postwar boundary arrangements constituted the biggest exercise in the reshaping of the political geography of Europe ever undertaken (Thompson, 1966, p. 626) and, according to some writers, possibly one of the most disastrous (Hobsbawm, 1994, p. 31). The process involved the greater part of the Continent and the only countries not affected were Holland, Spain, Luxembourg, Switzerland and Portugal. Large tracts of land and their populations and resources were reallocated, about a dozen new or reconstituted states were brought into being, while political frontiers were lengthened by some 12 500 miles (Gordon, 1941, p. 19).

The mundane details of the new geographical configuration need not detain us here. What is important is to assess the implications for the future stability of Europe. Possibly the most important factor was the power vacuum which arose in East-Central Europe. It was in this region that most of the new or reconstituted states emerged (Austria, Hungary, Czechoslovakia, Yugoslavia and Poland, for example) in place of the former Austro-Hungarian Empire. The latter was certainly a troublesome empire to administer and towards the end of the war it was in an advanced state of terminal decay. But for all its faults it did have a certain degree of economic coherence and during the nineteenth century it had acted as an important stabiliser in the European balance of power, one reason, no doubt, why the Allied powers were reluctant to witness its disintegration. Unfortunately they had very little choice in the matter since even before the end of hostilities nationalist groups were laying claim to territories, many of which were later confirmed by the Allied statesmen.

In the process the former equilibrium of Europe was destroyed. Most of the new states which emerged out of the ruins of the former empires (German, Romanov, Austro-Hungarian and Turkish) were chronically weak in every sense of the word and each suffered from acute political and social tensions. The resulting vacuum in the centre set the stage for later conflict. Newman (1968, pp. 27, 58, 105–6, 201) for example stresses the crucial role of the region in determining the subsequent distribution of power within Europe and ultimately the fate of the Continent. Given time the vacuum was bound to be filled by a predator nation since the states in question were 'extremely weak reeds to place in the path of Germany, and they possessed few features that could lead to any hope of their being anything but satellites ... of Germany, Hitler or no Hitler'. Almost from the very beginning of the interwar period France and Germany were locked in battle for the control of the East, the final outcome of which paved the way for the Second World War.

This raises the question: why Germany? Conceivably another power could have filled the gap, though on reflection there was no obvious candidate. Perceptively it was Lenin who envisaged what might arise out of the ruins of the peace. He foresaw two major powers with but a single aim: Germany wanted revenge, Russia wanted revolution: 'When our ways part', he said, 'they will be our most ferocious and our great enemies. Time will tell whether a German hegemony or a Communist federation is to arise out of the ruins of Europe' (Flood, 1989, p. 259). In other words, Germany had the strength and the motives to achieve domination (see below), both of which were plainly visible before Hitler came to power. One should also bear in mind that during the First World War the Germans had conceived a definite plan to colonise the East by setting up a chain of puppet monarchies in the conquered states from the Baltic to the Black Sea (Summers and Mangold, 1987, pp. 274–5, 397). On this interpretation therefore, there is no need to invoke a *deus ex machina* in the guise of Adolf Hitler to explain the Second World War because the seeds of a future conflagration had already been sown by the postwar peace settlement. As Overy (1995, p. 289) writes, 'Hitler played a part already written for him'.

The path of conquest was obviously facilitated by the weakness of the new configuration. It was also exacerbated by the lack of cohesion and cooperation among the new states, partly because of the frictions and rivalry arising out of the territorial changes and population displacements, and partly because of the activities of the major powers in the area for purposes of their own self-interest. Yet none of the European powers was prepared to back the new system fully or to promote the cause of Danubian federation, despite a British proposal for a Danubian customs union (Dockrill and Goold, 1981, pp. 128–30; League of Nations, 1932; Stambrook, 1963). Thus, in contrast to the position after 1945, national sovereignties dominated the scene in the 1920s, to the extent that there was little prospect of achieving unity and stability in Europe (Jacobson, 1983, pp. 603–4).

The new states in fact became little more than pawns in a game of European high politics and were allowed 'to exist and function as sovereign units for reasons which had little in common with economic considerations' (Momtchiloff, 1944, p. 84). It is true that the inherent weakness of many of the new states and their incompetent governments, together with the corruption of many politicians and state officials, left them highly vulnerable to loss of independence. Parliamentary democracy was a sham in many cases, though even when it thrived, as in the case of Czechoslovakia, it was no guarantee of safety. As Sontag (1971, p. 68) noted, the seeds of democracy fell on stony ground in Eastern Europe which lacked any real experience of political pluralism, and where political instability arising from graft, corruption, interethnic rivalry and nationalistic sentiments, was widespread and endemic from the start. It is not surprising to find, therefore, that most of the new states drifted towards authoritarian regimes during the course of the interwar period (Gilberg, 1992, pp. 278–83; Lee, 1987, p. 254). By 1938, 16 of the 28 European states had authoritarian regimes. Indeed, Schwartz (1973, pp. 11–12) is puzzled that anyone should have expected democracy to flourish in the region after the war because of so little past experience with democratic institutions coupled with the acute internal divisions based on class and nationality. Yet the European powers did little to ease the transition. It has been argued that the lack of understanding and foresight on the part of the Allied nations as to the significance of the region in terms of the future balance of power ultimately 'paved the way for Hitler's aggressive policy in Eastern Europe and eventually opened wide the door for Russian penetration' (Kiraly, Pastor and Sanders, 1982, p. 43). In short, there were too few good Europeans (Ross, 1983, p. 53).

The weakness of the East European states bore testimony to past economic deprivation for which the new European configuration could provide little answer. Economically the new states were worse off than before the war since they not only inherited a 'gigantic backlog of backwardness' (Spulber, 1966, p. 75), but they also suffered from the chaos following hostilities, the loss of a large internal market and the impact of new boundaries. Komlos (1983, p. 6) reckons that the consequences of the destruction of the central European market for the splintered territories was little short of disastrous, and this view would seem to be confirmed by what we now know about the economic viability of the Habsburg Empire (Good, 1984, p. 256). The potential trade losses might not have been so serious had economic factors been accorded greater priority when redefining the new shape of Europe. They were not totally ignored of course, but they were certainly never at the top of the agenda. Nor were the treaty clauses drafted with the intent of promoting any pan-European objective, economic or otherwise. According to Friedman (1974, p. 12), they caused the maximum disruption to the European productive system.

Even a brief perusal is sufficient to show that the new territorial arrangements lacked any economic logic since their economic potential bore little relation to the inheritance of land, people and resources (Berend and Ranki, 1969, p. 170). Most of the states fared badly in this respect, apart from Czechoslovakia which acquired a large part of the industrial assets of the former empire. Each nation received whatever resources and equipment happened to be located in the territories assigned to it. The inexorable rise of nationalism fed by the collapse of the

Habsburg Empire and legitimised by the selective application of Wilson's Fourteen Points in the Versailles settlement, threw economic coherence out of the window (cf. Marks, 1976, pp. 15, 22). Frequently this meant the complete break-up of former trading patterns and lines of communication and the splitting up of mutually dependent branches of industry. Yugoslavia, for example, inherited five different railway systems with four different gauges; each system served different centres so that they were practically unconnected with one another and unifying the disparate parts took the best part of a decade. In the case of Austria the textile industry was literally split asunder. The spindles were situated in Bohemia and Moravia, which became part of the new Czech Republic, while the weaving looms were located mainly in and around Vienna (Pasvolsky, 1928, pp. 527, 548). Hungary's main problem, on the other hand, was the excessive loss of raw materials which served her developing industries. She lost most of her iron ore, salt, copper and other non-ferrous metals, timber and water power. The loss of industrial capacity was less severe so that Hungary emerged from the war as a more industrialised country than hitherto (Berend and Ranki, 1974, pp. 92–3; Janos, 1982, pp. 205–6; Macartney, 1937, pp. 461–2). Regional concentration of industry also increased markedly, with Greater Budapest accounting for some two-thirds of those employed in manufacturing in 1920, as against only one-quarter before the war (Bencze and Tajti, 1972, pp. 19–28). In addition, the Treaty of Trianon (1920) destroyed Hungary's integrated transport system, especially the waterway network, the major part of the management of which was transferred to Prague, Bucharest and Belgrade (Halasz, 1928, p. 26). Such changes did more to hinder than to promote economic recovery after the war, and in the longer term they created resentment and frustration which added strength to the forces of nationalism and revisionism in the interwar period.

One of the most difficult tasks arising out of the new territorial configuration was that the new states were faced with the problem of building new economic systems and integrating the different fragments of territory and populations which they had inherited. In the case of the losers this meant adapting their systems to the much reduced level of resources, whereas the major beneficiaries encountered the problem of assimilating territories at different stages of development, often with varied fiscal and monetary systems and different legal and administrative practices. In practice it entailed the creation of new administrative systems, new currency and fiscal systems, new lines of communication, and the forging of fresh economic and trading links to replace those that had been destroyed. Poland faced one of the most difficult tasks since she had to integrate three very different segments of territory previously owing allegiance to alien rulers into one single state. Zweig (1944, p. 13) described the situation in the following terms:

> On the day of their political unification the three parts of Poland did not constitute a single economic unit. They had different systems of civil, commercial, and fiscal legislation. They belonged to differing customs units, to differing money and credit systems. Nor did they constitute a unity in the sense that they had developed after an organised pattern by constant and mutual testing. On the contrary some parts were over- and some under-developed.

The task was complicated further by the fact that Poland was in conflict with all her neighbours after the war, she had no natural frontiers, no government agencies to serve the whole country, very few established financial and monetary institutions to meet the needs of the new state and little in the way of highly developed industry except for that part of Upper Silesia awarded to her by the plebiscite of 1921 (Kitchen, 1988, p. 106).

Yugoslavia, or the new Kingdom of Serbs, Croats and Slovenes as it was originally called, faced an even greater diversity of interests to assimilate and consolidate: six customs areas, five currencies, five railway systems, three different banking systems and a host of different nationalities and religions (Lampe, 1980 p. 139). For Czechoslovakia the main task was that of reconciling the Czech lands with the less developed Slovak and Ruthenian territories, while Romania had to integrate its greatly enlarged domain. Austria and Hungary, on the other hand, had the reverse task of making sense out of the remnants left to them of their old empire, shorn of some of the most valuable assets. Only Bulgaria was spared major integration problems arising from territorial changes and ethnic heterogeneity, though she did have a large number of refugees from ceded lands to accommodate and a substantial reparations bill equivalent to one-quarter of her total national wealth (Bell, 1977, pp. 164, 194).

Ethnic divisions

However daunting the task of economic reconstruction and integration may have been, it was perhaps the social issue which was to prove the most intractable. Not that is the immediate social distress and disturbance arising from the war, but the long-term ethnic problem which was to haunt Europe for the rest of the century. As Hobsbawm (1994, p. 31) recently observed: 'The national conflicts tearing the continent apart in the 1990s were the old chickens of Versailles once again coming home to roost.' In all fairness the conflict and rivalry between different ethnic groups were not a new creation since their roots go back deep in history (Banac, 1988; Job, 1993, p. 53). But as Lentin (1991, p. 16) points out, the Versailles settlement, 'by exalting the primacy of national sentiment and encouraging its expression and satisfaction, revived old antagonisms and sparked off new ones'. Not surprising therefore that one of the guiding principles of Woodrow Wilson should be a call for national self-determination coupled with a reduction in ethnic intermingling in Europe. Though the postwar settlement is reckoned to have halved the number of people living under alien rule in Europe, this still left some 30 million in Central and Eastern Europe with minority status and about one quarter of the population of East European states consisting of minorities (Pearson, 1983, pp. 147–8; Sharp, 1991, p. 155). Some of the successor states were no less multinational than their predecessors (Hobsbawm, 1994, p. 33).

In fact the ethnographic map in postwar Europe was in some ways more complicated than previously. This was partly because the intermingling of populations occurred in a number of states with stronger national sentiments than hitherto now that statehood had become a reality. Virtually all countries in East-Central Europe were polyethnic to some degree and in some cases, such as Yugoslavia, Czechoslovakia and Romania, up to a dozen nationalities and as many religions coexisted unhappily together. Significantly there were pockets of Germans in all the new states (Polonsky, 1975, pp. 158–63). And at the end of the day it was German nationalism, rather than that of the successor states, which was to determine the fate of Europe. Germany kept alive the issue of her own minority grievances which became a useful tool in the quest to subvert the provisions of the Versailles Treaty and to find living space in the East. In this respect therefore the fragmentation of territories under the postwar settlement provided her with a golden opportunity to satisfy her ambitions to achieve a Greater Germany once the time was ripe.

By far the largest concentration of minorities was to be found in Czechoslovakia and Yugoslavia; Romania and Poland were above average; while Austria, Hungary and Bulgaria had the smallest incidence. In addition, some countries had large expatriate populations arising from the relocation of boundaries. Altogether, over 21 million people, or some 7–8 per cent of the dominant populations of Central and Eastern Europe, lived outwith the state of their inherited nationality, about half of whom consisted of Germans, Magyars and Bulgarians (Macartney, 1934, p. 268). Apart from the Albanians, the Hungarian expatriate situation was by far the worst, with one in three Hungarians living under alien rule as against one in ten Germans and one in sixteen Bulgarians (Kiraly, Pastor and Sanders, 1982, p. 73; Pearson, 1983, pp.

148, 170–71). Greece also had a massive expatriate population, mainly in Turkey, but most of these Greeks, 1.5 million or one-quarter of Greece's population, were exchanged for some 400 000 Turks resident in Greece following the latter's defeat in Asia Minor in 1923 (Herschlag, 1968, p. 24; Pentzopoulos, 1962, p. 18).

Tiltman (1934, p. 266) described the situation in terms of an 'ethnological soufflé', the problems arising from which have persisted to this day. The postwar territorial and population dispositions were bound to lead to squabbles since most minority groups were not happy with their lot, while the dominant populations of each state were more than willing to dispose of or discriminate against the minorities. It is true that under the League of Nations' minority treaties countries were enjoined to observe good behaviour towards their minority residents, but in practice they were generally reluctant to follow the good code guide. According to Robinson et al. (1943, p. 264) 'the states were mainly concerned with interpreting the provisions in the most restrictive possible sense and used every device to vitiate their effect'. Only rarely were minority groups accorded equality of treatment with the dominant nationality in such things as politics, education or economics.

The position of minority groups was particularly bad in the multinational states of Czechoslovakia, Yugoslavia and Romania (Donald, 1928, p. 131). Ironically, in the case of the first two countries there was not even a majority nationality since the Czechs and Serbs accounted for less than half of the respective populations. The Czechs were probably the most ruthless, though the Serbs ran them a very close second. As Pearson (1983, p. 155) noted 'in operating what was in practice a Czech empire, the Czechs broke all their earlier promises to the "subordinate minorities" in a manner almost calculated to antagonise them'. The Czechs in fact succeeded in alienating virtually all their important minorities – the Germans, Magyars, Slovaks, Ruthenes and Poles – by their discriminating practices. The most acute friction occurred between the Czechs and Slovaks; the former regarded the Slovaks as ignorant 'hillbillies', while in their turn the Slovaks perceived the Czechs as arrogant oppressors who were not prepared to recognise Slovakia's just claims. The Sudeten Germans, on the other hand, saw the Czechs as an inferior race, while the Czechs for their part regarded the Germans as invaders intent on subjugating them (Schwartz, 1973, p. 11; Wiskemann, 1938, pp. 118–20). The Germans as well as the Magyars were especially incensed by their loss of status in Czechoslovakia so that it occasions no surprise that Hitler sought to capitalise on the plight of the Sudeten Germans as a prelude to the acquisition of Czechoslovakia in 1938 (Pearson, 1983, p. 153).

The Yugoslav ethnic mix was even more complex. The major components (with percentages of total population in brackets) of the new state were as follows: Serbs (43), Croats (23), and Slovenes (8.5), but there were also fair sprinklings of Bosnian Moslems (6), Macedonian Slavics (5), Albanians (3.6), Germans (3.6) and Magyars (3.4), with Romanians, Jews, Gypsies, Vlachs and Turks bringing up the rear (Jelavich, 1983, p. 151). So fragmented was the new kingdom that none of these peoples ever really regarded themselves as belonging to one nation with the result that a distinct and common Yugoslav identity failed to materialise. From the inception of the new state the Serbs, even though inferior economically to the Slovenes and Croats, sought to impose their domination on the motley collection by establishing centralised control, while the Croats and other minorities struggled to gain greater power and autonomy. Though Serbian protagonists have sought to mitigate the charges of Serbian exploitation and discrimination, there is no doubt that both were practised frequently. Ethnic conflict therefore became a serious problem from the start (Dragnich, 1983, pp. 135–51). The most bitter rivalry was between the Serbs and Croats which at times virtually paralysed the country and left it vulnerable to foreign control (Jelavich, 1983, p. 151). Yugoslavia would be Nazi Germany's last major conquest to be carried out in a matter of weeks.

Ethnic rivalry and conflict were endemic throughout a large part of Europe in the interwar years, which not only weakened the fledgling states but also gave rise to irredentism on the part of expatriate populations, and this in turn was fanned by the revisionist policies of the ex-enemy countries, especially Germany and Hungary. Refugees from lost territories also added their weight to the claim for boundary revisions while at the same time creating assimilation problems for the host countries. Bulgaria, for example, faced an influx of 450 000 refugees from territories ceded to Greece and Yugoslavia, while 426 000 Hungarians returned from Czechoslovakia, Romania, Yugoslavia and Austria between 1918 and 1924 (Bell, 1977, p. 164; Donald, 1928, p. 266; Mocsy, 1983, p. 10). Greece, as already noted, absorbed a large migration from Turkey. It was the Hungarians, however, who remained the most committed to the restoration of lost territory even though there was little prospect that the beneficiary states would agree to a revision of the Trianon boundaries (Apponyi, 1928). In the longer term Hungary's recalcitrant attitude, like Germany's, was fraught with dangers for as Mocsy (1983, p. 195) notes: 'The resulting cool relations between Hungary and its neighbours weakened them all, increased their isolation, and prepared the way for domination of the entire region by a great power.' Little wonder, therefore, that Hungary became an ally of Nazi Germany.

The treatment of Germany

Very few nations, if any, were very happy with the postwar settlement, least of all Germany. As the principal antagonist Germany was dealt harsh terms. These included substantial loss of assets, territory and population in Europe and overseas, severe reparations penalties, restraints on rearmament and the occupation of key zones, all of which were designed to contain German ambitions in the future. Germany was also loaded with a war guilt clause by dint of the infamous Article 231 of the Treaty of Versailles. All these impositions, and especially the war guilt clause and the large reparations exactions, caused burning resentment and provided Germany with a strong motive to try and whittle away the onerous obligations and expand her empire eastwards. Even the fledgling Weimar Republic refused to guarantee its eastern borders in the Treaty of Locarno of 1925, in which its pledges were confined to its western frontiers. This was no accident. Revisionism to the east was implicit in German foreign policy even before Hitler arrived on the scene (see above). What he brought that was new was a fanatical racial doctrine which demanded 'lebensraum' (living space) in the East.

That Germany and not another power became the predator in East-Central Europe was almost a foregone conclusion. Germany had the strength and the motives to achieve territorial domination. Despite the exactions imposed by the Allies, Germany was potentially the strongest power on the Continent after the war. It certainly could not be written off as a great power since it still had enormous potential and it was only a matter of time before that potential was unleashed (Weinberg, 1969). That it took the form it did owes much to the policy of the Allied powers towards Germany following the war.

Given time and an easing of the terms of the peace settlement, there would be little to check Germany's ambitions. Germany felt she had good cause to reassert herself given the rebuff at Versailles. This was soon reflected in the attempt to modify or have removed the restrictive provisions of the peace settlement and the desire to regain recognition of great power status by restoring lost territories and expanding eastwards. These objectives were evident in Germany's foreign policy throughout the 1920s, that is, well before Hitler came to power.

The position was made easier for Germany by the fact that there was no one to champion effectively the cause of the East. The two most likely candidates, Britain and France, were unable to tackle the question satisfactorily, either from a security or economic point of view. To complicate matters the British and French had fundamentally opposing views on the Versailles settlement. London favoured gradual revision whereas Paris wanted the terms to be rigidly upheld. Britain assumed, mistakenly as it turned out, that after the Locarno settlement of 1925, the main feature of which was a mutual security pact among the western powers (including Germany) to respect the existing frontiers between France and Germany including the demilitarised Rhineland, that German ambitions would be contained. But Locarno, though originally inspired by Germany, proved little more than a smokescreen devised to pacify the French by her allies who by then were losing interest in the upholding of the postwar settlement (Klein-Ahlbrandt, 1995). In practical terms 'The era of Locarno suffused the international scene with an unreal glow which hid the fatal lesions in the European body politic' (Birdsall, 1941, p. 302). It no doubt heralded the start of Germany's reintegration into Europe but it also strengthened her position as far as revision of the terms of the peace settlement were concerned (Bretton, 1953; Henig, 1995, p. 44; Lentin, 1991, p. 27). Britain subsequently adopted an attitude of benign indifference to the fate of Central and Eastern Europe until it was too late. This was understandable given Britain's extensive imperial interests outwith Europe which resulted in 'a policy that was vital to the balance of power (being) neglected in favour of policies in support of traditional historical national interests' (Newman, 1968, p. 202). France took a more active role, concluding a series of mutual security treaties in Eastern Europe, since she rightly feared the resurgence of Germany, but unfortunately she received weak and intermittent support from her former western allies, especially on the security and containment issues. Worse still, the climate of opinion outside France tended to move in favour of German appeasement and France herself was not strong enough to take matters into her own hands even with the help of her entente allies in the East. And when she did, as in the case of the Ruhr invasion of 1923, things ended in disaster for all concerned.

Meanwhile Germany was quick to take advantage of Allied equivocation on the future balance of power in Europe. She chipped away steadily at the provisions of the peace settlement, especially those relating to zonal occupation, rearmament and reparations. In fact, during the 1920s much clandestine activity on the military front was already taking place in Germany in defiance of the peace treaty provisions (Lentin, 1991, p. 26). In this respect therefore, implementation of the provisions proved ineffective in containing Germany's ambitions.

Arguably it was the reparations issue, coupled with the political instability of the Weimar Republic, which provided the catalyst for the strengthening of Germany's strategy. Initially Germany was requested to pay what appeared to be an exorbitant sum by way of compensation, with provisional payments amounting to over 10 per cent of national income in the years 1919–22. The interim settlement was subsequently replaced by a longer-term arrangement when the Reparations Commission presented the final bill in May 1921. Though the annual annuities were modified, they still remained large and until postwar recovery had taken place they were probably outside Germany's ability to pay. The real problem therefore was not the fact that reparations were too high but that they were imposed too hastily. Germany was quite capable of paying a large indemnity providing she had time to recover her economic potential first. The big mistake the Allies made was to expect large payments before Germany was in a position to meet these without undue strain. It was the premature imposition of heavy demands for recompense which left the Germans feeling that they had been 'kicked in the teeth'.

On the other hand, it can also be argued that the actual sums involved were largely irrelevant since by then the damage had been done. What really mattered was not the sheer size of the bill but the political and psychological unwillingness of the Germans to accept the burden of reparations and war guilt in the first place (Fischer, 1974, p. 47). And it very soon became clear that they were not going to acquiesce without strong protest. When verbal onslaught appeared to fail, it took the form of an overt demonstration that Germany could not meet the sums demanded by resorting to the printing press. According to Holtfrerich (1986, p. 153) 'threatened by Allied sanctions on the one hand and by the disintegration of the Reich on the other, no German government could have complied with Reparations demands in any way other than resort to the printing of money'. The final outcome is well known: hyperinflation and the collapse of the currency in the latter half of 1923, exacerbated by the occupation of the Ruhr by France and Belgium on the pretext of a minor shortfall in reparation deliveries in kind, principally telegraph poles!

Whether an earlier and more judicious settlement of the reparations issue would have eased the situation given Germany's bitterness on the matter is debatable. What matters, however, is that no one gained from the episode. France lost face from the débâcle, while Germany's recovery was adversely affected by the horrific consequences of hyperinflation despite short-term initial gains (Hardach, 1984, p. 210; Petzina, 1977, pp. 13–15). But more to the point were the longer-term political and social consequences of the episode. It convinced many Germans more than ever that the disarmament and occupation restrictions of the peace treaty must be removed (Fergusson, 1975, pp. 123, 215). It is perhaps significant that it was during this period of turmoil that Hitler made his first major political impact. Subsequently his cause was to benefit from the victims of inflation. By destroying the savings base of most middle-class and lower middle-class families, inflation effectively served to undermine the political consensus of Weimar Germany. Not that Weimar parliamentary democracy was, as was similarly true in many of the successor states, a particularly robust child. Having been created by the German military leadership in the vain hope that Wilson's Fourteen Points would be extended to a democracy, it was then saddled with the onerous terms of a dictated peace. But in any case, the Weimar constitution did little to help the cause of democracy in that it encouraged the proliferation of political parties which made it practically impossible to form strong governments capable of taking decisive action on issues of major importance (Abraham, 1981; Jones, 1972, 1979, p. 148; Scheele, 1946; Willis and Chapman, 1935, pp. 200–201). Trying to reconcile the different and conflicting interests helped to contribute to the Government's financial weakness which in turn made it more difficult to stabilise Weimar's social system (McNeil, 1986, p. 278). Policy failure on one matter, however, was decisive in terms of later political events: in particular, the failure to implement a fair and equitable system of compensation for the victims of inflation. This left many middle-class households bitterly resentful and hence they became increasingly disenchanted with the traditional parties of bourgeois centre and right (Childers, 1983a, p. 382, 1984). Initially this dissatisfaction manifested itself in the emergence of splinter parties and a renewed burst of political instability. When these in turn failed to satisfy the grievances over compensation the alienated middle groups transferred their political affiliations to the right. Members of the *Mittelstand*, which included most of those who had borne the losses of inflation, probably accounted for over half of the Nazi Party's electoral support in the early 1930s, providing Hitler with the necessary backing to secure control of the country (Childers, 1983b, 1984). Thus inflation may be seen as an important cause of the political disintegration of Weimar Germany (Carsten, 1984, pp. 741–2). In short, the seeds of decay were sown well before the great depression and rising unemployment which some believe to have been the catalyst for the success of Nazi power (Fleisig, 1976, p. 56).

The relief of Europe

One of the major shortcomings of the postwar settlement was the failure to establish a proper programme for the relief and reconstruction of Europe (Silverman, 1982, p. 230). Much of the Continent was destitute of food, raw materials and equipment at the end of hostilities, and more to the point lacked hard currency with which to purchase essential supplies abroad (Aldcroft, 1977, pp. 56–7; League of Nations, 1943b). Many parts of Europe, especially Central and Eastern Europe, urgently required external assistance, not only to deal with the immediate needs of starving populations, but also for purposes of facilitating the reconstruction of the many devastated areas. Apart from the task of consolidating new territories, many countries were on the verge of economic collapse and were faced with the task of averting famine and social disorder. The position was further aggravated by continued military conflict along disputed borders and social and political instability verging on revolution in some countries.

Conditions throughout the Continent varied a good deal and the worst affected areas were those which had been used extensively for military operations. Some idea of the enormous tasks involved in reconstruction can be seen from the case of Poland which had been badly mauled by the warring powers. At one time or another some 80–90 per cent of Polish territory had been the scene of battle (Wellisz, 1938, pp. 39–40). The occupying powers – Russia, Germany and Austria – had literally ransacked the country and laid it waste. Direct material losses were enormous, with one-half or more of the assets (including livestock) destroyed or pillaged in some cases, while many villages were raised to the ground (Roszkowski, 1986, pp. 287–9). Thus by the end of the war stocks were low and output had sunk to negligible levels, especially in the Kingdom of Poland where industrial production was little better than in the Soviet Union at a mere 15 per cent of the prewar level (Kitchen, 1988, p. 106; Rose, 1939, p. 100; Teichova, 1985, p. 224; Wynot, 1983, p. 57). To make matters worse the administrative and financial apparatus was in a state of extreme chaos because of the different fiscal and currency systems in operation, the virtual collapse of the banking system based on former links with Berlin, St Petersburg and Vienna, the immobilisation of the transport system and the pernicious effects of inflation and border hostilities (Leslie, 1980, p. 140; Taylor, 1952, pp. 140–42; Zweig, 1944, pp. 29–33).

Poland was therefore in a desperate situation in the immediate postwar period. Everything, and especially food, was in short supply, unemployment was high and malnutrition and disease were widespread. For some years after the war the country verged on the brink of civil war such were the conditions of life as described by the British Director of Relief:

> The country ... had undergone four or five occupations by different armies, each of which combed the land for supplies. Most of the villages had been burnt down by the Russians in their retreat (of 1915); land had been uncultivated for four years and had been cleared of cattle, grain, horses and agricultural machinery by both

> Germans and Bolsheviks. The population here was living upon roots, grass, acorns and heather. The only bread obtainable was composed of those ingredients, with perhaps about 5 per cent of rye flour. Their clothes were in the last stages of dilapidation; the majority were without boots and shoes and had reached the lowest depths of misery and degradation. The distribution of food in the towns was very unequal. It was possible to buy almost anything in the restaurants at a price, and cafés and cake shops were well supplied, but in other parts of the same towns it was impossible to obtain food.
>
> (Quoted in Clough, Moodie and Moodie, 1965, p. 100)

The returning soldiers swelled the ranks of the unemployed, exacerbated the food problem and spread disease. Half the population of Warsaw was in receipt of unemployment relief and nearly all that of Lodz. In some areas children were dying for lack of milk and in many parts of eastern Poland famine conditions prevailed. Disease was also fairly general, especially typhus brought in by returning soldiers, and up to 60 per cent of the population was affected in some way. Malnutrition and disease pushed up the rate of mortality to more than 40 per thousand, while birth rates in Warsaw dropped to just under 12 per thousand.

Despite the appalling conditions over much of Europe there was little concerted effort to promote the reconstruction of Europe by the allied powers. In contrast to the position after the Second World War, the United States had little desire to get embroiled in European affairs, while allied cooperation disintegrated soon after the war partly because of Anglo-American rivalry (Artaud, 1973, p. 17). Thus apart from the provision of famine and relief deliveries in the armistice period, which were totally inadequate, little was done to promote European recovery.

Most of the relief in fact consisted of food supplies, with small sums disbursed to cover clothing needs, provided under the auspices of the American Relief Administration which had been established early in 1919 as the executive agency of the Allied Supreme Council responsible for European relief. Food to the value of $1 250 million was delivered to some 20 European countries under these arrangements, most of it being granted on a credit basis rather than as outright gifts. Soon after the signing of the peace treaty with Germany in June 1919 official relief programmes were sharply curtailed. The Supreme Council was wound up in that month and the American Relief Administration became an unofficial body responsible for relief. In effect, therefore, subsequent relief activities were largely confined to private and semi-official organisations which managed to distribute a further $500 million of foodstuffs over a period of two to three years, mostly in the form of gifts (League of Nations, 1943b, p. 34).

Given the scale of the requirements the relief deliveries were to prove grossly inadequate. Except for deliveries to Belgium and northern France, supplies on any scale never really got under way until February 1919 and they came to an abrupt halt in the summer of that year, long before the problems of hunger and poverty had been solved. On average every child in Central and Eastern Europe was fed for one month only by the American relief organisation which accounted for 80 per cent of the total relief aid disbursed. Child poverty alone remained acute in many areas. Even in the case of Czechoslovakia, one of the more advanced countries of East-Central Europe, a medical report in March 1921 found that 60 per cent of the children remained undernourished or lacking in vitality (League of Nations, 1943c, pp. 21–3).

The relief programme was a paltry affair compared with that under the United Nations Relief and Rehabilitation Administration (UNRRA) after the Second World War and it scarcely skimmed the surface of the problem. In any case, the real extent of the needs was never properly surveyed, the whole exercise was hastily improvised and there were innumerable difficulties in coordinating the relief efforts of the Allied countries. There is no evidence that those most in need of food fared better than others, while ex-enemy countries were discriminated against in that they were expected to pay cash for any deliveries received. Hungary, for example, received very little (Nötel, 1974, pp. 69–70).

Relief of famine and distress was, of course, only the first element in the process of reconstruction. Most European countries were also urgently in need of raw materials and equipment so that they could restore capacity to supply their own needs. But there was no equivalent to Marshall aid for this purpose. Indeed, international action to assist in the longer-term reconstruction of Europe was conspicuous by its absence, despite official recognition, on the American side at least, that something ought to be done to encourage the revival of Europe (Costigliola, 1976; Hogan, 1975, 1977; Leffler, 1979).

The failure to take effective action concerning raw materials to ensure adequate supplies for the devastated areas in Europe has been seen as one of the major tragedies of the early postwar period (Hill, 1946, pp. 16–17). For a time it did look as though there might be a positive response on raw materials. Some attempt to preserve and even extend the wartime allied cooperation for raw materials seemed likely with the establishment of the Supreme Economic Council in February 1919. Its main functions were to examine measures which might ensure an adequate supply of raw materials and other commodities for the devastated areas of Europe, including ex-enemy countries, and the Council duly established special sections to deal with various aspects of the problem. Unfortunately its executive powers were very limited; it had no specific authority to control the distribution of raw materials, while its mandate ran out at the end of the armistice period. The Council's effectiveness was further reduced by the abrupt withdrawal of economic controls, especially in Britain and the United States, in 1919, and America's clear desire to disengage herself as rapidly as possible from inter-allied organisations and any form of international control (Ministry of Munitions, 1922, p. 72; Zimmern, 1936, p. 157). Consequently the prospects of worthwhile action appeared extremely bleak and efforts to form new organisations bore little fruit. A European Coal Commission was established in August 1919 to coordinate coal production and its distribution throughout Europe but, lacking the necessary authority to put its recommendations into effect, it devoted most of its time to the pressing problem of supplying Austria with coal until this task was taken over by an organ of the Reparations Commission (League of Nations, 1946, pp. 17–18; Wallace and Edminster, 1930, pp. 320–21).

Nor did the peace treaties have much to say on this matter. They dealt with the problem of raw materials only incidentally in connection with commercial policy and reparations deliveries in kind from the ex-enemy states. They contained no provisions for ensuring an adequate supply of raw materials to newly created states or the defeated powers. Little more was heard about raw materials until October 1920, when the International Financial Conference at Brussels recommended the ter Meulen Plan, which was designed to provide international credits for the import of raw materials and primary necessities. But though viewed favourably by the main creditor countries the scheme was never put into operation. In any case, by 1920 it was already too late, since the rot had gone too far for the successful application of any kind of general scheme (Hill, 1946, p. 26). The scramble for raw materials in the boom of 1919–20 had left many Central and East European countries with a minimal supply. As the League of Nations (1946, p. 71) later observed 'the major part of continental Europe continued to be starved of primary products'. Consequently rehabilitation was seriously retarded, economies were further weakened, and exchange depreciation and inflation began to assume serious dimensions. Eventually the situation became so serious in some countries that a country-by-country approach was required, with credits linked to a definite and comprehensive plan of financial reconstruction under supervision. This approach was eventually adopted by the League of Nations for several countries, notably Austria and Hungary. But had a bold attempt been made at an earlier date to deal with the problems of reconstruction the economic chaos which befell some countries in Central and Eastern Europe might well have been avoided.

Failing concrete action most countries had to struggle as best they could to obtain imports by arranging credits with willing borrowers on a private basis, though after 1920 the major source of credit, the United States, almost dried up (League of Nations, 1943d, p. 68). Those countries most in need fared badly in the scramble for imports in the crucial years of 1919 and 1920. Data on import volumes for Europe indicate that Germany and Eastern Europe obtained only about one-third of their 1913 level of imports, the neutral countries fell short by some 20 per cent, while the western allies slightly exceeded their peacetime imports. The most serious shortfall was in the import of raw materials and semi-finished goods (Orde, 1990, p. 111).

The inability to secure essential supplies was clearly an important factor accounting for the slow recovery of many European countries. Some improvement was recorded over the very low levels of output at the end of hostilities, but by 1920 industrial production was still well below prewar levels in many areas, up to 50 per cent in some East European countries, and even in agriculture there was a serious shortfall compared with 1913 (League of Nations, 1943a, p. 12, 1943b, pp. 7–10).

International efforts to promote reconstruction in Europe after the First World War were very inadequate, a lesson which was appreciated by those responsible for the same task after 1945. A coordinated plan for the reconstruction of Europe was never conceived at any stage, and what relief was given was very limited given the scale of requirements. Moreover, relief tended to be regarded as a form of charity which could be extended to some countries and not to others. Political considerations rather than need determined whether cash payments for supplies were demanded, and the probable effects of cash payments or the issue of relief loans on a country's capacity to acquire raw materials had little influence on policy.

What is perhaps most disheartening about the whole episode is that the Allied powers, having devised a new configuration of Europe and given birth to several new states, then decided it was time to withdraw from the scene and leave the countries to fend for themselves. The consequences of the failure to organise an adequate reconstruction programme were especially serious, not only for the countries themselves, but also because of the policies to which they were eventually forced to resort in an effort to overcome their problems. Since many countries failed to secure adequate supplies of essential goods, recovery was delayed, factories remained idle and unemployment high. Unemployment benefits, domestic relief programmes, and a continued high level of military spending, coupled with the low taxable capacity of the population, meant that balanced budgets were out of the question. In Austria, for example, over one-half of public spending in 1921 went on food subsidies (Pasvolsky, 1928, p. 97). Furthermore, inadequate foreign credits to finance imports meant pressure on the demand for foreign exchange and a consequent depreciation of currency values and inflation. Faced with insurmountable problems and a sheer lack of resources governments were forced into extreme measures, such as trade control, currency depreciation and inflation, to ease the situation. For a time these gave a temporary fillip to economic activity, exports and employment and no doubt in the process helped to avert the threat of social disorder, but the final consequences were disastrous, especially in Germany, Hungary, Austria and Poland where hyperinflation took hold. The price paid for the short-term boost to activity through currency depreciation and inflation, was declining real income for the bulk of the population, erosion of savings, loss of confidence and, eventually, the flight of capital. Ultimately it led to the disintegration of the whole economic and social fabric of several countries. The situation was neatly summarised by the League of Nations (1943d, p. 70) in one of its later reports when it observed that for several years the whole economic and social organisation of many countries had been allowed to rot away and 'when it was finally faced, it had ceased to be a general problem of transition and reconstruction and had become a problem of cutting the gangrene out of the most affected areas one by one'.

Thus the breakdown in many European countries in the early 1920s can be attributed in part to the absence of speedy and effective international action to deal with the problems of European relief and reconstruction. It required adequate provision for stricken areas to permit more rapid recovery and hence obviate the need for exchange depreciation and inflation, and the immediate support for currencies seriously weakened by inflation, rather than waiting, as the League of Nations did, until the collapse was well under way. As Denise Artaud (1973, p. 16) notes, the delay in financial reconstruction was the root of the problem since the delay in bridging the dollar gap proved fatal: 'Le capital américain, britannique et neutre n'a pu encore trouver le chemin des régions où il fait défaut, et c'est dans une Europe où le crédit est encore largement paralysé que la crise économique de 1920–21 se propage.' [American, British and neutral capital did not flow to the regions where it was most lacking in the early postwar crisis years when much of Europe suffered from a credit deadlock.] Moreover, had the Allies taken action to curb the scramble for raw materials and control the boom in prices in 1919–20 this would have eased the burden for the destitute regions of Europe. Henig (1995, pp. 39–40) believes that the failure of the United States to assist the regeneration of Europe through liberal credit facilities was a significant factor in the failure to establish a lasting peace in Europe.

The leadership issue and the role of the United States

The European settlement as it emerged in the course of the 1920s had two main defects: it did not satisfy anyone, and it lacked firm leadership. France, Germany and Italy, for different reasons, were extremely disgruntled: France over compensation and the security issue, Germany because of the harsh treatment inflicted on her by the victors, and Italy as a result of unfulfilled promises of territory for joining the war. None of these countries was willing to promote the European cause. The remnants of the Austro-Hungarian Empire, and the new and reconstituted states each in their turn had their grievances, all of which led to fragmentation rather than unity. This left Russia and Britain. The former, not having been invited to the Paris Peace Conference, was not particularly happy with the territorial arrangements arising from the peace settlement, but in any case her exclusion policy and domestic problems precluded her from playing a European role of any significance. And even when she did at a later date it took the form of clandestine communist infiltration into East European countries. Britain, the one country which might have been in a position to take an active role, was more concerned with her imperial connections, which meant that she preferred to view the affairs of Europe with benign indifference when it suited her to do so. The independence of the new states was welcomed so long as it did not involve active intervention. The attitude was summed up by the British Foreign Secretary (Simon) in a communication to the Prime Minister (MacDonald) in July 1934 over the question of Austria: 'Our policy is quite clear. We must keep out of trouble in Central Europe at all costs ... There are circumstances in which Italy might move troops into Austria. There are no circumstances in which we would ever dream of doing so' (Carsten, 1986, p. 215). In fact a year later Simon was of the view that the ramshackle regime was only worth tolerating 'for fear of meeting something worse' (Carsten, 1986, pp. 225–6).

The result of this fissiparous tendency, in contrast to the situation after 1945, was that competitive national sovereignties dominated the scene in the 1920s to such an extent that there was little prospect of achieving unity and stability in Europe (Jacobson, 1983, pp. 630, 644). Schulz (1972) believes that blind nationalism and self-interest thwarted effective cooperation in the execution and subsequent revision of the peace settlement.

The question is why did America not take over the European mantle and reshape the destiny of Europe as she was to do after the Second World War? America's entry into the war and Woodrow Wilson's grandiose designs for Europe initially augured well for the future. Yet the

United States was subsequently to play a very equivocal role in the affairs of Europe. She refused to ratify the Versailles Treaty, failed to endorse the League of Nations, abandoned the relief of Europe with almost indecent haste, and rejected proposals to link reparations and inter-allied war debts. Moreover, though America professed a belief in the importance of European recovery, her own economic policy often ran counter to the interests of European countries, for example on matters of tariffs, immigration, overseas lending and monetary policy. It is true that her attitude towards Germany was more lenient than that of either Britain or France, but this only served to antagonise the French since it offered little in the way of security against a recalcitrant Germany.

America's isolationist approach towards Europe has to be seen within the context of her domestic politics. The United States had entered the war reluctantly in April 1917. After the conclusion of hostilities there was a wave of revulsion against war and military activity, together with an unwillingness to get involved in the affairs of other countries which might lead to further conflict. This largely explains why the United States found herself in such a low state of military preparedness at the outbreak of the Second World War (Overy, 1995, p. 190). The United States also felt remote from the European scene, both geographically and politically, and her own domestic interests were affected only marginally by what happened in Europe. Unlike the situation after the Second World War, America did not perceive any immediate power threat from Europe, and though European recovery was regarded as intrinsically important it was never seen as crucial to her own well-being. Thus, when it suited her own needs, the United States could afford to turn a blind eye to the problems of Europe, especially as these seemed likely to entail direct involvement in the affairs of that continent.

One should not, however, exaggerate America's isolationist stance, or at least one should distinguish between the public and private domain. American foreign economic policy has been described as selectively interventionist: to encourage prosperity in Europe through informal private channels, that is businessmen and diplomats (Costigliola, 1976). The nomination of Parker Gilbert as reparations agent and the massive flow of private capital to Europe, and especially to Germany, in the later 1920s, are indicative that the Americans had not washed their hands of Europe completely. Gilbert's work, in association with the banks, was instrumental in devising a revised reparations plan and for the gradual fusion of the whole issue of reparations and inter-allied debts (Wandel, 1971).

On the other hand, as Costigliola (1976, p. 501) notes, US policy was designed to maximise America's enlightened self-interest while minimising foreign entanglements. It came too late to ensure a stable world order and left Europe and Germany in particular in a very vulnerable position once private credits were withdrawn at the end of the 1920s. In any case, the real problem occurred earlier when allied cooperation on European reconstruction was required and might well have come to fruition had America been willing to assume a larger purpose in Europe (Trachtenberg, 1979). This she was not prepared to do, nor was she prepared to consider any remission on war debts or linking these to the reparations issue (Artuad, 1979; Orde, 1990, p. 82). On this score, Kent (1989, pp. 9, 286, 373) reckons that all the creditors are to blame for refusing to make concessions to each other. He also sees the network of claims as a ruse or 'diversionary smokescreen' devised by the Allied statesmen to take the heat out of popular clamour for genuine postwar reconstruction which would have entailed heavy taxation. This argument seems somewhat extreme and in any case it would not fully explain America's intransigent stance on debts which at the end of the day was at the root of the matter (McDougall, 1979, p. 23).

America's refusal to assume a hegemonic role had several unfortunate consequences. It meant first of all, that certain aspects of the postwar settlement, such as reparations and territorial rights, emerged as international issues. Secondly, it left Europe stranded in the early and later 1920s when American credits ceased to flow. Eventually private benefaction in the form of international lending emerged to fill the gap, but over which the there was little control. As Hogan (1977, p. 47) comments: 'The toothless loan control programme left the American government with no way to insure that capital exports really contributed to recovery.' Thirdly, it robbed Europe of the leadership it so badly needed in the 1920s, especially with regard to security, currency matters and greater European integration. McDougall (1979, pp. 12, 23), while recognising that the self-determination element in the peace treaties was an obstacle to integration, also believes that the Anglo-American refusal to sanction Franco-German integration through effective restrictions on German superiority as the French advocated, left the way open for Germany to apply in due course her own brand of European integration. Fourthly, the absence of US backing meant that the League of Nations played a diminutive role in the affairs of Europe, especially with regard to security and disarmament (Henig, 1973, p. 175). Apart from its work in rescuing several countries on the point of disintegration, perhaps its most lasting contribution was the large number of papers and documents it produced for the benefit of later historians. Finally, had America assumed a more positive role in Europe it might have been possible to reduce the inter-allied conflict on both political and economic issues and secure greater cooperation in re-ordering the affairs of Europe (Borass, 1994, pp. 232–3). Birdsall (1941, p. 297) believed that the American withdrawal was largely responsible for the subsequent fate of Europe:

> The defection of the United States destroyed the Anglo-American preponderance which alone could have stabilised Europe. It impoverished the authority and prestige of the League at its birth and it precipitated an Anglo-French duel which reduced Europe to the chaos from which Hitler emerged to produce a new chaos which he ... christened the 'New Europe'. Practically and immediately, it destroyed the Anglo-American treaty of military guarantee which was to have been one of the main props of French security, and it removed every prospect of material American support for all other guarantees of French security.

References

Abraham, P. (1981), *The Collapse of the Weimar Republic: Political Economy and Crisis*, Princeton, NJ: Princeton University Press.

Aldcroft, D. H. (1977), *From Versailles to Wall Street 1919–1929*, Harmondsworth: Penguin Books.

Apponyi, A. (1928), *Justice for Hungary: Review and Criticism of the Treaty of Trianon*, London: Longmans Green.

Artaud, D. (1973), *La reconstruction de l'Europe (1919–1929)*, Paris: Presses Universitaires de France.

Artaud, D. (1979), 'La question des dettes interalliées et la reconstruction de l'Europe', *Revue Historique*, 261.

Banac, I. (1988), *The National Question in Yugoslavia: Origins, History, Politics*, Ithaca, NY: Cornell University Press.

Bell, J.D. (1977), *Peasants in Power. Alexander Stambolski and the Bulgarian Agrarian National Union, 1899–1923*, Princeton: Princeton University Press.

Bencze, I. and Tajti, E. V. (1972), *Budapest: an Industrial-Geographical Approach*, Budapest: Akademiai Kiado.

Berend, I. T. and Ranki, G. (1969), 'The economic problems of the Danube region at the break-up of the Austro-Hungarian monarchy', *Journal of Contemporary History*, 4.

Berend, I. T. and Ranki, G. (1974), *Hungary: a Century of Economic Development*, Newton Abbot: David and Charles.

Birdsall, P. (1941), *Versailles Twenty Years After*, London: Allen and Unwin.

Boross, E. A. (1994), *Inflation and Industry in Hungary 1918–1929*, Berlin: Haude and Spener.

Bretton, H. L. (1953), *Streseman and the Revision of Versailles*, Stanford, CA: Stanford University Press.

Carsten, F. L. (1984), *Britain and the Weimar Republic: the British Documents*, London: Batsford.

Carsten, F. L. (1986), *The First Austrian Republic 1918–1938: a Study Based on British and Austrian Documents*, Aldershot: Gower.

Childers, T. (1983a), 'Inflation and electoral politics in Germany, 1919–29' in N. Schmukler and E. Marcus (eds), *Inflation through the Ages*, New York: Brooklyn College Press.

Childers, T. (1983b), *The Nazi Voter: the Social Foundation of Fascism in Germany, 1919–1933*, Chapel Hill, NC: University of North Carolina Press.

Childers, T. (1984), 'Who indeed did vote for Hitler', *Central European History*, 17.

Clough, S. B., Moodie, T. and Moodie, C. (eds) (1969), *Economic History of Europe: Twentieth Century*, London: Macmillan.

Costigliola, F. (1976), 'The United States and the reconstruction of Germany in the 1920s', *Business History Review*, 50.

Dockrill, M. L. and Goold, J. D. (1981), *Peace without Promise: Britain and the Paris Peace Conference, 1919–1923*, London: Batsford.

Donald, R. (1928), *The Tragedy of Trianon*, London: Thornton Butterworth.

Dragnich, A. N. (1983), *The First Yugoslavia: Search for a Viable Political System*, Stanford, CA: Hoover Institution Press.

Fergusson, A. (1975), *When Money Dies: the Nightmare of the Weimar Collapse*, London: William Kimber.

Fischer, W. (1974), 'Die Weimarer Republik unter dem weltwirtschaftlichen Bedingungen der Zwischenkriegszeit', in H. Mommsen, D. Petzina and B. Weisbrod (eds), *Industrielles System und politische Entwicklung in der Weimarer Republik*, Düsseldorf: Droste Verlag.

Fleisig, H. (1976), 'War-related debts and the great depression', *American Economic Review, Papers and Proceedings*, 66.

Flood, C. B. (1989), *Hitler: the Path to Power*, Boston: Houghton Mifflin.

Friedman, P. (1974), *The Impact of Trade Destruction on National Incomes: a Study of Europe, 1924–1938*, Gainsville, FL: University Presses of Florida.

Gilberg, T. (1992), 'The multiple legacies of history: Romania in the year 1990', in J. Held (ed.), *The Columbia History of Eastern Europe in the Twentieth Century*, New York: Columbia University Press.

Good, D. F. (1984), *The Economic Rise of the Habsburg Empire, 1750–1914*, Berkeley, CA: University of California Press.

Gordon, M. S. (1941), *Barriers to World Trade: a Study of Recent Commercial Policy*, New York: Macmillan.
Halasz, A. (1928), *New Central Europe in Economical Maps*, Budapest: R. Gergely.
Hardach, G. (1984), 'Banking and industry in Germany in the interwar period, 1919–1939', *Journal of European Economic History*, 13.
Henig, R. (ed.) (1973), *The League of Nations*, Edinburgh: Oliver and Boyd.
Henig, R. (1995), *Versailles and After 1919–1933*, London: Routledge.
Herschlag, Z. Y. (1968), *Turkey: the Challenge of Growth*, Leiden: E. J. Brill.
Hill, M. (1946), *The Economic and Financial Organisation of the League of Nations: a Survey of Twenty-Five Years*, Washington, DC: Carnegie Endowment for International Peace.
Hobsbawm, E. (1994), *Age of Extremes: the Short Twentieth Century 1914–1991*, London: Michael Joseph.
Hogan, M. J. (1975), 'The United States and the problem of international economic control: American attitudes toward European reconstruction, 1918–1920', *Pacific Historical Review*, 44.
Hogan, M. J. (1977), *Informal Entente: the Private Structure of Cooperation in Anglo-American Diplomacy, 1918–1928*, Columbia, MO: University of Missouri Press.
Holtfrerich, C.-L. (1986), *The German Inflation 1914–1923*, Berlin: Walter de Gruyter.
Jacobson, J. (1983), 'Is there a new international history of the 1920s?' *American Historical Review*, 88.
Janos, C. (1982), *The Politics of Backwardness in Hungary 1825–1945*, Princeton, NJ: Princeton University Press.
Jelavich, B. (1983), *History of the Balkans*. Vol. 2 *Twentieth Century*, Cambridge: Cambridge University Press.
Job, C. (1993), 'Yugoslavia's ethnic furies', *Foreign Policy*, (92).
Jones, L. E. (1972), 'The dying middle class: Weimar Germany and the fragmentation of bourgeois politics', *Central European History*, 5.
Jones, L. E. (1979), 'Inflation, revaluation and the crisis of middle class politics: a study of the dissolution of the German party system', *Central European History*, 12.
Kent, B. (1989), *The Spoils of War: the Politics, Economics and Diplomacy of Reparations, 1918–1932*, Oxford: Clarendon Press.
Keynes, J. M. (1920), *The Economic Consequences of the Peace*, London: Macmillan.
Kiraly, B. K., Pastor, P. and Sanders, I. (eds) (1982), *War and Society in East Central Europe*, Vol. VI, *Essays on World War I: Total War and*

Peacemaking, a Case Study of Trianon, New York: Brooklyn College Press.

Kitchen, M. (1988), *Europe between the Wars: a Political History*, London: Longman.

Klein-Ahlbrandt, W. L. (1995), *The Burden of Victory: France, Britain and the Enforcement of the Versailles Peace, 1919–1925*, New York: University Press of America.

Komlos, J. (1983), *The Habsburg Monarchy as a Customs Union*, Princeton, NJ: Princeton University Press.

Lampe, J. R. (1980), 'Unifying the Yugoslav economy 1918–1921: misery and early misunderstandings', in D. Djordjevic (ed.), *The Creation of Yugoslavia, 1914–18*, Santa Barbara, CA: Clio Books.

League of Nations (1932), *Conference for the Restoration of Central and Eastern Europe*, Stresa: League of Nations.

League of Nations (1943a), *Agricultural Production in Continental Europe during the 1914–18 War and the Reconstruction Period*, Geneva: League of Nations.

League of Nations (1943b), *Europe's Overseas Needs 1919–1920 and How They Were Met*, Geneva: League of Nations.

League of Nations (1943c), *Relief Deliveries and Relief Loans 1919–1923*, Geneva: League of Nations.

League of Nations (1943d), *The Transition from War to Peace Economy: Report of the Delegation on Economic Depressions Part I*, Geneva: League of Nations.

League of Nations (1946), *Raw Material Problems and Policies*, Geneva: League of Nations.

Lee, S. J. (1987), *The European Dictatorships 1918–1945*, London: Methuen.

Leffler, M. P. (1979), *The Elsuive Quest: America's Pursuit of European Stability and French Security, 1919–1933*, Chapel Hill: University of North Carolina Press.

Lentin, A. (1991), *The Versailles Peace Settlement: Peacemaking with Germany*, London: Thc Historical Association.

Leslie, R. F. (ed.) (1980), *The History of Poland since 1863*, Cambridge: Cambridge University Press.

Macartney, C. A. (1934), *National States and National Minorities*, Oxford: Oxford University Press.

Macartney, C. A. (1937), *Hungary and her Successors: the Treaty of Trianon and its Consequences 1919–1937*, London: Oxford University Press.

Marks, S. (1976), *The Illusion of Peace: International Relations in Europe 1918–1933*, London: Macmillan.

McDougall, W. A. (1979), 'Political economy versus national sovereignty: French structures for German integration after Versailles', *Journal of Modern History*, 51.
McNeil, W. C. (1986), *American Money and the Weimar Republic: Economics and Politics on the Eve of the Great War*, New York: Columbia University Press.
Ministry of Munitions (1922), *Official History of the Ministry of Munitions*, vol. 7, London: HMSO.
Mocsy, I. I. (1983), *War and Society in East Central Europe*. Vol. XII. *The Effects of World War I, The Uprooted: Hungarian Refugees and their Impact on Hungary's Domestic Politics, 1918–1921*, New York: Brooklyn College Press.
Momtchiloff, N. (1944), *Ten Years of Controlled Trade in South-Eastern Europe*, Cambridge: Cambridge University Press.
Newman, W. J. (1968), *The Balance of Power in the Interwar Years, 1919–1939*, New York: Random House.
Nötel, R. (1974), 'International capital movements and finance in Eastern Europe, 1919–1949', *Vierteljahrschrift für Sozial-und Wirtschaftsgeschichte*, 61.
Orde, A. (1990), *British Policy and European Reconstruction after the First World War*, Cambridge: Cambridge University Press.
Overy, R. (1995), *Why the Allies Won*, London: Jonathan Cape.
Pasvolsky, L. (1928), *Economic Nationalism of the Danubian States*, London: Allen and Unwin.
Pearson, R. (1983), *National Minorities in Eastern Europe 1848–1945*, London: Macmillan.
Pentzopoulos, D. (1962), *The Balkan Exchange of Minorities and its Impact on Greece*, Paris: Mouton.
Petzina, D. (1977), *Die Deutsche Wirtschaft in der Zwischenkriegszeit*, Wiesbaden: Franz Steiner.
Polonsky, A. (1975), *The Little Dictators: the History of Eastern Europe since 1918*, London: Routledge and Kegan Paul.
Robinson, J., Karbuch, O., Laserson, M. M., Robinson, N. and Vichniak, M. (eds) (1943), *Were the Minorities Treaties a Failure?* New York: Antin Press.
Rose, W. J. (1939), *Poland*, Harmondsworth: Penguin Books.
Ross, G. (1983), *The Great Powers and the Decline of the European States System 1914–1945*, London: Longman.
Roszkowski, W. (1986), 'Poland's economic performance between the two world wars', *East European Quarterly*, 20.
Scheele, G. (1946), *The Weimar Republic: Overture to the Third Reich*, London: Faber.

Schulz, G. (1972), *Revolutions and Peace Treaties 1917–1920*, London: Methuen.

Schwartz, H. (1973), *Eastern Europe in the Soviet Shadow*, New York: The John Day Company.

Sharp, A. (1991), *The Versailles Settlement: Peacemaking in Paris, 1919*, Basingstoke: Macmillan.

Silverman, D. P. (1982), *Reconstructing Europe after the Great War*, Cambridge, MA: Harvard University Press.

Sontag, R. J. (1971), *A Broken World, 1919–1939*, New York: Harper and Row.

Spulber, N. (1966), *The State and Economic Development in Eastern Europe*, New York: Random House.

Stambrook, F. G. (1963), 'A British proposal for the Danubian states: the customs union project of 1932', *The Slavonic and East European Review*, 42.

Summers, A. and Mangold, T. (1987), *The File on the Tsar*, London: Gollancz, paperback edn.

Taylor, J. (1952), *The Economic Development of Poland 1919–1950*, Ithaca, NY: Cornell University Press.

Teichova, A. (1985), 'Industry', in M. C. Kaser and E. A. Radice (eds), *The Economic History of Eastern Europe 1919–1975*, Vol. I, *Economic Structure and Performance between the Wars*, Oxford: Oxford University Press.

Thompson, D. (1966), *Europe since Napoleon*, Harmondswoth: Penguin.

Tiltman, H. H. (1934), *Peasant Europe*, London: Jarrolds.

Trachtenberg, M. (1979), 'Reparation at the Paris Peace Conference', *Journal of Modern History*, 51.

Wallace, B. B. and Edminster, L. R. (1930), *International Control of Raw Materials*, Washington, DC: Brookings Institution.

Wandel, E. (1971), *Die Bedeutung der Vereinigten Staaten von Amerika für das deutsche Reparationsproblem, 1924–9*, Tübingen: J. C. B. Mohr.

Weinberg, G. L. (1969), 'The defeat of Germany in 1918 and the European balance of power', *Central European History*, 2.

Wellisz, L. (1938), *Foreign Capital in Poland*, London: Allen and Unwin.

Willis, H. P. and Chapman, J. (1935), *The Economics of Inflation*, New York: Columbia University Press.

Wiskemann, E. (1938), *Czechs and Germans: a Study of the Struggle in the Historic Provinces of Bohemia and Moravia*, London: Oxford University Press.

Wynot, E. D. (1983), *Warsaw between the World Wars: Profile of the Capital City in a Developing Land, 1919–1939*, Boulder, CO: East

European Monographs, distributed by Columbia University Press, New York.

Zimmern, A. (1936), *The League of Nations and the Rule of Law, 1918–1935*, London: Macmillan.

Zweig, F. (1944), *Poland between the Wars: a Critical Study of Social and Economic Changes*, London: Secker and Warburg.

CHAPTER TWO

Postwar Instability in the European Economy

The decade bounded by the aftermath of the great war and the beginnings of a severe economic crisis and one dominated by major economic and political problems, has been described in various terms: a period of 'false stability' (Ross, 1983, p. 54), 'an era of illusions' (McDougall, 1979, p. 4), 'a period of surface harmony and apparent economic prosperity' (Marks, 1976, p. 108), and 'years of hope and vigour' which 'ended in despair' (Beyen, 1951, p. 3). All denote one thing, a failure to regain stability and composure. It ended in despair because the hope remained unfulfilled, namely that of recreating the prewar economic stability.

The reason why, according to Keynes in his vitriolic attack on the peace settlement, was that the statesmen of the time failed to appreciate the fragility of the international economic and financial mechanism that had been shattered by war, or the fact that the pre-1914 international economy was inherently unstable:

> Very few of us realise with conviction the intensely unusual, unstable, complicated, unreliable, temporary nature of the economic organisation by which Western Europe has lived for the last half century. We assume some of the most peculiar and temporary of our later advantages as natural, permanent, and to be depended on, and we lay our plans accordingly.
>
> (Keynes, 1920, p. 1)

In the meantime the war had done much to destroy the framework of the prewar system. The free and multilateral trading and financial system on which Europe and the periphery had depended was severely dislocated, the gold standard had been suspended or abandoned, currencies became debased, banking and credit systems were badly strained, while politically and geographically the map of Europe underwent violent change. Much of Europe had also been rendered destitute by over four years of hostilities. The situation therefore demanded, said Keynes, a settlement which would avert the threat of revolution in Europe by restoring international stability.

Keynes may have been somewhat naïve in his assumptions as to what was politically feasible at the time, but his assessment of the economic and social situation and its consequences was remarkably accurate. It was bad enough that contemporaries did not realise the extent to which the old order had been damaged by war, but when it led them to assume that it would be a relatively simple matter to restore the normal pattern of things by free trade and gold – perhaps a slight exaggeration but not far from the truth – that was even worse.

Thus it can be argued that the failure of Europe to reassert itself and regain its prewar eminence was not due simply to the direct consequences of war, serious though these undoubtedly were. After all, the even more traumatic experience of the 1940s did not leave Europe immobilised for long. A decade or so after the Second World War found Europe in a much stronger and more viable position than she had ever been in the 1920s. It is true that the American contribution to European reconstruction was far stronger than it was after 1918 but this cannot explain all the difference in the two experiences. Rather one has to relate to the differing policy reactions to understand the situation. Whereas after 1945 there was generally a constructive approach to the problems associated with the aftermath of war, this was generally not the case following the conclusion of hostilities in 1918. Statesmen and politicians, bankers and diplomats made many mistakes and it was their actions which were largely responsible for Europe's weakened state and left her vulnerable to external shocks.

The key issues of the postwar period, for example the creation of the new map of Europe, reparations and war debts, the reconstruction programme or rather lack of it, currency stabilisation and structural factors, were never satisfactorily resolved. The policy reactions on these matters did more to divide and destabilise Europe than to unite it and in the longer term they helped to set the stage for the Second World War. Several of these issues have already been covered in the first chapter of this volume and here we shall concentrate on currency problems and structural impediments, and the way in which the weaknesses in the European and international economy were concealed for a time by the more favourable political and economic climate of the later 1920s and the flow of American lending to Europe.

Monetary reconstruction: a lost opportunity

Currency issues were rarely out of the news in the 1920s and for most of the decade much energy was devoted to trying to restore a workable international exchange system. The restoration of the prewar liberal economic order – embracing freedom from economic controls, free trade and, above all, fixed exchange rates under the gold standard system – was regarded almost universally as a basic priority of policy

(Arndt, 1944, p. 223). In fact right through to the depression 'Ministers, officials, economists and businessmen alike continued to think about the broad issues of commercial policy in the light of the economic and political conditions obtaining in the prewar era and desired the general re-adoption of long-run policies appropriate to these conditions.' (League of Nations, 1942, pp. 154–5). The gold standard in particular exercised an almost mystic faith in the minds of contemporaries who regarded its restoration as the key to the return of European and world prosperity. The virtues of the gold standard were never questioned. Both the Brussels and Genoa International Conferences of 1920 and 1922 stressed the urgency of returning to fixed gold parities (Fink, 1984, p. 235; Kemmerer, 1944, pp. 109–10; Orde, 1990, p. 299). The same message had already been transmitted loud and clear to the world by the Cunliffe Report of 1918, such that the return to gold 'devint une affaire de prestige, un point de dogme, presque une question de religion' [became a question of prestige, a matter of principle, almost a religious faith] (van der Wee and Tavernier, 1975, pp. 79–80).

Whether the stabilising properties of the prewar monetary standard were as powerful as many contemporaries imagined is to be doubted. Recent research has cast doubt on some of the former conventional wisdom of the gold standard (Bordo, 1981; Cooper, 1982; Ford, 1989; Fremling, 1986; Giovannini, 1986; McCloskey and Zecher, 1976; McKinnon, 1993). The apparent success of the system probably owed more to the economic harmony among the major gold standard countries, together with the hegemonic leadership exercised by Britain (Triffen, 1968; Yeager, 1966). On the other hand, faith in the former system possibly led to an insufficient awareness of the enormous structural changes that had taken place in the world economy and world finance through 1914–20, especially the wide variations in cost/price relationships among countries, the weakened position of Britain and the emergence of the United States as a major creditor, all of which were to effect the working of a restored standard.

Notwithstanding any reservations on the working of the prewar monetary system, there were also sound reasons, apart from the suggestion that it was a ruse to assert Anglo-American hegemony over the international financial system (Silverman, 1982, p. 58), why the restoration of fixed rates of exchange based on gold should be strongly desired. Some countries, notably France and Italy, saw it as an important prestige symbol, while Britain regarded it as a way of maintaining the pre-eminent position of the City of London to compensate for industrial decline (Kunz, 1987, p. 4). Rather more important was the fact that the floating exchange rates which followed the general abandonment of gold had given rise to large and erratic swings in exchange rates and these in turn had tended to exacerbate the inflationary potential in Europe. Admittedly many of the more violent movements in the exchanges were a product of lax monetary and fiscal policies in the constrained conditions of the period, but that did not alter the fact that they were seen as a major impediment to reconstruction and recovery. Pigou, in his memorandum to the Brussels Conference of 1920, had warned that wide fluctuations in exchange rates were a great hindrance to trade and credit transactions (Pigou, 1920, p. 12). Keynes was also in favour of a modicum of exchange stability to encourage international trade and investment. In a memorandum of 1922 he advocated that the principal European exchanges should be stabilised against gold with other countries following later. He also believed that stabilisation should be related to current market rates rather than prewar parities though with wider bands than under the prewar gold standard, and that competitive depreciations should be avoided (Moggridge, 1992, pp. 377–8, 382–3). The head of the League of Nations Intelligence Service was even more emphatic about the need for stable exchanges; trade could scarcely flourish, he argued, when 'European exchanges ... danced and jumped with spasmodic and tireless energy ... That instability has not only rendered the transaction of business from day to day extraordinarily difficult and risky, but has for years excluded the possibility of laying down any elaborate economic programme for the future' (League of Nations, 1920, p. ix; Loveday, 1931, p. 31). There was also a belief that speculative activity exacerbated fluctuations in exchange rates and led to overtracking from true equilibrium levels (League of Nations, 1944). The extent of this may have been exaggerated but more recent experience with the vagaries of floating exchange rates now affords greater sympathy with the motives of statesmen in the 1920s for restoring some order to exchange rates.

Unfortunately, in contrast to the negotiated settlement following the Second World War, the process of currency stabilisation in the 1920s was little short of disastrous. There was no systematic plan to stabilise currencies simultaneously and insufficient attention was paid to the vast changes which had taken place in the world economy and relative prices since 1914. In the conditions of the time it must be admitted that it would have been difficult to formulate a coherent plan but this was partly because there was no general programme devised for European reconstruction which would have allowed this to happen. Thus the process of currency stabilisation was a long-drawn-out affair with some countries only managing to stabilise formally shortly before the general collapse of the gold standard in the early 1930s (see Table 2.1). For the most part countries acted independently of one another and stabilised their exchange rates at different times throughout the 1920s as and

Table 2.1 Dates and levels at which currencies stabilised

Country	*Stabilisation date*[1]	*% of prewar value*
Austria	1922	new currency
Belgium	1926	14.3
Bulgaria	1924 (1928)	3.7
Czechoslovakia	1923	14.3
Denmark	1926	prewar parity
Estonia	1924 (1927)	1.1
France	1926 (1928)	20.0
Finland	1926	12.5
Germany	1923 (1924)	new currency
Greece	1928	6.7
Hungary	1924	new currency
Italy	1927	25.0
Japan	1930	prewar parity
Latvia	1921	0.8
Netherlands	1924	prewar parity
Norway	1928	prewar parity
Poland	1926 (1927)[2]	new currency
Portugal	1929 (1931)	4.6
Romania	1927 (1929)	3.0
Sweden	1922	prewar parity
Switzerland	1924	prewar parity
United Kingdom	1925	prewar parity
Yugoslavia	1925 (1931)	9.1

Notes:
1. Dates of *de jure* stabilisation where different from those of *de facto* stabilisation are shown in brackets.
2. Poland initially stabilised the gold value of its currency in 1924 but was forced to abandon it the following year.

Source: League of Nations (1946), pp. 92–3.

when it best suited their needs, which usually meant when they had managed to regain control of their domestic financial systems. Only limited recognition was given to the relative shift in costs and prices which had taken place since 1914 when choosing a new rate. The chief objective was to select a rate that was felt to be defensible, though even this maxim was disregarded when questions of prestige or honour were at stake. Only a few countries such as the UK, The Netherlands, Switzerland, Denmark, Norway and Sweden, managed to restore their old parities; most countries had to make do with much devalued rates (League of Nations, 1946, pp. 91–4).

The majority of countries in fact adopted a modified form, the gold exchange standard, by which a country's monetary authority tied its currency to gold indirectly by dealing on the foreign exchange market to maintain a fixed exchange rate with a foreign currency on either a gold coin or gold bullion standard. The British were largely responsible for getting the gold exchange standard accepted at the Genoa Conference of 1922 ostensibly on the pretext that it would economise on the use of gold of which there was expected to be a growing shortage, but also because it would help sterling to regain its former pre-eminence as a key currency. Accordingly, Britain was instrumental, through the Financial Committee of the League of Nations which it dominated, in getting the gold exchange standard adopted in those European countries in which the Bank of England assisted with stabilisation plans (Kooker, 1976, pp. 86–7). Many other countries also adopted the same form. Of the 51 nations on some form of gold standard between 1919–37, 32 adopted the gold exchange standard in which their reserves consisted primarily of foreign exchange. The gold exchange system no doubt facilitated the process of currency stabilisation and helped to economise on the use of gold, but since many countries harboured the ideal of moving to a full gold standard eventually, this posed a threat to central banks of the key currencies should there be a general move to convert their foreign exchange holdings into gold (Mouré, 1992, p. 264). The French in particular never regarded it as more than a temporary expedient and suspected that it was a ruse to secure Anglo-American hegemony in international finance.

The upshot was a largely unworkable system of exchange rates, since many were in disequilibrium from the start. The most glaring examples were the undervaluation of the French and Belgium currencies, the overvaluation of sterling, the lira and the Scandinavian currencies. Those countries with undervalued currencies no doubt secured some initial gains, but conversely this threw an extra burden on countries with overvalued currencies which depressed activity and entailed restrictive domestic policies. Any fixed exchange rate system is only as good as the individual components and it was bound to disintegrate in time. As the League of Nations commented in one of its later reports (League of Nations, 1944, p. 117): 'The piecemeal and haphazard manner of international monetary reconstruction sowed the seeds of subsequent disintegration. It was partly because of the lack of proper coordination during the stabilisation period of the 'twenties that the system broke down in the 'thirties.'

Given the initial disequilibrium in exchange rates it is not altogether surprising that the new standard functioned less smoothly than before the war when international stability was more in evidence. Indeed, it is true to say that no system of fixed exchange rates can hope to operate satisfactorily if the alignment of currencies, especially major ones, is out of kilter from the start. The choice of wrong exchange rates magnified balance of payments problems and the system was called upon to make adjustment on a far greater scale than previously and for which it was never designed, and at a time when the adjustment mechanism, for various reasons, was less easy to operate. As Condliffe (1941, pp. 102–3) noted more than a century ago, the restoration of the gold standard was a futile gesture since the necessary conditions were not present for its successful operation. In particular he mentioned the growing impediments to international trade, migration and capital movements, the increasing inflexibility of price systems, and the emergence of nationalistic monetary policies designed to deal with increasing pressures on domestic economies. Few countries were now prepared to sacrifice the stability of their domestic economies for the sake of external equilibrium to the extent that had been the case before 1914. This meant that the so-called traditional 'rules of the game', however much they may have been observed in the breach, could not be adhered to (hence the increasing concentration of gold in Paris and New York), while the division of financial power among rival financial centres (London, Paris and New York) and the pyramiding of short-term claims on these centres, none of which was prepared to defend the system in the final analysis, created further operational difficulties. The system was bereft of a hegemonic leader which some see as crucial to a successful international monetary system (Llewellyn and Presley, 1995). Thus Paris played her own game, New York was an absentee landlord and London was too weak to orchestrate the system as she had done before 1914, partly because of sterling's changed liquidity position as a reserve currency (Foreman-Peck, 1983, p. 236).

Given the form in which it was restored and the way in which it was subsequently operated, it was inconceivable that the postwar monetary standard could have provided a solution to the instability problems of the 1920s. Once the pattern had been set moreover, there was little hope of readjustment in the absence of international cooperation, and in any case the rates eventually chosen tended to be regarded as sacrosanct. It was only a matter of time therefore before the system itself disintegrated since, once subject to pressures, countries were not prepared to sacrifice domestic stability on the altar of the exchanges. Thus, far from being a stabilising force, the restored monetary standard itself has been seen as a source of instability (Fearon, 1979, p. 25). In so far as it made it more difficult for adjustment to take place between creditors and debtors, together with the imbalances in reserve holdings which emerged through dishonouring the 'rules of the game', then it can certainly be seen as a destabilising element. Though whether it can also be regarded as a significant causal factor for the initial slide into depression in 1929, is another matter. The origins of the great contraction are of course part of another story. But what should be noted is that once the depression got under way the influence of the gold standard was crucial. For, as Friedman and Schwartz and others have confirmed, no major contraction involving a substantial fall in prices can develop in any one country without the links forged by the gold standard reinforcing the transmission and spread effects of depression to other countries tied to gold through international deflation (Choudhri and Kochin, 1980; Friedman and Schwartz, 1963, p. 359). Once these pressures became too severe of course, relief was sought by going off gold.

No one would deny that the monetary reconstruction of the 1920s was far from ideal. A great opportunity was missed to achieve greater uniformity of currency units and a workable system of exchange rates. The number of different currency units had increased considerably compared with before the war, from 8 to 22 (Preston, 1931, p. 328). However, one should bear in mind that while governments with their increasingly nationalistic sentiments did little to foster the cause of improved international cooperation in monetary matters, behind the scenes the chief central bankers and other individuals were active in promoting the monetary reconstruction in Europe. Preston (1931, p. 329) stresses the important role of central bank cooperation in facilitating the restoration of the gold standard. But monetary reconstruction had a wider connotation than currency stabilisation *per se*. It also involved the establishment of central banks in countries which lacked them, the provision of loans and credits to help countries stabilise their currencies and bring their financial affairs into order, and technical advice to new central banks.

The two most influential bankers in this respect were Montagu Norman, Governor of the Bank of England and Benjamin Strong, Governor of the Federal Reserve Bank of New York until his death in 1928. Their collaborative work was probably instrumental in rescuing Europe from financial chaos. Einzig (1932, pp. 7–8, 72) reckoned Norman contributed more than anyone to the reconstruction of Europe and that the Bank of England under his guidance saved Europe from complete financial collapse. Norman's vision of Europe was probably more enlightened and constructive than that of many of his contemporaries. He was especially concerned that the European economy should be revitalised through financial and monetary reconstruction. For much of the decade he worked unremittingly to achieve this end by promoting the creation of central banks, arranging loans and credits to assist with currency stabilisation and financial reform, and providing expert advice on finance and banking to those in need. In one way or another the Bank of England under Norman's influence played an important role in assisting Austria, Belgium, Bulgaria, Germany, Greece, Hungary, the Free City of Danzig, Poland and Romania (Einzig, 1932, p. 55). Much of his work was done indirectly through the Financial Committee of the League of Nations on which British representatives preponderated. Outwith Europe, Norman's banking expertise was also in evidence in imperial countries where he did much to promote the cause of central banking throughout the interwar years, while in South America Dr E. W. Kemmerer, a Princeton University don and adviser to several governments in the postwar years, carried out similar activities. The latter was responsible for the setting up of central banks in several of the Latin American republics, including Peru (1922), Columbia (1923), Uruguay (1924), Chile and Guatemala (1925), Ecuador (1927) and Bolivia (1929). These new banks were to function within the framework of the gold exchange standard and, in fact, they became the instruments through which exchange stability and financial reform were carried out.

As the French suspected, not all this work was solely altruistic. Fears of an Anglo-American financial hegemony abounded, and not only in French circles. Norman would of course have been the first to admit that he also had Britain's interests at heart. More specifically, he was very anxious to ensure that sterling remained a key currency and that it did not play second fiddle to the dollar. This was the main reason why he was keen to promote the adoption of the gold exchange standard, apart from its additional advantage as a device for economising on the use of gold. Yet these reservations notwithstanding, it seems likely that Norman did have a wider vision than national motives dictated and that he more than anyone saw the urgency of regenerating Europe through monetary reconstruction and closer cooperation among European countries. He had, for instance, a notion for a federation in Eastern Europe which would incorporate most of the Danubian countries in a customs free zone (Péteri, 1992, p. 251).

Einzig (1932, p. 72) recognised how crucial Benjamin Strong's support was to Norman's work and his influence in helping to foster greater cooperation among central bankers (Clarke, 1967, p. 41). But there were limits to the extent of that cooperation. Norman was never able to formalise the role of the chief central bankers within an association in the 1920s, partly because of Strong's lukewarm attitude towards such a move and the ever-present suspicions of the French (Boyce,

1987, pp. 40–41, 167). When eventually a forum for inter-bank cooperation and discussion emerged, with the establishment of the Bank for International Settlements in 1930, time for effective cooperation was fast running out. By then politicians and bureaucrats were beginning to take over as national domestic priorities came to dominate the scene. As Mouré (1992, p. 278) comments:

> Central banks, tied as they were to national policy and politics, lacked the understanding, the power and, in some cases, the will necessary for more effective co-operation in rebuilding the international monetary system. By 1928, political rivalries and conceptual differences had arrested the development of central bank co-operation. The gold exchange standard did not command sufficient support to attract the continuous co-operation advocated by the Genoa resolutions.

By the time the 1931 crisis exploded, financial affairs in Europe were so enmeshed in politics and security that there was little hope of salvation through central bank initiatives. Two years later central bank cooperative efforts for the World Economic Conference fell foul of political expediency (Clavin, 1991, 1992, pp. 282, 310–11).

Structural problems

Of fundamental importance to the stability of the real economy in the long term were the severe structural problems which either originated in or were exacerbated by war. According to Svennilson (1954, pp. 44, 52), the interwar period can be seen as a prolonged structural transformation crisis for the European economy. Growth and stability were slowed down by formidable structural problems following the war and the slowness with which adjustment took place. At the end of the 1920s the European economy was in a state of incomplete transformation in relation to technical change and new developments in the international market. 'Europe', he writes 'was suffering from the arterio-sclerosis of an old-established, heavily capitalised economic system, inflexible in relation to violent economic change. Low productivity in agriculture and many manufacturing industries, and widespread unemployment kept national output and incomes low, and blocked the road towards rapid general expansion' (Svennilson, 1954, p. 52). Rostow (1978, p. 228, 1980, p. 92) paints a similar picture and argues that relatively low income growth retarded the structural change. High unemployment and low productivity levels in Europe made it difficult to generate the expansion in real consumer income required to move in a big way into new sectors of activity, especially motor transport, and thereby relieve the unemployment in the old staple industries. Even in America, where conditions were so much more favourable to sectoral shifts, depressed agrarian prices and the skewed distribution of income gains in the 1920s were to become increasing sources of weakness late in the decade.

For much of Eastern Europe, and for parts of Western Europe too, the big problem was the large share of resources locked up in inefficient agriculture at a time when the market for many of the products of this sector was weakening. The transfer of resources out of agriculture was slow and patchy and so rates of accumulation and income levels remained depressed compared with those of the West (see Aldcroft and Morewood, 1995; Kaser and Radice, 1985, 1986).

In the case of the mature industrial economies of Western Europe the main problem lay in the heavy commitment to what became the ex-growth staple trades and the slow emergence of new sectors of activity. There were signs before 1914 of emerging structural difficulties as some of the industrial economies failed to adjust to new technologies and new patterns of demand. The war tended to accentuate this tendency since it gave a boost to expansion of capacity in some of the traditional sectors of activity relative to subsequent peacetime requirements. The war also resulted in lost markets, import substitution in both old and new countries and technical changes in competing products. Such developments left European staple industries with excess capacity, high unemployment and declining markets. Shipbuilding, iron and steel, engineering, coal, textiles and, of course, agriculture were considerably expanded world-wide during the period of hostilities and inevitably excess capacity became a problem in the 1920s. World shipbuilding capacity, for example, almost doubled during the war and by the end of the postwar boom there was enough shipping in existence to last the rest of the decade without further construction. Iron and steel capacity in Europe (including the UK) was 50 per cent higher by the mid-1920s than it had been in 1913, yet for much of the interwar period output remained below the prewar level. Coal was another industry in which excess capacity prevailed and here the main causes were a sharp deceleration in the growth of world demand for coal, the opening up of new sources of supply and the competition from substitute fuels. Textiles was another problem area, especially cotton, with import substitution in developing countries being the main source of trouble.

The most extreme manifestation of the structural problem was to be found in Britain where export losses in traditional products to former markets were severe. But industrial Europe as a whole faced similar, if less acute, difficulties, and the delay in making the transition to a new technological base meant high unemployment and low incomes which in turn slowed down the shift to leading growth sectors based on the consumer market (Fischer, 1974, pp. 27–33; Milward, 1974, pp. 53–5; Rostow, 1978, pp. 228–9, 1980, p. 92). Resistance to change by vested interest groups and institutional constraints also retarded the pace of change. In Germany for instance, the banks, agrarian interests and the large concerns in heavy industry were instrumental in defending the *status quo* and for much of the time they secured the support of the government (James, 1986, p. 418; Petzina and Abelshauser, 1974, pp. 60, 64). Germany therefore failed to adapt to the shift in world economic relationships wrought by war and so her competitiveness declined. Instead, 'industry and agriculture ... responded primarily with defensive measures, using cartelization, tariffs, and government subsidies to avoid fundamental restructuring. Banks proved more willing to loan to stagnant industries than dynamic ones. The German economy had therefore not regained its prewar competitiveness on world markets' (Hughes, 1988, p. 93). In the case of Britain, institutional constraints have been seen as a major impediment to structural change (Elbaum and Lazonick, 1984, 1986).

If we examine the commodity structure of European manufacturing exports it becomes clear that Europe's ability to compete effectively in world markets was linked closely with its ability to adjust its production structure to changing patterns of demand for manufactures. Although the war undoubtedly helped to delay the adjustment process, it is apparent that many European countries were handicapped before hostilities commenced because of their heavy commitment to traditional sectors of activity coupled with the increasing rigidity of their industrial structures. As Table 2.2 indicates, the UK, Germany, France, Italy, Belgium and Switzerland had one-half or more of their exports in contracting sectors in world trade and relatively low shares in the expanding ones. Sweden and the United States, by contrast, were much more favourably placed. It is significant that the latter two countries were the ones that responded most rapidly to the changes in patterns of world demand after the war by altering still further their export structures in the direction of expanding product markets. Thus by the end of the decade the United States had 44 per cent of its exports in the machinery and transport equipment groups, and Sweden one-third, while shares in declining groups were well under one-half. For most European countries, however, changes in the export product mix were fairly marginal, and in some cases anyway they were the result of declines in the importance of textiles rather than a genuine attempt to expand in the dynamic sectors of world trade. In the case of Germany and the UK, machinery exports actually fell in volume during the period. Both countries had a very weak export performance, with exports

Table 2.2 Exports of manufactures from selected countries, 1913–28 (percentage shares of three major commodity groups)

	Expanding groups (machinery and transport equipment)		*Stable groups (metals and chemicals)*		*Contracting groups (textiles and miscellaneous manufactures)*	
	1913	*1928*	*1913*	*1928*	*1913*	*1928*
UK	15.9	19.5	21.6	19.2	62.5	61.3
Germany	16.9	19.4	33.6	35.6	49.5	45.0
France	10.0	12.1	15.6	21.7	74.4	66.2
Italy	7.6	9.8	8.4	7.6	84.0	82.6
Belgium	9.3	8.3	29.9	35.4	60.8	56.3
Switzerland	11.8	16.9	11.3	16.8	76.9	66.3
Sweden	18.8	33.4	35.9	25.2	45.3	41.4
US	23.8	44.3	38.9	24.9	37.3	30.8
Total eight countries	15.8	23.2	26.6	24.9	57.6	51.9

Source: Svennilson (1954), p. 295.

failing to regain the prewar volumes. Only France managed a creditable export performance but this was due more to her undervalued currency rather than to any great innovative dynamism of the economy.

The inflexibility of the export product structure takes on an added significance if we consider the effects of both import substitution and changes in competitive shares. The failure to modernise the production structure meant that industrial countries faced two adverse influences simultaneously: an inability to compete in expanding sectors in high income countries, and the effects of import substitution in contracting sectors in the lesser developing countries. Thus the heaviest setbacks after the war occurred in the expanding commodity groups of machinery and transport equipment, and only in a few protected markets was Europe able to maintain its relative position. In the contracting sectors, textiles were the main problem area, especially for Britain and Switzerland since these goods bulked large in their total exports in 1913. Textiles were severely hit by import substitution in Asia and Latin America and also from Japanese competition in third markets.

Overall, the biggest losses through import substitution and competitive market shares occurred in the larger countries – Germany, the UK and France. Britain suffered by far the worst in both respects because of her heavy dependence on textiles and other basic sectors vulnerable to import substitution, but also because of her general inefficiency in manufacturing and the effects of a high exchange rate after the return to gold in 1925. Germany also suffered quite badly from import substitution and competitive handicaps: losses were experienced in most major markets except non-industrial countries, and in most commodity groups though with some relative strength in the expanding sectors to Western Europe and non-industrial countries. French losses were mainly confined to import substitution since there was relative strength in trade with Western Europe and non-industrial countries in both expanding and stable sectors of world trade. The smaller European countries (Belgium, Italy, Sweden, Switzerland and The Netherlands) faced serious import substitution, but found some compensation in relative strength in competitive shares for the groups as a whole (Maizels, 1963, pp. 90–95, 153–4, 184, 191–9, 228).

Papering over the cracks

Despite the impediments to European stability in the first half of the 1920s, by the middle of the decade economic and political conditions had taken a turn for the better. The Locarno Pact of 1925, the revised reparations settlement of the previous year, and the negotiated agreements relating to Allied war debts, did much to boost international confidence and reduce political tensions and suspicions of war. Most of the great inflations had run their course and Britain's return to the gold standard in April 1925 helped to pave the way for currency stabilisation elsewhere. Primary commodity prices had firmed somewhat after the sharp downturn following the postwar boom. Above all, reconstruction and recovery had made some headway and 'real progress began to take the place of a painful struggle to regain a plateau of prosperity which had been lost' (Loveday, 1931, p. 41). If there were still signs of tension and weakness in the international economy, these were all but forgotten as the world looked forward to a period of sustained prosperity.

The boom in activity of the later 1920s was led by the United States. Most regions of the world shared in the prosperity and Europe regained some of the ground she had lost earlier. The improvement in Europe's performance prompted the observation by the author of the League of Nation's study into the world depression that the prewar equilibrium between Europe and the rest of the world had more or less been restored (Ohlin, 1931, p. 17). In retrospect this view appears rather wide of the mark. Below the surface there were still plenty of signs of maladjustment: notably large areas of unemployed or underemployed resources in certain sectors, especially agriculture and heavy industry; the failure of some of the larger countries, for example Germany and the UK, as well as several smaller ones, for example Austria, to achieve full recovery; the rise in primary inventories, especially food products, and renewed weakness in commodity prices; the patched up nature of the international currency system; and, above all, the dependence of many countries on the inflow of foreign capital. Such factors rendered the equilibrium a fragile one, leaving Europe vulnerable to external shocks.

In fact, prosperity in Europe and the world at large was heavily dependent on the health of the American economy and the continued flow of credit from the United States and, to a lesser extent, from Britain and France. But, at the same time, international lending played a crucial role in the instability crisis on more than one occasion. The failure of reconstruction in Europe in the early 1920s, as noted in the previous chapter, can be traced directly to the collapse in international credits, when aggregate net capital movements from the main creditors, principally the United States, declined by over 60 per cent between 1920 and 1923. Foreign lending on a large scale was resumed only after the first major currency stabilisation phase had been completed, rising from a low point in 1923 to a peak in 1928 (North, 1962, p. 48). Many countries benefited from this outflow, American investment being directed mainly towards Europe (with Germany by far the largest borrower), Latin America and Canada, while Britain favoured the Dominions, Africa and Asia.

While the massive flow of lending in the later 1920s undoubtedly facilitated developments of one sort or another in many parts of the world, it also created a false sense of security. It gave an impression of soundness and stability which in fact did not exist. Yet so long as the flow of lending continued, the cracks in the international economic structure were concealed. But at the same time the lending itself helped to widen the cracks through the burdens it imposed on the borrowers. Thus once the flow was turned off the fragile stability was undermined. As Dunning (1970, p. 20) commented: 'a climate of investment so radically different from that of pre-war days, combined with substantial short-term capital movements, powerfully contributed to the world economic collapse of 1931 and its aftermath.'

One of the main problems was that the debtor countries, sometimes with ample encouragement on the part of the creditors, borrowed too much relative to their ability to service loans. Postwar investments were no longer readily self-liquidating as most of them had been in the nineteenth century, largely because the borrowers were unable or unwilling to generate sufficient exchange earnings. Some borrowers squandered the proceeds on prestige projects or in maintaining consumption, instead of ensuring that they went into exchange-generating investments. The result was that many debtors were forced to continue borrowing simply to enable them to service past loans, thereby raising their debt burdens to intolerable levels.

Probably the worst excesses in this respect occurred in Central and Eastern Europe, including Germany, and in Latin America. Germany may have been a special case because of her reparations obligations but she borrowed far more than she required to meet the latter and much of the excess was used to finance domestic consumption and acquire assets abroad (Harris, 1935, pp. 6–10; Moulton and Pasvolsky, 1932, p. 285; Schmidt, 1934, p. 110). Schuker (1988, p. 123) has been highly critical of the misuse of funds by Germany, and even though he may have overstated the case there is no doubt that in a wider context the German debt problem was becoming unmanageable. As Moulton and Pasvolsky (1932, pp. 384–5) pointed out, German and European borrowing on such a scale could not go on indefinitely, nor fail to accentuate the existing maladjustments:

> Even if the world depression had not begun at the end of 1929 and international lending had not suddenly decreased almost to vanishing point, it was inconceivable that new loans could have continued to exceed the rising reparation and Allied debt instalments, plus interest charges on the vast volume of private indebtedness

> that had already been created. The loan policy which constituted the second phase of post-war reparation and inter-Allied debt policy thus did not solve the war debt problem nor lay the foundation for enduring world prosperity.

The situation was not dissimilar in East European countries which had incurred unmanageable debt levels by the later 1920s, with debt service payments accounting for one-quarter and sometimes up to one-half of the value of export receipts (Aldcroft, 1988, p. 597). Moreover, since servicing foreign loans required strong currency earnings obtainable from a limited range of exports, the actual strain was much greater than these figures indicate (Raupach, 1969, p. 80). Europe was by no means unique in this respect. Many Latin American and African countries as well as the White Dominions had seriously over-committed themselves and were engaged in an uphill struggle to meet the obligations on past loans (Schedwin, 1970, pp. 2–3, 68, 75; United Nations, 1955, p. 15).

In reality, therefore, the maintenance of the fragile equilibrium in both the European and the international economy was heavily dependent on the continued flow of funds from creditors to debtors (Costigliola, 1976, p. 501). Even had conditions in the United States not determined the subsequent course of events, a reaction was bound to have come in time simply because of the increasingly insupportable debt burdens of the borrowing nations. In fact, at the beginning of 1928 the Governor of the New York Federal Reserve Bank, Benjamin Strong, was said to be sceptical of the wisdom of making further loans to Europe (Schuker, 1988, p. 43). Even in that year debtor nations of the United States and Britain were paying nearly $700 million a year in interest, dividends and amortization more than they received in new loans, and by the following year this burden had almost doubled (Royal Institute of International Affairs, 1937, p. 284). Equilibrium in external accounts was often only maintained with the help of short-term credits, which later themselves became a destabilising force of some magnitude.

Much of the increase in the relative debt burden in 1929 can be attributed to the decline in lending. Net outward movements from the main creditors declined by over one-third, and by nearly half in the case of the United States, while in the following year the fall was even more dramatic (North, 1962). The most vulnerable areas were Germany, Eastern Europe, Latin America and Australia. Many primary producing countries in Eastern Europe and along the periphery faced severe difficulties. Coming on top of weakening commodity prices and followed by a downturn in the American economy in the summer of 1929 and the subsequent curtailment in American import demand, the drying up of capital imports placed intolerable burdens on their economies and balance of payments. The way out of the impasse was eventually sought through deflation, devaluation, debt default and trade control, the backwash effects of which eventually reverberated on the metropolitan economies (see Chapter 5).

Conclusions

Before the war Europe was a significant force in the world economy even though her relative strength was beginning to wane. Thereafter her standing slipped significantly. During the war itself several years of growth were sacrificed, trade volumes and markets collapsed and Europe emerged from the conflict in a prostrate condition both politically and economically. The balance of economic gravity shifted westwards and it was to be several decades before Europe was able to reassert itself.

The reconstruction and recovery process in the 1920s was a painful and protracted affair which did little to recapture her former glory. Europe's influence in the world diminished and her economy remained fragile. In terms of world industrial production, income and trade, Europe's relative importance declined. Her share of world exports fell from 58.9 to 48 per cent between 1913 and 1929, while that of manufactures dropped from 81.5 to 67.3 per cent (Yates, 1959, pp. 32–3, 48–50). The four major industrial countries – Germany, the UK, France and Belgium – experienced a decline from 37.5 to 29.5 per cent in their share of world manufacturing production (League of Nations, 1945, p. 13).

The war itself can only account for part of the setback. Though it undoubtedly caused severe dislocations and distortions to the economic system and interrupted the normal course of growth for several years, the argument here is that it was what followed in the aftermath that was primarily responsible for upsetting the stability of Europe. The policies pursued by national governments and the Allied powers effectively stifled Europe's full recovery and the restoration of equilibrium. In this and the previous chapter it has been shown how the new configuration of Europe and the failure to follow through with an adequate programme of reconstruction, together with the treatment of Germany and the reparations issue, and the absence of a coordinated plan for currency stabilisation, meant that the political and economic system of Europe was left in a highly fragile and vulnerable state. National rather than international policies gave rise to a legacy of missed opportunities and hence growth was dampened and structural transformation slowed down.

The failure to bring peace and stability to Europe can therefore be attributed largely to the inability of the Allied powers to reorganise the system of nation states in a way which would resolve long-standing problems. The failure was both an economic and political one. The inability to contain the revisionist ambitions of defeated states or to quell the march of national aspirations, coupled with the failure to ensure the economic viability of the new states, inevitably gave rise to unstable conditions. As Nautz (1994, p. 261) comments: 'The prevailing nationalism and the failure to establish basic rules for economic relations delayed peace on the continent.' It was not so much the defects of the terms of the peace settlement, but a failure to agree on how they should be carried out that fatally undermined the stability of Europe and left the way open for the emergence of a new hegemonic order. Perhaps had Britain and France been able to sink their differences under American leadership and agree on a programme of regeneration involving Germany things might have turned out differently. But once weaknesses in the Allied stance emerged Germany seized the opportunity to whittle away systematically at the restrictions imposed upon her.

Economically Europe became heavily dependent on the United States as the major country. Unfortunately the latter proved to be an unpredictable backer. She did little to provide the leadership that Europe required in this period and for much of the time American policies posed a constant threat to Europe's economic stability: for example the hasty withdrawal of reconstruction aid, restrictive import policies and gold sterilisation measures. Nor did she do much to secure a balance of power in Europe. For a time there appeared to be sufficient resilience in the European and international economy to withstand these setbacks provided the American economy remained healthy and it continued to pour dollars into Europe and the rest of the world. But once these supports were removed there was nothing left to prop up the system. As the United Nations (1949, pp. 66–77) commented in one of its early reports: 'The stage was thus set for the disturbances which culminated in the international financial crisis of 1931 and the subsequent disintegration of the international economy.'

References

Aldcroft, D. H. (1988), 'Eastern Europe in an age of turbulence, 1919–1950', *Economic History Review,* **41**.

Aldcroft, D. H. and Morewood, S. (1995), *Economic Change in Eastern Europe since 1918*, Aldershot: Edward Elgar.

Arndt, H. W. (1944), *The Economic Lessons of the Nineteen-Thirties*, London: Oxford University Press.

Beyen, J. W. (1951), *Money in Maelstrom*, London: Macmillan.

Bordo, M. D. (1981), 'The classical gold standard: some lessons for today', *Federal Reserve Bank of St Louis Review*, 63.
Boyce, R. W. D. (1987), *British Capitalism at the Crossroads 1919–1932: a Study in Politics, Economics and International Relations*, Cambridge: Cambridge University Press.
Choudhri, E. U. and Kochin, L. A. (1980), 'The exchange rate and the international transmission of business cycle disturbances: some evidence from the great depression', *Journal of Money, Credit and Banking*, 12.
Clarke, S. V. O. (1967), *Central Bank Cooperation 1924–31*, New York: Federal Reserve Bank of New York.
Clavin, P. (1991), 'The world economic conference 1933: the failure of British internationalism', *Journal of European Economic History*, 20.
Clavin, P. (1992), 'The fetishes of so-called international bankers: central bank cooperation for the world economic conference, 1932–3', *Central European History*, 1.
Condliffe, J. B. (1941), *The Reconstruction of World Trade*, London: Allen and Unwin.
Cooper, R. N. (1982), 'The gold standard: historical facts and future prospects', *Brookings Papers on Economic Activity*, 1.
Costigliola, F. (1976), 'The United States and the reconstruction of Germany in the 1920s', *Business History Review*, 50.
Dunning, J. H. (1970), *Studies in International Investment*, London: Allen and Unwin.
Einzig, P. (1932), *Montagu Norman: a Study in Financial Statesmanship*, London: Kegan Paul, Trench, Trubner and Co.
Elbaum, B. and Lazonick, W. (1984), 'The decline of the British economy: an institutional perspective', *Journal of Economic History*, 44.
Elbaum, B. and Lazonick, W. (1986), *The Decline of the British Economy*, Oxford: Clarendon Press.
Fearon, P. (1979), *The Origins of the Great Slump*, London: Macmillan.
Fink, C. (1984), *The Genoa Conference: European Diplomacy 1921–1922*, Chapel Hill, NC: University of North Carolina Press.
Fischer, W. (1974), 'Die Weimarer Republik under den weltwirtschaftlicher Bedingungen der Zwischenkriegszeit', in H. Mommsen, et al. (eds), *Industrielles System und politische Entwicklung in der Weimarer Republik*, Düsseldorf: Droste Verlag.
Ford, A. G. (1989), 'International financial policy and the gold standard, 1870–1914', in P. Mathias and S. Pollard (eds), *The Cambridge Economic History of Europe*, Vol. VIII, Cambridge: Cambridge University Press.
Foreman-Peck, J. (1983), *A History of the World Economy: International Economic Relations since 1850*, Brighton: Wheatsheaf Books.

Fremling, G. M. (1986), 'A specie-flow model of the gold standard', *Journal of Money and Finance, 5.*

Friedman, M. and Schwartz, A. J. (1963), *A Monetary History of the United States, 1867–1960*, Princeton, NJ: Princeton University Press.

Giovannini, A. (1986), 'Rules of the game during the international gold standard: England and Germany', *Journal of Money and Finance, 5.*

Harris, C. R. S. (1935), *Germany's Foreign Indebtedness*, Oxford, Oxford University Press.

Hughes, M. L. (1988), *Paying for the German Inflation*, Chapel Hill, NC: University of North Carolina Press.

James, H. (1986), *The German Slump: Politics and Economics, 1924–1936*, Oxford: Oxford University Press.

Kaser, M. C. and Radice, E. A. (eds) (1985), *The Economic History of Eastern Europe 1919–1975*, Vol. I, *Economic Structure and Performance between the Wars*, Oxford: Oxford University Press.

Kaser, M. C. and Radice, E. A. (eds) (1986), *The Economic History of Eastern Europe 1919–1975*, Vol. II, *Interwar Policy, the War and Reconstruction*, Oxford: Oxford University Press.

Kemmerer, E. W. (1944), *Gold and the Gold Standard*, New York: McGraw-Hill.

Keynes, J. M. (1920), *The Economic Consequences of the Peace*, London: Macmillan.

Kooker, J. L. (1976), 'French financial diplomacy: the interwar years', in B. M. Rowland (ed.), *Balance of Power or Hegemony: the Interwar Monetary System*, New York: New York University Press.

Kunz, D. (1987), *The Battle for Britain's Gold Standard in 1931*, London: Croom Helm.

League of Nations (1920), *Currencies after the War: a Survey of Conditions in Various Countries*, Geneva: League of Nations.

League of Nations (1942), *Commercial Policy in the Inter-War Period*, Geneva: League of Nations.

League of Nations (1944), *International Currency Experience: Lessons of the Inter-War Period*, Geneva: League of Nations.

League of Nations (1945), *Industrialisation and Foreign Trade*, Geneva: League of Nations.

League of Nations (1946), *The Course and Control of Inflation: a Review of Monetary Experience in Europe After the First World War*, Geneva: League of Nations.

Llewellyn, D. T. and Presley, J. R. (1995), 'The role of hegemonic arrangements in the evolution of the international monetary system', in J. Reis (ed.), *International Monetary Systems in Historical Perspective*, Basingstoke: Macmillan.

Loveday, A. (1931), *Britain and World Trade,* London: Longmans, Green.

Maizels, A. (1963), *Industrial Growth and World Trade*, Cambridge: Cambridge University Press.

Marks, S. (1976), *The Illusion of Peace: International Relations in Europe, 1918–1933*, London: Macmillan.

McCloskey, D. N. and Zecher, J. R. (1976), 'How the gold standard worked, 1880–1913', in J. A. Frenkel and H. G. Johnson (eds), *The Monetary Approach to the Balance of Payments*, London: Allen and Unwin.

McDougall, W. A. (1979), 'Political economy versus national sovereignty: French structures for German integration after Versailles', *Journal of Modern History,* 4.

McKinnon, R. I. (1993), 'The rules of the game: international money in historical perspective', *Journal of Economic Literature*, 31.

Milward, A. S. (1974), 'Bericht', in H. Mommsen et al. (eds), *Industrielles System und politische Entwicklung in der Weimarer Republik*, Düsseldorf: Droste Verlag.

Moggridge, D. E. (1992), *Maynard Keynes; an Economist's Biography*, London: Routledge.

Moulton, H. G. and Pasvolsky, L. (1932), *War Debts and World Prosperity*, Washington, DC: Brookings Institution.

Mouré, K. (1992), 'The limits to central bank cooperation 1916–36', *Contemporary European History*, 1.

Nautz, J. (1994), 'Between political disintegration and economic reintegration: Austrian trade relations with the successor states after world war I', in D. F. Good (ed.), *Economic Transformations in East and Central Europe: Legacies from the Past and Policies for the Future*, London: Routledge.

North, D. C. (1962), 'International capital movements in historical perspective', in R. F. Mikesell (ed.), *U. S. Private and Government Investment Abroad*, Eugene, OR: University of Oregon Books.

Ohlin, B. (1931), *The Course and Phases of the World Economic Depression*, Geneva: League of Nations.

Orde, A. (1990), *British Policy and European Reconstruction after the First World War*, Cambridge: Cambridge University Press.

Péteri, G. (1992), 'Central bank diplomacy: Montagu Norman and Central Europe's monetary reconstruction after world war I', *Contemporary European History*, 1

Petzina, D. and Abelshauser, W. (1974), 'Zum Problem der relativen Stagnation der deutschen Wirtschaft in den zwanziger Jahren', in H. Mommsen, et al. (eds), *Industrielles System und politische Entwicklung in der Weimarer Republik*, Düsseldorf: Droste Verlag.

Pigou, A. C. (1920), 'Memorandum on credit, currency and exchange fluctuations', Paper prepared in connection with the Brussels International Conference at the request of the Secretariat of the League of Nations, Geneva, Geneva, League of Nations.

Preston, H. H. (1931), 'Europe's return to gold', *Harvard Business Review*, 9.

Raupach, H. (1969), 'The impact of the great depression on Eastern Europe', *Journal of Contemporary History*, 4.

Ross, G. (1983), *The Great Powers and the Decline of the European States System 1914–1945*, London: Longman.

Rostow, W. W. (1978), *The World Economy: History and Prospect*, London: Macmillan.

Rostow, W. W. (1980), *Why the Poor Get Richer and the Rich Slow Down: Essays in the Marshallian Long Period*, London: Macmillan.

Royal Institute of International Affairs (1937), *The Problem of International Investment*, Oxford: Oxford University Press.

Schedwin, C. B. (1970), *Australia and the Great Depression: a Study of the Economic Development and Policy in the 1920s and 1930s*, Sydney: University of Sydney Press.

Schmidt, C. T. (1934), *German Business Cycles 1924–1933*, New York: National Bureau of Economic Research.

Schuker, S. A. (1988), *American Reparations to Germany 1919–33: Implications for the Third World Debt Crisis*, Princeton, NJ: Princeton University Press.

Silverman, D. P. (1982), *Reconstructing Europe after the Great War*, Cambridge, MA: Harvard University Press.

Svennilson, I. (1954), *Growth and Stagnation in the European Economy*, Geneva: United Nations.

Triffin, R. (1968), *Our International Monetary System: Yesterday, Today and Tomorrow*, New York: Random House.

United Nations (1949), *International Capital Movements during the Interwar Period*, New York: United Nations.

United Nations (1955), *Foreign Capital in Latin America*, New York: United Nations.

van der Wee, H. and Tavernier, K. (1975), *La Banque Nationale de Belgique: l'histoire monétaire entre les deux guerres mondiales*, Brussels: Banque Nationale de Belgique.

Yates, P. L. (1959), *Forty Years of Foreign Trade*, London: Allen and Unwin.

Yeager, L. B. (1966), *International Monetary Relations: Theory, History and Policy*, New York: Harper and Row.

CHAPTER THREE

Inflation, Currency Depreciation and Reconstruction in Europe

Introduction

For several years after the guns along the western front had ceased firing, most European countries experienced inflationary pressures of varying degrees of intensity and of varying duration (Preston, 1931, pp. 319–21). These ranged from the nightmare conditions of hyperinflation in Germany, Austria, Hungary, Poland and Russia, to the lengthy but somewhat milder inflations in France, Belgium, Italy and several other countries. By contrast, only in the UK and in the Scandinavian countries were orthodox deflationary policies adopted soon after the war to eradicate inflationary pressures and prepare the way for a return to the gold standard at the prewar parity.

From a technical point of view inflations of the magnitude experienced in Europe in the postwar period could only have arisen through loss of control over the money supply. It follows therefore that inflation could have been brought to a halt at any time had the money-creating proclivities of governments and central banks been curbed (Cagan, 1956). However, one must recognise that there were several factors which made it difficult to achieve this goal in the immediate aftermath of war. Economic, social and political conditions were such that rigid and orthodox financial policies were precluded in many cases. In several countries, especially in Germany, Hungary, Poland and Austria, conditions were so deplorable that draconian measures to check inflation with their attendant results in terms of depression and unemployment, would probably have caused a collapse of the social fabric (Einzig, 1935, p. 51; Feldman, 1975, 1977, p. 463). Weak governments, inefficient administrations, heavy spending and limited tax bases made it almost impossible to rein in public expenditure, apart from which the needs of reconstruction and recovery forced governments to pursue active fiscal policies. In Germany, of course, special factors such as reparations presented an additional problem.

While inflation may not have been deliberately chosen initially as a policy weapon to aid reconstruction, it soon came to be seen as a relatively painless way of easing some of the more pressing postwar problems (Feldman, 1993, p. 838). Maier (1975, p. 590) sees it as a tempting if spurious way of purchasing social peace. Schuker (1976, p. 12) notes that once hyperinflation was in full swing in Germany, business and government leaders found a serious practical reason to justify their reluctance to stabilise the currency. Stabilisation meant deflation, unemployment, reduced profits and possibly social unrest. Furthermore, the political balance was so precarious and the threats to the Weimar Republic so serious that until the final monetary collapse came in the autumn of 1923, fearful men in weak positions did not dare take the risks inherent in decisive action.

In broad terms, therefore, one could argue that the pressing problems of reconstruction and the need to maintain social harmony forced governments to pursue policies that exacerbated the inflationary momentum which had its origins in the methods adopted for financing wartime hostilities. However, it is not the purpose of this chapter to discuss the motives for inflation or the problems of stabilisation. The main issue here is to determine whether inflation was a help or hindrance to the reconstruction process and whether the costs outweighed the benefits. The mechanics of inflation along with the methods used to stabilise currencies in this period have already been discussed in some depth by various writers, especially with respect to Germany, but the contribution of inflation to the reconstruction and recovery of Europe has been less adequately explored, at least outside Germany, while in the latter case it has given rise to some controversy as to its impact (Eichengreen, 1986).

Most contemporary observers were more concerned about the adverse effects of inflation and currency depreciation than any potential benefits they might bestow on the economy (Loveday, 1931, p. 31; Pigou, 1920, p. 12). Keynes, for example, was well aware of the dangers to the revival of trade and investment after the war from extreme price and exchange instability, and in his memorandum on the exchanges of 1922 he advocated that the main European exchanges should be stabilised as soon as possible with other countries following later (Moggridge, 1992, pp. 377–8, 382–3). However, the contrast between inflating and deflating countries in terms of economic activity and employment in the early 1920s did not escape the notice of contemporary writers even though few were prepared to advocate unsound financial policies to achieve a boost to recovery. Later writers, no doubt conditioned by the inflationary experience of the postwar period, were inclined to follow the traditional wisdom of interwar commentators. There have been a few exceptions. The most remarkable, given popular conceptions about hyperinflation, was Laursen and Pedersen's (1964) study of Germany in which they argued that Germany secured a net gain from hyperinflation (see below). More recently, Eichengreen (1986) has argued the case for a favourable inflationary scenario: 'price-level changes exercised a powerful influence over the economic recovery of the industrial nations in the 1920s. Those countries marked by moderate inflation expanded more rapidly and recovered more quickly from the after-effects of the First World War than did those which endured deflation'. Based on a sample of 13 countries he finds a positive relationship between inflation and depreciated exchange rates on the one hand, and economic performance on the other. Three inflationary countries (France, Belgium and Italy) are juxtaposed against ten countries that did not experience sustained inflation: Canada, the United States, Australia, Japan and six European (Sweden, Denmark, Norway, the UK, The Netherlands and Spain). Two years earlier Broadberry (1984) concluded that overvalued exchange rates were largely responsible for the poor economic performance of the UK and Scandinavian countries. Finally, Solomou (1996, ch. 2) distinguishes between the short-run and long-term effects of exchange rate movements. He maintains that the cyclical recovery paths of France, Belgium and Italy were indistinguishable from countries such as the United States, Sweden and Japan which did not experience prolonged depreciation of their currencies. On the other hand, countries with depreciated rates relative to their 1913 parities received a favourable long-term stimulus compared with those countries constrained by prewar exchange rate values. However, one advantage for countries returning to gold at the prewar parity levels and averting sustained inflation was that they were less inhibited in their policy response to the great depression.

The general conclusion from more recent studies seems to be that inflation and currency depreciation were better than fiscal and monetary prudence in activating recovery. However, apart from Germany, the hyperinflationary countries are excluded from the accounts. Secondly, some of the studies use partial indicators of performance and it is not clear that a sharp distinction can be made between the prewar parity brigade of countries and those that experienced moderate inflations. Thirdly, there is very limited attempt to take account of the wider and longer-term implications of inflation, or to assess fully what happens when stabilisation takes place.

Here we shall deal with four hyperinflationary countries (Germany, Austria, Hungary and Poland) and two moderate inflators (France and Belgium) and then compare performance with European countries which avoided sustained inflation. Before turning to the case studies, a brief discussion of the ways in which inflation may influence real economic variables is apposite.

Inflation and growth

Whether inflation is good or bad for growth has been a much debated issue since the sharp acceleration in inflation during the 1970s. The experience of recent decades suggests that it has not been particularly favourable for the economy. However, the historical record on this issue throws up mixed findings. There appears to be no unambiguous relationship between inflation on the one hand and growth and employment on the other. Indeed, there are many examples in the post-1945 period where rapid inflation has been accompanied by high rates of economic growth (Dawson, 1992, p. 129). Nor is there any a priori consistency regarding the groups and individuals who are likely to gain or lose from inflation (Bootle, 1981; Higham and Tomlinson, 1982). However, this does not mean that inflation is always good for growth. Rather it suggests that what matters are the conditions under which inflation takes place that are important since it is these which will determine the probable outcome for the economy.

It is possible to specify the circumstances under which an economy will benefit, at least temporarily, from an inflationary regime. According to rational expectations theory, real effects can flow from an inflationary monetary policy providing the monetary shock is unanticipated. However, if the change in monetary regime is fully anticipated and all economic agents respond simultaneously there will be no change in relative prices and all that will happen is that the general level of prices will rise while real output remains the same. On the other hand, real output changes in the former scenario will only materialise providing economic agents respond differentially to an unanticipated monetary change. The most favourable situation will occur where capital responds more quickly than labour to the monetary shock.

Thus if capital has a higher learning curve and adjusts its selling prices faster than the price of labour it will gain at the expense of labour; capital's share of total income will rise and there is a good chance that output and employment will respond favourably. This situation is based on the assumption that firms' input costs rise more slowly than final product prices, principally because wage costs lag behind selling prices and the cost of living. An additional assumption is that price flexibility prevails with few administrative controls over price formation. In this situation profit margins improve and firms are willing to increase output and investment and recruit more labour. If inflation is rapid and interest rates turn negative, this will further encourage a shift of resources into fixed assets. Another important influence is the behaviour of the exchange rate. If this falls faster than the internal price level is rising, it will stimulate the export sector.

These conditions do not always hold under all inflationary conditions, in which case inflation can do more harm than good. For example, in the moderately inflationary experience of the 1970s, industry's selling prices lagged behind input costs, especially those of labour, because of the presence of strong real wage resistance and a slow learning curve on the part of employers with respect to the need for price adjustments. Labour therefore gained at the expense of capital, profits were severely squeezed and hence investment and employment were adversely affected. Moreover, the uncertainty prompted by the sudden upsurge in inflation also helped to check investment. Further adverse influences were the trends in consumption and savings. Consumption was depressed because savings ratios rose as people tried to restore the real value of their savings. Finally, after initial hesitation, governments adopted policies to bring inflation under control and this also tended to squeeze profits.

By contrast, the ingredients for a favourable response were present for the most part in both hyperinflationary and moderate inflationary countries in the 1920s. Capital gained at the expense of labour primarily because real wages were held back so that input costs lagged behind product prices and business made good profits. Rapid inflation and negative real interest rates also encouraged a flight into real assets, while periodic plunges in the exchange rate gave a boost to exports. Furthermore, until the stabilisation of currencies was instituted, there were few administrative controls to disturb market forces. In other words, business firms were free to adjust their prices and keep one step ahead of input costs. Though here one should contrast the situation with that of rentiers, whose ability to exploit the inflationary potential was thwarted by administrative controls on the level of rents, especially in Germany. Hence, landlords did very badly indeed.

A second main channel of influence was the public sector. For a time governments took advantage of the inflationary potential to ease their own financial problems and encourage the process of reconstruction. Technically inflation could have been brought to a halt at any time by resolute policies to check the growth in money supply. But in the difficult circumstances of the postwar years when governments were strapped for cash to meet the demands of reconstruction and social relief, monetising fiscal deficits or printing money was seen as a politically expedient way of providing the state with real resources at a time when governments lacked the strength or the will to impose adequate taxation systems to provide for their revenue needs. Issuing money was a less painful option than taxation in a difficult social climate since it provided revenue through a special kind of tax on real money balances. It was an attempt by governments to extract an additional amount of real revenue from the economy by means of an inflation tax (Jacobs, 1977, p. 295). The tax base was equivalent to the volume of real cash balances in public hands, while the tax rate was determined by the rate of depreciation in the value of money, which in turn was equivalent to the rate at which prices rose. In other words, the revenue collected in real terms was the product of the rate of increase in prices (the tax rate) and the volume of real cash balances (the tax base).

While politically more acceptable than conventional taxation in the conditions of the time, and also easier to administer, the effectiveness of this system of tax gathering tended to diminish over time and hence ever larger doses of monetary growth and inflation were required to keep the process going. As prices rose in response to an increase in the monetary stock then ever increasing volumes of money issue were required to maintain the desired level of real revenue. Webb (1989, p. 48) estimates that the revenue-maximising inflation rate averaged 30 per cent a month for the years 1919–23, with a range of 22–45 per cent. In other words, up to that ceiling governments could extract greater real resources from the economy by issuing more debt, but thereafter diminishing returns set in and so the real revenue from the inflation tax declined. Once the government exceeded the optimal limit, then the process exploded into hyperinflation. Thus taken to its limits, the state's ability to generate real revenue diminished sharply as it exceeded the optimum tax point, prices soared and the unit of currency became worthless (Brown, 1988, p. 122; Cagan, 1956, pp. 77–90; Horsman, 1988, p. 234; Jacobs, 1977).

Even under the favourable scenario outlined above one cannot, of course, automatically conclude that the temporary boost to output and employment generated by inflation is a good thing for the economy and society in the long term. For one thing the distribution of gains may be so skewed that a majority of the population lose out in the process. Secondly, in severe inflations the stampede to acquire assets of any sort to preserve values may lead to speculative accumulation which is not in the best long-term interests of the economy. Thirdly, when stabilisation finally takes place the economy will tend to move into recession so that many of the previous gains are wiped out. Historical experience with controlling inflation provides little reason to suppose that a real output crunch can be avoided in the immediate post-stabilisation period (Gordon, 1982, p. 11). Finally, severe inflations may have serious political and social consequences for society.

Germany

Germany's inflation was the most spectacular and one about which the most has been written. At the end of the period prices had risen by one million million times compared with 4 000 million in Russia, 2.5 million in Poland, 23 000 times in Hungary and 14 000 times in Austria. Though inflation had initially emerged as a result of inept wartime financing, the later stages of the drama can be seen not so much as an act of deliberate policy but rather as an attempt to exploit the inflationary potential arising from the monetary financing of the growth of government debt in the context of the very difficult conditions of the time (Feldman, 1993, p. 838; Webb, 1985, p. 490; cf. Ferguson, 1995, p. 476). Feldman (1992, pp. 78–9) sees the inflationary policies of the years 1918–23 as being motivated by the urgency of stabilising the political system and at the same time reconstructing the economy. However, the final stages in 1923 were very much determined by the reparations issue. Hardach (1980, p. 23) believes that this was primarily responsible for the ultimate catastrophe. Resort to the printing press was an overt demonstration that Germany could not meet the Allied demands for 'threatened by Allied sanctions on the one hand and by the disintegration of the Reich on the other, no German government could have complied with Reparation demands in any way other than resort to the printing press' (Holtfrerich, 1986, p. 153). The final collapse of the currency came in the autumn of 1923, following the Ruhr occupation by the French and Belgians on the pretext of a minor shortfall on reparation payments in kind.

Given the longer-term social and political consequences of this episode, one's immediate reaction is to say that it was a bad thing for all concerned and to conclude that the country made a net loss on the deal. Certainly many people suffered badly in the final phases of inflation and the experience left a lasting bitterness in many people's minds. However, opinion is still somewhat divided on this issue; some writers have been more favourably disposed to the beneficial impact of inflation, at least in terms of the way in which it stimulated activity and employment in contrast to the deflationary climate in the Anglo-Saxon countries in the early 1920s (Feldman, 1983, p. 388; Holtfrerich, 1986, chs 7–9). In fact one or two authors have even concluded that there was a net gain to society (Graham, 1930, pp. 320–24; Laursen and Pedersen, 1964, pp. 123–6).

The case in support of this claim rests substantially on a comparison with countries that carried out restrictive credit and fiscal policies. Had Germany adopted the latter policy approach after 1920, there would have been serious unemployment which, given the poverty of the

German population at the time coupled with its revolutionary mood, would probably have led to serious political and social upheavals. As it was, the outcome in terms of welfare was favourable in comparison with those countries which followed an anti-inflation strategy. A high level of employment was maintained, industrial production and real income were higher than under any alternative system proposed at the time (while its distribution was probably more egalitarian), capital accumulation was encouraged, probably more so than under a full employment non-inflationary state, and less was paid on reparations. Laursen and Pedersen do point out, however, that conditions could have been better without inflation if economic management had been able to find policies which would ensure full employment without inflation. In the absence of these, they argue, it was better to have inflation rather than sacrifice employment opportunities.

Their case appears to rest on tenuous grounds even though initially Germany gained from the inflationary conditions. Between 1919 and 1922 output, industrial production and exports all rose strongly and unemployment fell to small proportions. What is especially noteworthy is that Germany avoided the sharp postwar slump of 1921–22 that was such a marked feature of the countries pursuing deflationary policies. By the middle of 1922 unemployment in Germany was under 1 per cent as against double figure levels in Britain, Sweden, Norway and The Netherlands.

However, the performance was by no means as good as the unemployment figures would seem to imply. While Germany may have gained initially in so far as she did not suffer a contraction crisis after the postwar boom of 1919–20, she made up for this in 1923 when income and production were checked sharply. Industrial production collapsed in the latter part of that year and for the year as a whole it was only about half the 1913 volume, even less than in 1920 (Czada, 1974, pp. 386–95). The same was true of national income which by the end of 1923 was barely half that of the 1913 level. Estimates of total output and income for the crisis year vary somewhat but there is no doubt that the trend was sharply down. Maddison's estimate for total output for that year, at 79 per cent of 1913, is probably somewhat high given the disastrous setback in the latter part of that year (see Table 3.1 on p. 75). A more realistic income measure for 1923 as a whole would be around 70 per cent of the prewar figure (Schmidt, 1934, p. 14; Witt, 1974, p. 424).

The poor performance was not confined to 1923. Despite the inflationary boost to activity, income and production levels remained well below those of prewar throughout the years 1920–23, while exports were barely one-half their prewar volume (Angell, 1929, pp. 33–45;

Mendershausen, 1955, ch. 1; OEEC, 1960, p. 9). As a glance at Tables 3.1 and 3.2 (pp. 75 and 76) will demonstrate this dismal record cannot be matched by any of the major countries, not even those which pursued counter-inflationary policies on their way back to gold!

The working classes had no great cause for celebration despite the fact that most of them were employed for a time. They suffered from the slow adjustment of wages to inflation with the result that real wages fell almost continuously from 1919 to 1923, by which time they were barely two-thirds those of 1913. During the most intense phase of inflation real wages fell to 50 per cent of the prewar level (Bry, 1960, p. 230; Feldman, 1993, p. 614). Civil servants and salaried employees also fared badly (Kunz, 1982, pp. 371–2). Wages earners were also the biggest losers from the tax system since under current assessment (PAYE) they paid 100 per cent of their tax in real terms, while other taxpayers on lagged assessments paid very much less tax in real terms, 36 per cent in 1920 and 19 and 27 per cent respectively in the years 1921 and 1922 (Witt, 1983, pp. 459–62). For many therefore it meant poverty and even starvation. Since the main gainers tended to be debtors, businessmen and clever asset speculators, it follows that the distribution of income turned against the wage and salary earning classes.

Moreover, full employment was only a transitory phenomenon. It is true that unemployment was low in 1921 and 1922 when production was rising from a very low base at a time when the reverse was the case in the deflationary countries. However, partial unemployment was said to be fairly pervasive because of work-sharing practices encouraged by the government (Moulton and McGuire, 1923, p. 125). But even the good employment conditions did not last for ever. Germany reaped the harvest in 1923 and 1924. Unemployment among trade union members in 1923 shot up dramatically during the course of the year, from 4.2 per cent in January to 19.1 per cent in October, and to a peak of 26–28 per cent early in 1924, a rate which was more than double that of other west European countries. The real unemployment rate was probably much higher, however, since many workers were on short time or reduced pay (Ferguson, 1995, p. 384). For the decade as a whole the level of unemployment was no better than that of other countries (Bry, 1960, p. 230; Dornbusch, 1987, pp. 349–50; Fergusson, 1975, p. 208; Lundberg, 1968, p. 32; Wiggs, 1933, p. 210).

All the evidence seems to indicate that real wages and per capita consumption of basic commodities were much lower throughout the years of inflation than they had been before the war and that real wages, despite some improvement following stabilisation, did not regain their former level until as late as 1928. Bry's original conclusion is still basically sound:

> All in all, it can be said that both the index numbers of industrial production and the scattered data on per capita consumption tend to corroborate the broad findings on real wages during inflation. These levels were substantially below, and during the last phases of the crisis pitifully below, the real wages that prevailed before the outbreak of World War I.
>
> (Bry, 1960, p. 233)

The surprising thing is that German trade unions did not show any very resolute resistance to the government's financial and tax policies. Born (1977, p. 115) suggests that they were kept docile by the favourable employment conditions. Yet this seems a rather weak argument in view of the generally deteriorating conditions for the working classes during the inflation period and the sharp reversal of the favourable employment situation in 1923 and 1924. Moreover, it seems to conflict with the evidence on industrial strife. During the inflation years there were more working days lost by industrial disputes than at any other time through the period 1900–33 (Ferguson, 1995, p. 425). Contrariwise, if the bulk of the population had been relatively quiescent in these years there would be less strength in the argument that social revolution would have been caused by policies designed to bring an earlier end to inflation.

Perhaps the worst sufferers from inflation were rentiers and savers, or at least those who failed to shift their money into fixed assets which would be revalorised when the currency was stabilised. Property owners were very badly hit (Ferguson, 1995, pp. 426–7). Rent control coupled with inflation reduced the value of rents to less than 1 per cent of prewar values. One Hamburg landlord reckoned that in 1923 it required an entire month's taking from all his apartments to replace one broken toilet seat (Lyth, 1990, p. 135)! Many petty rentiers were left in dire straits and were forced to depend on public relief. Hughes (1988, p. 22) suggests that possibly as many as half a million were in this situation by the end of 1921. Liquid savings and social insurance contributions vanished without trace so that many middle- and lower middle-class families lost their entire life's savings. They received derisory compensation in the post-stabilisation period and it was this embittered *Mittelstand* group which was instrumental in bringing about the disintegration of the Weimar political system (see Childers, 1982, 1983a, 1983b; Hughes, 1982, 1988; Jones, 1972, 1979, 1980, 1989).

By contrast, the business community, and especially big business, was the principal beneficiary from inflation, largely at the expense of the workers, small traders and savers. Profits were buoyant since costs, especially wages, lagged behind selling prices, real interests rates were negative, debts were wiped out and exporters gained from currency depreciation. But the feverish industrial activity of the period, which has been so much acclaimed, was more apparent than real. Hardach (1980, p. 21) refers to it as 'a sham boom'. It is true that many new concerns came into being, bankruptcies were very low, while investment in plant and equipment appeared to be buoyant. However, though output rose from a very low base, it still remained well below the prewar level, while productivity declined (Schmidt, 1934, pp. 14–15). Exchange depreciation may have helped exports in the inflationary bursts, though here the benefits can be exaggerated. The main trade gain through currency depreciation occurred early on in 1919–20 when the gap between German and foreign prices was at its most favourable. Thereafter the relative price advantage was never as favourable despite further currency depreciation, while buoyant domestic activity sucked in imports faster than the rise in exports. Export volumes remained well below the prewar level in the inflation years and, in fact, rose faster during the post-stabilisation period (Ferguson, 1995, pp. 409–10; Maddison, 1991, p. 316). Given the surge in imports, currency depreciation probably did not overly protect German industrialists from foreign competition, but the lag in labour costs dampened technical progress and mechanisation, so that part of the gain in employment was at the expense of efficiency (Ringer, 1969, p. 85). In any case, the inflationary boom, such as it was, was nearing its end by the autumn of 1922 and it is clear that its collapse was well under way before passive resistance to the Ruhr occupation made it complete. The year 1923 was a total disaster when industrial output plunged to less than 50 per cent of the prewar level (Feldman, 1993, p. 838).

If for a time German industry benefited from inflation it is clear that the benefits were fast receding by late 1922, and from then on they became negative in the Ruhr occupation period and in the stabilisation crisis which followed. In the end inflation and its aftermath probably hindered rather than promoted industrial reconstruction since once stabilisation took place it had to begin afresh. As Hardach (1984, p. 210) notes: 'In the end, inflation had delayed the return to normal economic conditions in Germany by several years compared to other countries.' Webb (1989, p. 102) reckons that while it may have saved parliamentary government and eased the lot of the common man (though quite how is a mystery), it did not greatly advance the strength of the German economy. In the years following the currency reform and the new reparations arrangements (the Dawes Plan of 1924) Germany made a relatively slow recovery. Industrial output and national income did not regain prewar levels until 1927, unemployment remained high, and savings and investment were lower than before the war. The savings ratio was much lower than previously, averaging 8.5 per cent in 1925–29 as against 15.5 per cent in the decade or so before 1913 (Balderston,

1982). Though fixed debts had been cleared away many firms found themselves short of working capital since most liquid capital and savings had been destroyed in the inflation. With memories of the inflation close at hand, the propensity to save remained low after 1923, capital was short and interest rates high so that Germany was forced to borrow heavily abroad in the later 1920s. Restrictive monetary policy also helped to dampen recovery.

There are doubts too about the strength of investment activity during the inflationary period. Despite net depreciation during the war years, investment never regained its prewar share in spending, and it may even have grown faster before the war. Webb (1989, pp. 87–9) concludes that investment did not make an exceptional contribution to growth during the inflation period, while Ferguson (1995, pp. 410–11) marshals an impressive list of reasons to counter the traditional argument that inflation stimulated real investment by business firms. Case studies for iron and steel and the machine-building industries also provide some support for the impression that inflation was not particularly beneficial to industrial investment. Feldman in his seminal study (1993, p. 843) draws a suitably cautious conclusion:

> The condition of German industry certainly would have been worse without the inflationary reconstruction, but it would be a mistake to overestimate the depth of that reconstruction and an even greater mistake to think that its longer-term consequences were as positive as they could have been or should have been.

The qualitative aspects of the industrial expansion provide further grounds for a cautious stance. Though Webb (1989, p. 89) reckoned that there was no great long-term legacy of excess capacity, it would be surprising given the conditions of the time had the investment of this period been optimally structured. We know that much capacity was hastily installed and badly designed and that the inflation spawned many mushroom concerns and unwieldy trusts. The lagged response of interest rates to inflation encouraged the negotiation of loans for dubious projects and schemes, and thus gave rise to many rickety undertakings (Horsman, 1988, p. 13). Feldman (1993, p. 843) refers to the 'host of fly-by-night firms and dubious investments' most of which disappeared once the artificial conditions which had propagated them disappeared. The most spectacular, of course, was the collapse of the famous (infamous) Stinnes Combine whose huge debt structure crumbled once the mark was stabilised. But many other firms shared a similar fate as the soaring bankruptcy statistics demonstrate (Lyth, 1990, pp. 163–4). Thus the pattern of investment was certainly distorted during the inflationary years and not all the investment of this period was in the best long-term interests of the German economy.

Overall therefore, it is difficult to believe that the impact of inflation and stabilisation was anything but adverse for German society as a whole, or that the German position could have been much worse under a more orthodox financial policy (cf. Ferguson, 1995, p. 462, 1996, pp. 659–62). The latter argument would only hold if one believes that classical remedies would have brought on social revolution and a collapse of the regime, as some writers have hinted (Holtfrerich, 1986, p. 137; Schuker, 1976, p. 12; Webb, 1987, p. 430). But whether it was necessary to continue inflation much after 1919 to save German democracy has recently been questioned (Ferguson, 1995, p. 448). In point of fact, during these postwar years Germany had suffered more than five years of turmoil, poverty, starvation and tension which scarcely did much for the wealth and health of the German population (Ringer, 1969, pp. 112–18; Rowley, 1994). As Feldman (1993, p. 837) points out, the legacy of inflation was to be found in every corner of German society and many of the conditions to which it gave rise were to persist well into the future and were to play an important part in the destruction of Weimar democracy. Indeed, for a generation or more the Germans lived under the spectre of inflation and their policy reactions, and those of other inflationary countries, to the 1929–32 depression were conditioned in part by the disastrous episode. Moreover, the structural and financial weaknesses arising from the inflationary episode marked the beginning of the disintegration of Weimar capitalism which was completed in the slump of the early 1930s (Balderston, 1985). Thus, the sacrifices made for a temporary boost to activity and employment seem on balance to have been far too high, especially as Germany had then to suffer many of the stabilisation pangs which had been endured by those countries following deflationary policies from the start.

Austria

Austria's inflation was much less severe than the German and of shorter duration. Strong inflationary pressures had been inherited from the war and the subsequent course of inflation was influenced by weak government and lack of faith in the durability of the new republic which had continuous budgetary deficits between 1919 and 1922 (Rothschild, 1947, pp. 19–23).

Nevertheless, inflation did serve its purpose in the short term by providing a stimulant to the economy. There was a powerful investment, production and export boom which lasted for about three years from late 1919 until the second half of 1922. Industrial production and total output rose strongly from the very low levels recorded in the immediate aftermath of war, while unemployment fell from a peak of 186 030 in May 1919 to a low of 8 709 in November 1921, after which it began to rise again (Nötel, 1984, p. 148; Rothschild, 1947, p. 28).

Most sectors experienced recovery forces and there was an especially strong demand for investment goods, with some branches of industry almost regaining prewar levels of output. Company formation was buoyant: 'new companies shot out of the ground like mushrooms in these favourable conditions of low labour costs, high prices and insatiable consumer demand'. The number of joint stock and limited companies trebled between 1918 and 1923 and there was a big expansion in the capital base through frequent capital issues (Teichova, 1983, p. 556).

Austria became a haven for bargain basement hunters from neighbouring countries taking advantage of the depreciating crown: 'Huge crowds of foreigners exploited the opportunities provided by the convulsing corpse of the Austrian crown' (Brown, 1988, p. 121).

Though the short inflationary boom may well have averted social upheaval, the costs incurred were considerable. By August 1922 the boom had more or less spent itself, at which point the Austrian government appealed to the League of Nations for assistance in stabilising the country's finances and exchange. Nötel (1984, p. 148) describes the repercussions as appalling in terms of disorganisation, the distortion of price relatives and income inequalities. The distribution of gains and losses was very uneven. Throughout the inflation wages lagged well behind the cost of living so that real wages fell to less than one-half of prewar levels at their worst point and in some cases they were below subsistence (Carsten, 1986, p. 47; Rothschild, 1947, p. 27). Even with some recovery later in 1922 they still remained well below prewar standards. The worst affected groups were undoubtedly pensioners and those living on small fixed incomes or savings most of whom were reduced to abject poverty and had to resort to public assistance.

By contrast, huge profits were made by those in business who were adept at timing buying and selling and who moved into fixed assets promptly. Larger concerns had an advantage over the smaller in this process since the latter were less experienced and had fewer opportunities to exploit market conditions. Hence there was a tendency towards greater concentration in industry during this period.

Despite the strong boost to exports the balance of trade remained unfavourable, partly because of the limited supply capability of the economy initially and partly because of the high import content of exports. The fall in world prices 1920–21 also reduced Austria's competitive edge somewhat. On the other hand, the low value of the crown and the strong demand for foreign exchange encouraged the sale of capital assets, especially real estate and industrial shares, so that foreign control of industry increased (Rothschild, 1947, p. 30).

Once stabilisation was achieved in November 1922, stagnation set in, unemployment rose and bankruptcies became common. Within a year one-third of the existing companies had failed and unemployment rose to 167 000 in March 1923 compared with only 30 967 the previous August (Rothschild, 1947, pp. 37–8; Teichova, 1983, pp. 556–9). However, in contrast to the experience of some other countries, the check to activity was short-lived and fairly mild, though it should be noted that the large expansion in capacity in the years 1919–23 proved excessive since in 1924–26 output was only about two-thirds capacity and still some way below the prewar level (Layton and Rist, 1925, p. 15). It was the workers who bore the brunt of the stabilisation crisis. In February 1925 unemployment rose to 193 000 and a year later it was even higher (Mings, 1966, p. 21; Rothschild, 1947, p. 38; Sargent, 1982, pp. 55–6; Wicker, 1986, p. 355). One factor which exacerbated unemployment was the sharp cutback in employment in financial institutions, government service and construction, all major beneficiaries of inflation. In addition, a drive to improve industrial efficiency led to a reduction in manning levels as firms got rid of the excess labour they had taken on when it was cheap (Layton and Rist, 1925, pp. 16–17). In the later 1920s Austria did experience a somewhat firmer recovery, though total output barely surpassed the prewar mark and unemployment never fell below 5 per cent (Maddison, 1982, p. 174; Wicker, 1986, p. 355). In the aftermath of inflation domestic policy remained fairly tight and interest rates high. Private savings fell to negligible levels during the inflation and remained depressed thereafter so that rates of interest charged to industry were excessive: 22 per cent on first-class overdrafts in 1924 and 15 per cent in 1925 (Rothschild, 1947, p. 37).

Most commentators agree that the long-term structural problems of the Austrian economy were not solved by the inflationary episode. If anything it may well have exacerbated them as the character of inflation changed over time more towards that of asset speculation rather than investment in productive facilities. The main preoccupation of business and finance became the timing of transactions, and speculation was more profitable than the planning of long-term investment and technical improvements, hence, structural adjustment was delayed. As already noted, many of the mushroom concerns disappeared once the artificial conditions on which they had thrived evaporated, since they were based on insecure financial foundations. Even the export boom may have had detrimental consequences if Carsten's (1986, p. 47) supposition that it was based on a 'continuous consumption of the country's capital', is correct, though without more detailed knowledge of the course and structure of investment in this period it is impossible to verify this point.

The Austrian experience does not say very much for the benefit of inflation. A temporary boost to activity was secured but at considerable cost to the bulk of the population, serious distortions to income distribution and with little contribution to the restructuring of the economy. It is perhaps significant that overall Austria had one of the worst performing economies in the 1920s; this was in sharp contrast to her neighbour, Czechoslovakia which, admittedly had benefited handsomely from the peace settlement, recorded a strong recovery as a result of early currency stabilisation thereby averting the ravages of serious inflation.

Hungary

Hungary's inflation was greater than that of Austria but considerably less than either Poland's or Germany's. According to Berend and Ranki (1974b, p. 103) it passed from a spontaneous phenomenon to a conscious policy designed to finance reorganisation of the economy after the failure of the first attempt to stem inflation and stabilise the currency in the summer of 1921. Stabilisation was finally achieved three years later with the assistance of the League of Nations.

As in the case of Austria, economic activity and trade were stimulated by inflation though the extent and depth of the boom has sometimes been exaggerated. It is true that virtually every industry apart from clothing recorded an expansion in capacity and many new enterprises were founded (Pasvolsky, 1928, pp. 159–60, 350–52). Cheap loans and a sharp decline in real wages to less than one-half of the prewar level, gave a boost to industrial activity and employment (Berend and Ranki, 1974b, p. 103; Ranki, 1983a, p. 527). The steel, metal and coal industries were especially favoured, while employment and output in manufacturing as a whole rose by about one-third (Berend and Ranki, 1974a, p. 199).

However, the main impact was concentrated in one year, 1922, after which manufacturing activity relapsed quite sharply. Even by 1924, after some recovery, it was still only around 65 per cent of the prewar level while between 1921 and 1924 it had risen by a mere 5 per cent (Boross, 1994, p. 129; League of Nations, 1945, pp. 134–7). Real wages remained depressed and unemployment rose sharply following monetary reform in the summer of 1924; estimates vary but Wicker (1986, pp. 350, 356–7) suggests unemployment among trade unionists doubled within a year, to 12 per cent or more, and remained high until late 1926. As in the case of Austria, there was a big shake-out of labour from financial institutions and government service.

Though there was undoubtedly some increase in industrial capacity during the inflation, as the value of currency declined capital moved away from the productive sector and investment was diverted increasingly into speculative financial activities including share transactions on the stock exchange (Berend and Ranki, 1974a, p. 198). The major beneficiaries were the property-owning classes who could protect themselves from the ravages of inflation, while large landowners were able to pay off their prewar debts in worthless paper money (Ranki, 1983a, p. 527). Those dependent on wage earnings and income from savings fared very badly indeed.

Thus the benefit from inflation was relatively short-lived and did little to solve the fundamental problem of capital shortage in Hungary. The post-stabilisation recession was quite severe and further delayed readjustment of the country to its new boundaries. On the other hand, Hungary's situation was never as serious as that of Austria since it had a more balanced economy and in the later 1920s it performed somewhat better than Austria (Boross, 1994, p. 221).

Poland

Given Poland's desperate state after the war it is scarcely surprising that monetary chaos occurred. Few countries were devastated as badly as Poland since much of the country had been affected by war operations in one way or another, added to which the new republic had the difficult task of welding together three disparate segments formerly under the control of Germany, Russia and Austro-Hungary, at a time of continuing border hostilities and limited resources. Large budgetary deficits therefore arose and these could only be covered by the issue of money as governments came to recognise this as a useful tool in the reconstruction process (Roszkowski, 1989, p. 107). Several attempts were made to stabilise the currency and eliminate inflation before success was finally achieved in 1927. However, after 1923 the main inflationary thrust was over to all intents and purposes (League of Nations, 1946, pp. 106–11).

Since economic activity was so depressed in the immediate postwar years, with industrial output a mere 35 per cent of the prewar level (Roszkowski, 1986, p. 288), inflation could scarcely fail to have a favourable impact. By all accounts physical reconstruction proceeded rapidly in the early 1920s and was nearing completion by the middle of the decade, while steady progress had been made towards unifying the country since inflation had a positive influence in levelling costs and wages throughout the country (Landau, 1992, pp. 152–3). Industrial employment rose by 135 per cent between 1920 and 1922, to around 82 per cent of the prewar level, while unemployment had been virtually eliminated by the time hyperinflation took hold in the latter half of 1923 (Ranki, 1983b, p. 481). Currency depreciation helped Poland to re-establish itself in the domestic market and also to exploit the markets of more stable currencies. The inflation tax was an important source of government income, accounting for two-thirds of budgetary revenues in the years 1918–23. A large part of the proceeds was distributed by the State in the form of subsidies and credits, many of which became more or less outright gifts due to the rapid decline in the value of money. The main beneficiaries were business and the propertied classes who gained at the expense of the rest of the population. The impact on the peasant community was somewhat mixed, with gains arising from diminished tax and debt burdens offset by losses on savings and deteriorating terms of trade (Landau, 1983, pp. 514–18, 1984; Zweig, 1944, p. 32).

Landau (1983, p. 513) reckons that the overall balance sheet is difficult to determine, though it would seem apparent that the majority of the population paid the price for a temporary increase in employment opportunities. Wage, salary and professional workers, as well as those living on fixed, unearned incomes, could not easily protect themselves against inflation. Initially the burden of inflation appears to have been fairly evenly distributed, but by late 1923 this was no longer the case. The working classes bore a large share of the inflation tax (40 per cent), while real wages fell dramatically after 1921, to about half the prewar level in 1923 compared with 98 per cent in the first half of 1921, though even this was better than the 30 per cent recorded in 1919 (Landau, 1983, pp. 517–18). Judging by the amount of social unrest in Poland in the latter half of 1923, when waves of revolutionary activity broke out in the country, inflation had certainly lost any appeal it might have once had for the working classes.

The prolonged stabilisation process resulted in stagnation. Manufacturing output fell sharply in 1924, rose slightly in 1925 and dropped again in the following year by which time it was barely 60 per cent of the prewar level. Even by the end of the decade it was still only 86 per cent, the worst performance of any East European country (Aldcroft and Morewood, 1995, p. 44; League of Nations, 1945, pp. 134–7). Unemployment rose to over 350 000 by early 1926, as against a low of 52 000 at the peak of inflation (October 1923), which was worse than that recorded in the immediate postwar period (Jack, 1927, p. 187; Landau, 1983, p. 518).

France and Belgium

So far we have only considered countries which experienced runaway inflation. If we turn to some of the countries that had moderate to strong inflations there is some evidence to suggest that the impact was more beneficial and lasting than in the case of the hyperinflationary countries. Of the western powers the two most severely affected by wartime devastation were France and Belgium.

France emerged from the war almost bankrupt with large debts and most of her foreign investments either lost or liquidated. Around 10 per cent of French territory was actually devastated, including some of her most valuable resources; while industrial and agricultural output fell to between 30 and 40 per cent below that of 1913, and exports were but a fraction of the prewar level. The French economy was probably more severely crippled than those of her adjacent neighbours with the possible exception of Belgium (Ogburn and Jaffé, 1929, pp. 20–23). By 1919 the franc had lost 50 per cent of its former purchasing power and much worse was to follow. The main consolation was that France recovered the important industrial area of Alsace-Lorraine and could look forward to reparations from Germany.

Despite the setback France made a remarkable recovery. By 1923 the volume of exports had recovered to the prewar level, while two years later they were almost one-quarter larger than in 1913. Industrial output nearly doubled between 1921 and 1924 by which time the previous peak had been surpassed. Estimates of real income or output are open to debate but it seems likely that these were some 10 per cent greater than prewar by the middle of the 1920s (League of Nations, 1945, pp. 134–7; Maddison, 1982, pp. 174–5, 250–1; Markovitch, 1966, p. 170; Sauvy, 1965, p. 282). Agriculture did not share in the recovery to the same extent and so declined in relative importance.

There is little doubt that, despite periodic financial and currency difficulties, France made a fairly good recovery in the first half of the 1920s when inflation and currency depreciation proceeded apace. By all accounts physical reconstruction was achieved quite rapidly, helped along by generous government assistance on the assumption that Germany would foot the bill through reparation payments. At the end of 1921, 80 per cent of the damaged industrial establishments of any size had recommenced operations, and a start had been made in erecting new capacity in the devastated areas of the north (Davis, 1921, p. 224). By 1925 a large part of the reconstruction work had been completed. Much importance is usually attached to the considerable transformation and modernisation of France's industrial structure during these years, especially in metallurgy, chemicals and the new potential growth sectors. Heavy investment in new equipment and modern technology made French industry somewhat more efficient than before 1914 (Martin, 1927; Kemp, 1972, pp. 67–71; Ogburn and Jaffé, 1929, p. 120). The adoption of new techniques and mechanisation were encouraged by the shortage of labour which was partly eased by immigration. The government contributed substantially to the reconstruction and modernisation programme which helped to 'shake up' French industrialists and reduce their resistance to change. Though the extent of the transformation has probably been exaggerated, there is no doubt that French industry was very active in this period.

Inflation and currency depreciation had an important role to play in the process of reconstruction and recovery of the French economy during this period. The decline of the franc helped to counteract the impact of the world recession of 1921 which was much less severe in France than in the counter-deflationary countries. It imparted a strong stimulus to exports and the tourist trade. Exports rose by no less than 56 per cent between 1922 and 1926 and by the latter date they were about one-third higher than in 1913. This was a remarkable achievement given that at the end of the war they were less than a one-third of the prewar level (Maddison, 1982, pp. 250–51). Kemp (1972, p. 97) asserts that it was not until the later 1920s that an export boom took over from one based on reconstruction and the home market. This is surely incorrect and is possibly based on the plateau in export volumes between 1920 and 1922 after the immediate postwar surge. The main spurt to French exports occurred in the first half of the decade and formed part of the reconstruction process, whereas by the later 1920s export growth had flattened out.

On the domestic front inflation certainly proved beneficial to the business community. According to Landes (1969, p. 464), the sharp decline in the value of the franc 'made borrowing so profitable that even those entrepreneurs imbued with the traditional abhorrence of credit learned to sacrifice commercial morality to pecuniary advantage'. The cheapening of money eased the burden of industrial debt and stimulated the rapid growth of industrial capacity in the devastated regions (Clough, 1939, p. 318). Nor does inflation appear to have posed a serious liquidity problem for the business community. On the contrary, Wasserman (1934, p. 234) in a study of six major industries found that French business emerged from the inflationary period in a relatively strong position. Most industries were able to earn large profits, increase their working capital, use excess liquid funds for purposes of increasing their fixed assets, find a ready market for the issue of new securities, and in general improve their financial position. He concludes that 'possibly the *worst* effect which inflation may be said to have had upon enterprise in France was the urge toward expansion which it engendered, for the increase in fixed assets is one of the outstanding results in this analysis'.

More generally, the population as a whole suffered less than in countries which experienced extremes of deflation and hyperinflation. Throughout the period there was fairly full employment of resources and rising real wages, even though non-wage incomes gained at the expense of wage-earners. Fixed income groups and savers did not suffer the same disastrous consequences as their Central European counterparts. Nor did the stabilisation phase cause undue problems. It is true that production fell by some 20 per cent between its peak in October 1926 through to the trough of the following spring, while unemployment more than quadrupled in the two months to February 1927 (Horsman, 1988, p. 84). But these were temporary setbacks and overall the recession following stabilisation was mild and short-lived.

Eleanor Dulles (1933, pp. 59–61), writing before the war, could see very little benefit to the economy from inflation:

> there seems to have been no marked improvement in the activity of French factories and mines, no brilliant response of productive energy to the injection of an artificial stimulus. The upward swing of some of the curves was no more marked than that which was almost certain to come with the recovery from the business depression of 1921, and resulted in no large increase in national wealth. Reconstruction still played a part in the business revival of 1923, but it came to have less effect on general conditions in 1924; and the upward surge of prices did not take its place as a mechanism for increasing the output of real wealth.

She concluded therefore that there was 'certainly no decisive argument for inflation as an aid to industry, agriculture or commerce ... based on what happened in France'.

Her strictures are certainly too strong. It is true that the French economy still suffered from many traditional weaknesses inherited from the previous century; that France nearly paid the price of inflationary financing in a collapse of the currency; and that there was nothing especially remarkable about the performance of the French economy in the 1920s when compared with that of other countries (see below). However, most writers would probably agree that France was one of the few countries to benefit on balance from inflation and currency depreciation (Horsman, 1988, p. 84). In fact Clough (1939, p. 318) suggested that its success led at times to it being advocated as a national policy.

The Belgian case has many similarities to that of France, though the recovery effort was not quite as impressive. War damage was very severe and by 1919 industrial production and exports were less than 50 per cent of the prewar level (Baudhuin, 1946, pp. 91–104). The government readily assumed much of the cost of reconstruction in the belief that compensation would be forthcoming from Germany. As with French experience, this resulted in a considerable amount of new plant based on modern techniques being installed in some industries. The iron and steel industry, which was almost obliterated during the war, was one of the major beneficiaries. Generous government assistance coupled with the erosion of fixed debts through inflation enabled Belgian ironmasters to re-equip their undertakings with modern plant on relatively easy terms. Output of pig iron surpassed the 1913 level in 1924 and by 1927 Belgium had 50 per cent more blast furnace capacity than when the war started, and some of it was the most technically advanced in Europe (Landes, 1969, p. 462).

By 1925 the reconstruction process was more or less completed. Most of the farms had been restocked and nearly every square foot of devastated area was again under the plough. Belgian agricultural production showed a better record than the average for Western Europe in the early 1920s and by 1924 it had regained the prewar level. All the devastated houses and most of the damaged public buildings had been completely rebuilt or restored (Pringle, 1927, p. 137). However, it was not until the middle of the decade that industrial production managed to regain prewar dimensions (Shepherd, 1936, p. 16). One reason for the weaker performance than France was that Belgium suffered more severely in the depression of 1921, though recovery from this setback was quite strong. Perhaps more important was the poor export performance despite the benefits of an undervalued currency (Mings, 1966, p. 23). Currency depreciation, though on par with that of France, did not give much of a fillip to exports which languished badly in the early 1920s (van der Wee and Tavernier, 1975, p. 72). Belgium, like Britain, failed to regain the markets she had lost in wartime and by the mid-1920s export volume was still 27 per cent below the prewar level (Maddison, 1982, pp. 250–51).

Comparisons

The six countries considered in detail above may now be compared with six countries which undertook monetary and fiscal contraction in order to restore their prewar parities, that is Denmark, The Netherlands, Norway, Sweden, Switzerland and the UK. In Tables 3.1–3.3 data are given for gross domestic product, export volumes and manufacturing production for all 12 countries for the 1920s. Three addi-

Table 3.1 Volume of gross domestic product (1913 = 100)

	1918	*1919*	*1920*	*1921*	*1922*	*1923*	*1924*	*1925*	*1929*
Austria	73.3	61.8	66.4	73.5	80.1	79.3	88.5	94.5	105.1
Germany	82.0	72.3	78.6	87.5	95.2	79.1	92.6	103.0	121.3
Belgium	67.8	79.2	92.5	94.1	103.3	107.0	110.5	112.2	125.5
France	63.9	75.3	87.1	83.5	98.5	103.6	116.6	117.1	134.4
Italy	133.3	111.0	101.3	99.8	104.9	111.3	112.4	119.8	131.1
Finland	67.0	80.9	90.5	93.5	103.4	111.0	113.9	120.4	145.6
Denmark	93.8	105.9	110.9	107.7	118.6	131.1	131.5	128.5	153.0
Netherlands	90.7	112.4	115.8	122.9	129.6	132.8	142.5	148.5	177.4
Norway	96.3	112.6	119.7	109.8	122.6	125.3	124.7	132.4	158.6
Sweden	84.5	89.4	94.6	91.1	99.7	105.0	108.3	112.3	135.9
Switzerland	89.4	95.3	101.5	99.0	108.5	114.8	119.1	127.8	154.5
UK	113.2	100.9	94.8	87.1	91.6	94.5	98.4	103.2	111.9

Source: Maddison (1995), pp. 148–50.

Table 3.2 Volume of exports (1913 = 100)

	1918	*1919*	*1920*	*1921*	*1922*	*1923*	*1924*	*1925*	*1929*
Austria	—	—	—	—	—	—	75.6	82.1	86.3
Germany	15.0	17.0	36.7	44.4	61.3	52.9	50.8	65.3	91.8
Belgium	—	—	—	—	—	—	—	72.8	107.2
France	28.0	45.0	86.0	83.0	86.0	103.0	119.0	124.0	147.0
Italy	48.9	75.1	105.5	70.7	80.8	93.7	117.3	127.4	122.7
Finland	11.4	51.2	77.6	72.4	102.7	108.7	124.9	138.9	161.4
Denmark	39.9	38.6	77.9	87.2	96.6	123.2	142.5	138.4	181.0
Netherlands	23.8	81.3	87.4	83.0	93.4	103.7	124.6	134.9	171.2
Norway	61.1	67.1	90.5	76.0	97.8	104.5	110.8	121.8	167.1
Sweden	65.1	66.5	75.8	59.1	81.2	79.7	95.8	106.0	156.1
Switzerland	—	—	—	62.6	70.1	74.4	87.3	89.7	100.7
UK	37.7	54.7	70.7	49.3	68.0	74.7	76.0	74.7	81.3

Source: Maddison (1991), pp. 316–18.

Table 3.3 Indices of manufacturing production (1913 = 100)

	1920	*1921*	*1922*	*1923*	*1924*	*1925*	*1926*	*1927*	*1928*	*1929*
Austria	48.0	64.0	76.0	81.0	82.0	95.0	95.0	106.0	116.0	118.0
Germany	59.0	74.7	81.8	55.4	81.8	94.9	90.9	122.1	118.3	117.3
Hungary	—	64.0	80.0	56.6	66.6	76.7	83.4	98.7	108.0	113.9
Poland	35.1	46.8	73.9	71.2	56.8	63.1	58.9	76.1	86.1	85.9
Belgium	67.3	55.8	80.6	92.1	104.4	100.0	117.4	127.7	137.4	139.9
France	70.4	61.4	87.8	95.2	117.9	114.3	129.8	115.6	134.4	142.7
Italy	95.2	98.4	108.1	119.3	140.7	156.8	162.8	161.2	175.2	181.0
Denmark	127.8	106.9	112.6	125.1	136.2	126.4	126.4	127.9	138.3	148.7
Netherlands	—	109.9	115.2	117.4	127.5	141.8	147.4	159.9	174.5	187.3
Norway	101.9	71.8	90.0	99.8	107.2	117.0	104.2	106.5	118.2	131.2
Sweden	97.2	74.7	87.2	96.8	100.9	112.7	123.5	126.8	136.0	150.8
Switzerland	94.5	71.4	76.9	86.7	93.3	95.5	90.0	103.2	109.8	117.5
UK	92.6	55.1	73.5	79.1	87.8	86.3	78.8	96.0	95.1	100.3
Czechoslovakia	69.8	100.0	91.8	96.7	129.0	136.4	130.4	153.8	166.0	171.8
Finland	87.4	88.5	104.5	119.7	123.6	152.5	164.7	186.1	202.6	197.6
World	93.2	81.1	99.5	104.5	111.0	120.7	126.5	134.5	141.8	153.3

Source: League of Nations (1945), pp. 134–7.

tional countries, Italy, Czechoslovakia and Finland, are also included for comparative purposes.

As far as total output is concerned (Table 3.1) the inflationary countries performed worse relative to 1913 than the parity countries both through to 1925 and thereafter. Apart from the UK, all the parity countries had a better record than the inflationary group. The worst case was Austria which barely managed to exceed its prewar level of total output by the end of the decade. The same holds true in the case of exports, with the exceptions of the UK and Switzerland. Even in the case of Norway, which experienced a check to manufacturing activity in the mid-1920s prior to her return to gold, there was no impact on export earnings which suggests that the krona was not being forced into overvalued territory (Nordvik and Grytten, 1994, p. 144). On average the inflationary group had a weaker record, with Austria and Germany failing to recover their prewar volumes (Table 3.2).

In the case of manufacturing production, there is greater variability but a similar pattern is repeated. It is true that the inflationary countries avoided the sharp contraction in activity of the early 1920s experienced by the parity brigade. On the other hand, by 1925 the hyperinflationary countries and Belgium had failed to regain their prewar levels of production, whereas only the UK and Switzerland were in the same position. By the end of the decade the hyperinflationary countries were still falling behind the parity group, again with the exception of the UK and Switzerland. France and Belgium had a better record though even they were surpassed by Denmark, Sweden and The Netherlands.

On balance, therefore, the countries which experienced serious inflation did not have a particularly impressive economic record compared with most of the confirmed stabilisers. Accordingly, there would seem to be no strong case for arguing that inflation and currency depreciation were the winning combination in the recovery effort.

The best performers were those that stabilised at an early date with devalued currencies and thereby avoided the adverse effects of sustained inflation. The prime examples here are Czechoslovakia and Finland, both of which experienced substantial inflation through to the early 1920s and sharp fluctuations in exchange rates in 1921 and 1922. However, tight financial and monetary control was implemented promptly and by 1923 inflationary forces had been brought under control and exchange rates stabilised at rates one-seventh and one-eighth respectively of prewar levels (Gruber, 1924, pp. 183–9; Hjerppe, 1996, p. 159; League of Nations, 1925, p. 53; Pryor, 1973, pp. 194–5). Keynes (1923, pp. 146–7) criticised the harsh policy in Czechoslovakia which caused an industrial setback and serious unemployment for a short time, but recognised that the country was better placed than most other European nations to reconstruct her economy on the basis of a sound and fixed currency. The main exception is Italy which experienced inflation and a depreciating exchange until the lira was stabilised in 1927. The record in this case is mixed. Her total output expansion was weaker than that of most of the parity countries, but manufacturing production forged ahead strongly throughout the decade, partly as a result of the policy promotion efforts of the new fascist state.

Conclusions

There appears to be some support for the view that inflation did ease the process of reconstruction and recovery in several European countries in the first half of the 1920s, at least in the short term. Most of the countries which experienced sustained inflation, whether moderate or hyperinflationary, had a higher-level activity and employment than the Anglo-Saxon countries which deflated sharply soon after the war in order to eradicate inflation. On the other hand, while the inflating countries gained an initial stimulus, over the longer term their performance does not compare favourably with countries returning to parity apart from the UK. By 1929 the Scandinavian countries and The Netherlands recorded a better performance relative to 1913 than virtually any of the countries that had experienced sustained inflation. By far the worst performance was recorded by the hyperinflationary countries, whereas those experiencing moderate inflation had more to show for it. But the best performers were those countries, such as Czechoslovakia and Finland, which sorted out their financial affairs at an early date and were therefore able to make strong progress under stable financial conditions.

Bearing in mind that economic and social conditions varied so much from country to country in the postwar years, it is difficult to draw axiomatic conclusions regarding the impact of alternative policies. Nevertheless, the evidence would seem to indicate that the best policy option was one that favoured early stabilisation at a favourable exchange rate.

The crucial question is whether the temporary stimulus to economic activity was worthwhile when set against the costs involved. The bulk of the population probably lost out. The distribution of income became more unequal and tended to favour a small segment of the population such as businessmen, landowners, speculators and anyone fortunate enough to shunt their savings into fixed assets. Those deriving income from employment and interest-bearing deposits fared badly, since real wages and earnings were severely squeezed while most small savings became worthless. In Germany real wages fell almost continuously between 1919 and 1923 and by the latter date real weekly earnings were well below those of 1913. It was not until the end of the decade that real wages and real per capita income regained or surpassed the prewar levels. The situation was even worse in Hungary and Poland where real wages fell to around one-half the levels of 1913. Salary earners, especially those engaged in public service, also experienced losses of similar magnitude, with the added disadvantage that their employment opportunities were less buoyant than those for wage earners. For the peasant community inflation was something of a mixed blessing. It wiped out much of farm indebtedness, but it also destroyed rural savings, while the terms of trade of the agrarian sector deteriorated during inflation. Furthermore, much of the inflationary tax burden was borne by the poorer sections of the community including, of course, the peasantry.

In addition, many lower middle-class groups on fixed incomes and with small savings suffered badly. Savings were all but wiped out and there was little compensation for them in the post-stabilisation period. One consequence of this suffering was the rise of right-wing radical movements.

In many East European countries production did not manage to regain prewar levels even at the peak of the inflation boom. Moreover, inflation did little to solve their long-standing problems of backwardness caused by low rates of accumulation, lack of capital, low levels of productivity and severe structural imbalances.

Though most countries experienced high levels of activity and investment during the inflationary period, much of the investment became speculative in the later stages when capital was diverted from productive uses into any kind of assets which would retain some intrinsic worth. The feverish scramble into assets, even productive ones, was not necessarily beneficial in the long term. Inflation probably caused a serious misallocation of resources in so far as it led to a haphazard creation of enterprises many of which were inefficient, and a flight of savings into any kind of physical assets for the sake of maintaining some real worth. Had there been a conscious attempt to direct resources and investment into constructive endeavours, the final outcome might have been more favourable from the point of view of subsequent requirements. Einzig (1935, pp. 77–8) pointed out that: 'In the almost complete absence of economic planning, the beneficial effects of unorthodox finance were reduced to a minimum, and its destructive effects were increased to a maximum.' Many of the inflation-inspired enterprises collapsed like a pack of cards once the artificial conditions were removed, leaving a trail of abandoned assets the quality of which left much to be desired (Kavka, 1960, p. 115). Others had to be propped up by state protection and assistance once stabilisation was imposed (Einzig, 1935, p. 77). The sub-optimal nature of many investments was an inevitable outcome of the feverish scramble for assets in the inflationary conditions of the time. The real gains from inflation became gradually weaker and eventually negative as resources and savings were diverted from productive capital assets into speculative activities in attempts to beat inflation. This involved not only a flight into tangible assets and commodities, but also a move into gold and more stable foreign currencies, together with speculation in company shares which were issued in ever larger quantities during the inflationary boom in company formation (Berend and Ranki, 1974a, p. 198).

The final consequences, that is post-stabilisation, were as serious, if not more so, than for countries which undertook a policy of retrenchment before inflation got out of hand. In some cases the implementation of orthodox deflationary policies checked normal economic activity for up to two years (Ranki, 1983b). In effect stabilisation measures brought inflationary countries back to square one so that they had to begin the task of reconstruction and recovery again. Most of the hyperinflationary countries recorded a poor economic performance in the 1920s, especially Austria and Poland.

Thus if we take full account of the aftermath of inflation and the misery it created for the bulk of the population (Rowley, 1994), one has doubts as to whether the temporary and artificial stimulus derived from inflation was really worthwhile. And the longer-term consequences are worth bearing in mind. This is especially true in the case of Germany where the shift to the right in politics and the policy reaction in the subsequent depression of 1929–32 were both conditioned by the inflationary experience of the 1920s. Indeed, Solomou (1996, ch. 2) argues that countries which had retrenched early were less inhibited than those experiencing sustained inflation in their policy response to depression.

One final point is worth bearing in mind: that is, monetary manipulation cannot solve real economic problems. Depending on particular circumstances, monetary inflation may for a time impart a favourable stimulus to economic activity, but over the long term there is little to be gained and much to lose, compared with countries that follow a prudent financial course. It is fanciful to imagine that monetary forces can have a permanent and lasting beneficial influence on the real fundamentals of an economy on which long-term development ultimately depends.

References

Aldcroft, D. H. and Morewood, S. (1995), *Economic Change in Eastern Europe since 1918*, Aldershot: Edward Elgar.

Angell, J. W. (1929), *The Recovery of Germany*, New Haven, CT: Yale University Press.

Balderston, T. (1982), 'The origins of economic instability in Germany 1924–1930: market forces versus economic policy', *Vierteljahrschrift für Sozial-und Wirtschaftsgeschichte*, 69.

Balderston, T. (1985), 'Links between inflation and depression: German capital and labour markets 1924–1931', in G. D. Feldman and E. Müller-Luckner (eds), *Die Nachwirkungen der Inflation auf die deutsche Geschichte 1924–1933*, Munich.

Baudhuin, F. (1946), *Histoire économique de la Belgique, 1914–1939*, vol. I, Brussels: Emily Bruylant.

Berend, I. T. and G. Ranki (1974a), *Economic Development in East Central Europe in the 19th and 20th Centuries*, New York: Columbia University Press.

Berend, I. T. and G. Ranki (1974b), *Hungary: a Century of Economic Development*, Newton Abbot: David and Charles.

Bootle, R. (1981), 'How important is it to defeat inflation? – the evidence', *The Three Banks Review*, December.

Born, K. E. (1977), 'The German inflation after the first world war', *Journal of European Economic History*, 6.

Boross, E. A. (1994), *Inflation and Industry in Hungary, 1918–1929*, Berlin: Haude and Spener.

Broadberry, S. N. (1984), 'The North European depression of the 1920s', *Scandinavian Economic History Review*, 32.

Brown, B. (1988), *Monetary Chaos in Europe: the End of an Era*, London: Croom Helm.

Bry, G. (1960), *Wages in Germany, 1871–1945*, Princeton, NJ: Princeton University Press.

Cagan, P. (1956), 'The monetary dynamics of hyperinflation', in M. Friedman (ed.), *Studies in the Quantity Theory of Money*, Chicago: University of Chicago Press.

Carsten, F. L. (1986), *The First Austrian Republic 1918–1938: a Study Based on British and Austrian Documents*, Aldershot: Gower.

Childers, T. (1982), 'Inflation, stabilisation and political realignment in Germany 1924–1928', in G. D. Feldman, C.-L. Holtfrerich, G. A. Ritter and P.-C. Witt (eds), *The German Inflation Reconsidered: a Preliminary Balance*, Berlin: Walter de Gruyter.

Childers, T. (1983a), 'Inflation and electoral politics in Germany, 1919–

29' in N. Schmukler and E. Marcus (eds), *Inflation through the Ages*, New York: Brooklyn College Press.

Childers, T. (1983b), *The Nazi Voter: the Social Foundation of Fascism in Germany, 1919–1933*, Chapel Hill, NC: University of North Carolina Press.

Clough, S. B. (1939), *France: a History of National Economics, 1789–1939*, New York: Charles Scribner's Sons.

Czada, P. (1974), 'Grosse Inflation und Wirtschaftswachstum', in H. Mommsen, D. Petzina and B. Weisbrod (eds), *Industrielles System und politische Entwicklung in der Weimarer Republik*, Düsseldorf: Droste Verlag.

Davis, J. S. (1921), 'Recent economic and financial progress in France', *Review of Economic Statistics, 5*.

Dawson, G. (1992), *Inflation and Unemployment: Causes, Consequences and Cures*, Aldershot: Edward Elgar.

Dornbusch, R. (1987), 'Lessons from the German inflation of the 1920s', in R. Dornbusch, S. Fischer and J. Bossons (eds), *Macroeconomics and Finance: Essays in Honor of Franco Modigliani*, Cambridge, MA: MIT Press.

Dulles, E. L. (1933), *The Dollar, the Franc and Inflation*, New York: Macmillan.

Eichengreen, B. (1986), 'Understanding 1921–1927: inflation and economic recovery in the 1920s', *Rivista di Storia Economica*, 3.

Einzig, P. (1935), *World Finance since 1914*, London: Kegan Paul, Trench, Trubner.

Feldman, G. D. (1975), 'Economic and social problems of the German demobilization, 1918–19', *Journal of Modern History*, 47.

Feldman, G. D. (1977), *Iron and Steel in the German Inflation, 1916–1923*, Princeton, NJ: Princeton University Press.

Feldman, G. D. (1983), 'The historian and German inflation', in N. Schmukler and E. Marcus (eds), *Inflation through the Ages*, New York: Brooklyn College Press.

Feldman, G. D. (1992), 'Industrialists, bankers, and the problem of unemployment in the Weimar Republic', *Central European History*, 25.

Feldman, G. D. (1993), *The Great Disorder: Politics, Economics and Society in the German Inflation, 1914–1924*, Oxford: Oxford University Press.

Ferguson, N. (1995), *Paper and Iron: Hamburg Business and German Politics in the Era of Inflation, 1897–1927*, Cambridge: Cambridge University Press.

Ferguson, N. (1996), 'Constraints and room for manoevre in the German inflation of the early 1920s', *Economic History Review*, 49.

Fergusson, A. (1975), *When Money Dies: the Nightmare of the Weimar Collapse*, London: William Kimber.
Gordon, R. J. (1982), 'Why stopping inflation may be costly: evidence from fourteen historical episodes', in R. E. Hall (ed.), *Inflation: Causes and Effects*, Chicago: University of Chicago Press.
Graham, F. D. (1930), *Exchange, Prices and Production in Hyperinflation Germany, 1920–23*, Princeton: Princeton University Press.
Gruber, J. (1924), *Czechoslovakia: a Survey of Economic and Social Conditions*, New York: Macmillan.
Hardach, G. (1984), 'Banking and industry in Germany in the interwar period 1919–1939', *Journal of European Economic History*, **13**.
Hardach, K. (1980), *The Political Economy of Germany in the Twentieth Century*, Berkeley: University of California Press.
Higham, D. and Tomlinson, J. (1982), 'Why do governments worry about inflation?', *National Westminster Bank Quarterly Review*, May.
Hjerppe, R. (1996), *Finland's Historical National Accounts 1860–1914: Calculation Methods and Statistical Tables*, Jyväskylä: Kari-Pekka Kivirauma.
Holtfrerich, C.-L. (1986), *The German Inflation 1919–1923*, Berlin: Walter de Gruyter.
Horsman, G. (1988), *Inflation in the Twentieth Century: Evidence from Europe and North America*, Hemel Hempstead: Harvester-Wheatsheaf.
Hughes, M. L. (1982), 'Economic interest, social attitudes, and creditor ideology: popular responses to inflation', in G. D. Feldman et al. (eds), *The German Inflation Reconsidered: a Preliminary Balance*, Berlin: Walter de Gruyter.
Hughes, M. L. (1988), *Paying for the German Inflation*, Chapel Hill, NC: University of North Carolina Press.
Jack, D.T. (1927), *The Restoration of European Currencies*, London: P. S. King and Son.
Jacobs, R.L. (1977), 'Hyperinflation and the supply of money', *Journal of Money, Credit and Banking*, **9**.
Jones, L. E. (1972), 'The dying middle class: Weimar Germany and the fragmentation of bourgeois politics', *Central European History*, **5**.
Jones, L. E. (1979), 'Inflation, revaluation and the crisis of middle class politics: a study of the dissolution of the German party system', *Central European History*, **12**.
Jones, L. E. (1980), 'The dissolution of the bourgeois party system in the Weimar Republic', in R. Bessel and E. Feuchtwanger (eds), *Social Change and Political Development in the Weimar Republic*, London: Croom Helm.
Jones. L. E. (1989), 'Democracy and liberalism in the German inflation:

the crisis of a political movement, 1918–1924', in G. D. Feldman (ed.), *Consequences of Inflation*, Berlin: Colloquium Verlag.

Kavka, F. (1960), *An Outline of Czechoslovak History*, Prague: Orbis.

Kemp, T. (1972), *The French Economy, 1919–1939: the History of a Decline*, London: Longmans.

Keynes, J. M. (1923), *A Tract on Monetary Reform*, London: Macmillan.

Landau, Z. (1983), 'Inflation in Poland after world war I', in N. Schmukler and E. Marcus (eds), *Inflation through the Ages*, New York: Brooklyn College Press.

Landau, Z. (1984), 'Poland's finance policy in the years of the Great Depression (1930–35)', *Acta Poloniae Historica,* **49**.

Landau, Z. (1992), 'The economic integration of Poland, 1918–23', in P. Latawski (ed.), *The Reconstruction of Poland, 1914–23*, Basingstoke: Macmillan.

Landes, D. S. (1969), *The Unbound Prometheus: Technological Change and Industrial Development in Western Europe from 1750 to the Present*, Cambridge: Cambridge University Press.

Laursen, K. and Pedersen, J. (1964), *The German Inflation, 1918–23*, Amsterdam: North Holland Publishing Company.

Layton, W. and Rist, C. (1925), *The Economic Situation of Austria*, Geneva: League of Nations.

League of Nations (1925), *Memorandum on Currency and Central Banks 1913–1924*, vol. 1, Geneva: League of Nations.

League of Nations (1945), *Industrialisation and Foreign Trade*, Geneva: League of Nations.

League of Nations (1946), *The Course and Control of Inflation: a Review of Monetary Experience in Europe after World War I*, Geneva: League of Nations.

Loveday, A. (1931), *Britain and World Trade*, London: Longmans, Green.

Lundberg, E. (1968), *Instability and Economic Growth*, New Haven: Yale University Press.

Lyth, P. J. (1990), *Inflation and the Merchant Economy: the Hamburg Mittelstand*, Oxford: Berg Publishers.

Maddison, A. (1982), *Phases of Capitalist Development*, Oxford: Oxford University Press.

Maddison, A. (1991), *Dynamic Forces in Capitalist Development*, Oxford: Oxford University Press.

Maddison, A. (1995), *Monitoring the World Economy 1820–1992*, Paris: OECD.

Maier, C. S. (1975), *Recasting Bourgeois Europe: Stabilisation in France, Germany and Italy in the Decade after World War One*, Princeton, NJ: Princeton University Press.

Markovitch, T. J. (1966), 'L'industrie française de 1789 à 1964: conclusions générales', in *Histoire quantitative de l'économie française*, Paris: Institut de Science Économique Appliqué.

Martin, G. (1927), 'The industrial reconstruction of France since the war', *Harvard Business Review*, 5.

Mendershausen, H. (1955), *Two Postwar Recoveries of the German Economy*, Amsterdam: North Holland Publishing Company.

Mings, T. R. (1966), *An Inter-Country Comparison of the Factors Determining Cyclical Behaviour in Sweden, Canada, Austria and Belgium, 1929–1937*, Ann Arbor, MI: University Microfilms.

Moggridge, D. E. (1992), *Maynard Keynes; an Economist's Biography*, London: Routledge.

Moulton, H. G. and McGuire, C. E. (1923), *Germany's Capacity to Pay: a Study of the Reparations Problem*, New York: McGraw-Hill.

Nordvik, H. W. and Grytten, O. H. (1994), 'The labour market, unemployment and economic growth in Norway, 1920–1939', *Scandinavian Economic History Review*, 42.

Nötel, R. (1984), 'Money, banking and industry in interwar Austria and Hungary', *Journal of European Economic History*, 13.

OEEC (1960), *Industrial Statistics 1900–1959*, Paris: OEEC.

Ogburn, W. F. and Jaffé, W. (1929), *The Economic Development of Postwar France: a Survey of Production*, New York: Columbia University Press.

Pasvolsky, L. (1928), *Economic Nationalism of the Danubian States*, London: Allen and Unwin.

Pigou, A. C. (1920), 'Memorandum on credit, currency and exchange fluctuations', paper prepared in connection with the Brussels International Conference at the request of the Secretariat of the League of Nations, Geneva, Geneva, League of Nations.

Preston, H. H. (1931), 'Europe's return to gold', *Harvard Business Review*, 9.

Pringle, W. H. (ed.) (1927), *Economic Problems in Europe Today*, London: A. and C. Black.

Pryor, Z. P. (1973), 'Czechoslovak economic development in the interwar period', in V. S. Mamatey and R. Luza (eds), *A History of the Czechoslovak Republic 1918–1948*, Princeton, NJ: Princeton University Press.

Ranki, G. (1983a), 'Inflation in Hungary', in N. Schmukler and E. Marcus (eds), *Inflation through the Ages*, New York: Brooklyn College Press.

Ranki, G. (1983b), 'Inflation in post-World War I East-Central Europe', in N. Schmukler and E. Marcus (eds), *Inflation through the Ages*, New York: Brooklyn College Press.

Ringer, F. K. (ed.) (1969), *The German Inflation of 1923*, New York: Oxford University Press.
Roszkowski, W. (1986), 'Poland's economic performance between the two world wars', *East European Quarterly*, 20.
Roszkowski, W. (1989), 'The growth of the state sector in the Polish economy in the years 1918–1926', *Journal of European Economic History*, 18.
Rothschild, K. W. (1947), *Austria's Economic Development between the Two Wars*, London: Frederick Muller.
Rowley, E. E. (1994), *Hyperinflation in Germany*, Aldershot: Scolar Press.
Sargent, T. J. (1982), 'The end of four big inflations', in R. E. Hall (ed.), *Inflation: Causes and Effects*, Chicago: University of Chicago Press.
Sauvy, A. (1965), *Histoire économique de la France entre les deux guerres, 1918–1931*, Paris: Fayard.
Schmidt, C. T. (1934), *German Business Cycles 1924–1933*, New York: National Bureau of Economic Research.
Schuker, S. A. (1976), *The End of French Predominance in Europe: the Financial Crisis of 1924 and the Adoption of the Dawes Plan*, Chapel Hill, NC: University of North Carolina Press.
Shepherd, H. L. (1936), *The Monetary Experience of Belgium*, Princeton, NJ: Princeton University Press.
Solomou, S. (1996), *Themes in Macroeconomic History: the UK Economy, 1919–1939*, Cambridge: Cambridge University Press.
Sommariva, A. and Tullio, G. (1987), *German Macroeconomic History, 1880–1979: a Study of the Effects of Economic Policy on Inflation, Currency Depreciation and Growth*, London: Macmillan.
Teichova, A. (1983), 'A comparative view of inflation of the 1920s in Austria and Czechoslovakia', in N. Schmukler and E. Marcus, (eds), *Inflation through the Ages*, New York: Brooklyn College Press.
van der Wee, H. and Tavernier, K. (1975), *La Banque Nationale de Belgique et l'histoire monétaire entre les deux guerres mondiales*, Brussels: Banque Nationale de Belgique.
Wasserman, M. J. (1934), 'Inflation and enterprise in France, 1919–1926', *Journal of Political Economy*, 42.
Webb, S. (1985), 'Government debt and inflationary expectations as determinants of the money supply in Germany 1919–1923', *Journal of Money Credit and Banking*, 17.
Webb, S. (1986), 'Fiscal news and inflationary expectations in Germany after world war I', *Journal of Economic History*, 46.
Webb, S. (1987), 'The German inflation and foreign business cycles, 1920–1922', *Explorations in Economic History*, 24.
Webb, S. (1989), *Hyperinflation and Stabilization in Weimar Germany*, Oxford: Oxford University Press.

Wicker, E. (1986), 'Terminating hyperinflation in the dismembered Habsburg Monarchy', *American Economic Review,* 76.

Wiggs, K. I. (1933), *Unemployment in Germany since the War*, London: P. S. King.

Witt, P.-C. (1974), 'Finanzpolitik und sozialer Wandel in Krieg und Inflation 1918–1924', in H. Mommsen, D. Petzina and B. Weisbrod (eds), *Industrielles System und politische Entwicklung in der Weimarer Republik*, Düsseldorf: Droste Verlag.

Witt, P.-C. (1983), 'Tax policies, tax assessment and inflation: toward a sociology of public finances in the German inflation, 1914–1923', in N. Schmukler and E. Marcus (eds), *Inflation through the Ages*, New York: Brooklyn College Press.

Zweig, F. (1944), *Poland between the Wars: a Critical Study of Social and Economic Changes*, London: Secker and Warburg.

CHAPTER FOUR

The Decline of Europe: Trade and Reconstruction in the 1920s

There were already signs before 1914 that Europe's relative economic strength was beginning to wane, but it was the war which effectively shattered her economic supremacy. Several years of growth were sacrificed, trade volumes collapsed and Europe emerged from the conflict in a prostrate condition, both economically and politically. The balance of economic gravity shifted westwards and it was to be half a century before Europe was able to reassert itself. The reconstruction and recovery process of the 1920s was a painful and protracted affair which did little to recapture former glory. In the first half of the decade many countries were struggling even to regain their prewar levels of activity, while trade volumes lagged behind. Conditions were not conducive to rapid revival since scarcely a year passed without some event or series of events intervening to hold back the rate of progress. The second half of the decade saw a more sustained revival against the background of an improved international environment. But the equilibrium was more apparent than real. There were deep-seated problems in Europe and the international economy which left Europe vulnerable to external shocks. It was only a matter of time before its resilience was tested and found wanting. The traumas of the next two decades can be related back to the economic and political vacuums which were the legacy of the war and its aftermath.

Determinants of international trade

To a large extent it is changes in national incomes which determine changes in foreign trade. Changes in national output tend to evoke similar movements in foreign trade unless these are deliberately checked by commercial policy. Thus for the world as a whole there has been a strong tendency for output and trade to move in tandem, while over the longer term trade has usually grown faster than total incomes. The spread of industrialisation and the growing proportion of services (often non-tradeable) in total output have not been sufficient to offset the trade generation effects of rising real incomes, as some economists once thought would be the case (Deutsch and Eckstein, 1961; Grassman, 1980).

A second important factor, at least from the point of view of the individual country, is the structural composition of output. Fast-growing countries tend to have dynamic trade sectors largely because their economies are continually adapting to changing patterns of demand and new markets. Thus their product mix tends to be slanted towards fast-growing trade sectors and hence they do an increasing share of their business in expanding markets. The converse is true for slow-growing countries. Thus the composition of output and trade direction are crucial to success.

A third relevant factor, and one related to the second, is competitiveness. Fast-growing countries tend to be competitive because their supply capability is constantly improving, both in price and non-price terms, by dint of rapid growth, high rates of investment and innovation and structural transformation. Slow-growing countries, on the other hand, tend to lose out in international trade because the supply side does not respond rapidly enough to changing market conditions, unit costs therefore rise and volume is lost to competitors.

For the world as a whole one can argue that trade is essentially demand determined, but that for the individual country it is more likely to be supply driven. In the latter case, a single country cannot hope, in the long term, to gain trade share in an expanding world market unless it has the correct supply positioning.

The above factors are relevant to Europe's trade position in the interwar years. Europe lost out to the rest of the world after 1913 because the war administered a shock which destroyed both income and trade growth for several years. Furthermore, the war and its aftermath slowed down the adaptation of the economic structure with the result that it did not respond rapidly enough to changes in world demand patterns following hostilities. Consequently, Europe as a whole lost market share in world trade. This was probably only to be expected given the difficult economic conditions in the first few years after the war. By the time reconstruction and recovery were more or less complete there were but a few years, until the next cataclysm, for Europe to try and regain lost ground.

The world trade position

In the half century or so before 1914 the volume of international trade expanded at roughly the same rate as world production (both manufacturing and primary commodity production), while trade volumes increased much more rapidly than total output (Table 4.1). There was a rise therefore in the trade–income ratio (exports plus imports as a share

Table 4.1 Rates of growth of output (GDP) and exports (X)

	1870–1913		*1913–1929*		*1929–1950*		*1950–1973*	
	GDP	*X*	*GDP*	*X*	*GDP*	*X*	*GDP*	*X*
Austria	2.4	3.5	0.3	–0.9	0.2	–1.3	5.3	10.5
Belgium	2.0	4.2	1.4	0.4	0.7	0.2	4.1	9.1
Denmark	2.7	3.3	2.7	3.8	2.4	1.4	3.8	6.9
Finland	2.8	3.9	2.3	3.0	2.0	1.0	4.7	7.2
France	1.6	2.8	1.9	2.4	0.6	0.1	5.1	8.2
Germany	2.8	4.1	1.2	–0.6	0.9	–4.7	6.0	12.3
Italy	2.0	2.2	1.6	1.3	1.4	0.1	5.6	11.3
Netherlands	2.2	3.3	3.6	3.4	1.5	0.0	4.7	10.4
Norway	2.1	3.2	2.9	3.2	2.9	2.3	4.1	7.3
Sweden	2.2	3.1	1.9	2.8	3.4	2.8	3.7	6.9
Switzerland	2.4	3.9	2.9	0.0	2.4	0.6	4.5	8.1
UK	1.9	2.8	0.7	–1.3	1.7	1.0	3.0	3.9
Australia	3.5	4.3	1.3	0.4	2.9	1.9	4.7	5.6
Canada	4.0	4.1	2.5	4.2	3.2	2.3	5.1	7.0
Japan	2.3	8.5	3.7	6.1	1.1	-0.9	9.2	15.1
USA	4.0	4.9	3.1	2.9	2.7	1.7	3.9	6.3

Sources: Calculated from data in Maddison (1991), pp. 316–23, (1995), pp. 148–51.

of GNP) in most of the major countries (Grassman, 1980). This was no longer true in the interwar years. Trade growth slowed down and it no longer kept pace with production. Trade growth also fell behind that of income growth and there was a sharp decline in trade–income ratios (Table 4.1; Grassman, 1980).

The break in trend, which was not to be re-established until after the Second World War, was largely a product of wartime disruption, even though there was a fairly close correspondence between industrial output and exports during the recovery period of the 1920s. The war destroyed several years of normal income and trade growth. Trade in particular was badly hit. By the end of the war world trade volume was substantially less than prewar despite large gains by North America and Japan (Table 4.2). Europe bore the brunt of the burden; for many countries international trade had almost ceased to exist. The contraction was partly a function of reduced incomes, but even more important were the restrictions imposed on trade during hostilities and continued for some time thereafter. The reconstruction aftermath delayed recovery

Table 4.2 Indices of output (GDP) and exports (X): 1913 = 100

	1918		*1920*		*1921*		*1925*		*1929*	
	GDP	*X*	*GDP*	*X*	*GDP*	*X*	*GDP*	*X*	*GDP*	*X*
Austria	73.3	—	66.4	—	73.5	—	94.5	82.1	105.1	86.3
Belgium	67.8	—	92.5	—	94.1	—	112.2	72.8	125.5	107.2
Denmark	93.8	39.9	110.9	77.9	107.7	87.2	128.5	138.4	153.0	181.0
Finland	67.0	11.4	90.5	77.6	93.5	72.4	120.4	138.9	145.6	161.4
France	63.9	28.0	87.1	86.0	83.5	83.0	117.1	124.0	134.4	147.0
Germany	82.0	15.0	78.6	36.7	87.5	44.4	103.0	65.3	121.3	91.8
Italy	133.3	48.9	101.3	105.5	99.8	70.7	119.8	127.4	131.1	122.7
Netherlands	90.7	23.8	115.8	87.4	122.9	83.0	148.5	134.9	177.4	171.2
Norway	96.3	61.1	119.7	90.5	109.8	76.0	132.4	121.8	158.6	167.1
Sweden	84.5	65.1	94.6	75.8	91.1	59.1	112.3	106.0	135.9	156.1
Switzerland	89.4	—	101.5	—	99.0	62.6	127.8	89.7	154.5	100.7
UK	113.2	37.7	94.8	70.7	87.1	49.3	103.2	74.7	111.9	81.3
Australia	95.6	79.9	101.9	93.2	111.9	101.5	127.9	98.5	122.8	107.2
Canada	106.5	154.8	97.3	118.5	86.8	110.5	118.7	192.5	149.5	193.2
Japan	127.8	211.5	132.1	145.0	146.6	128.3	156.6	183.6	178.8	257.9
USA	114.8	119.7	114.7	141.8	112.1	113.4	141.2	128.0	163.0	158.2

Sources: Maddison (1991), pp. 316–18, (1995), pp. 148–50.

in Europe so that it was some years before world trade recovered to its prewar level despite growth elsewhere. In fact it was not until the mid-1920s that world trade volumes approached former levels. In the later 1920s world trade expanded rapidly and by 1929 it was around one-third higher in volume than it had been in 1913. On the other hand, if we take the prewar base year of 1913 through to 1929, then trade growth was considerably lower – about half that of the period 1870–1914 – while the rate of export growth fell below that of total output for the first time since the beginning of modern economic growth. Only in the restrictionist era of the 1930s and during the Second World War did the trade–income ratio decline further (Table 4.1; Grassman, 1980).

Europe's decline

The main burden of the disruption fell upon Europe. As a producer and trader Europe lost substantial ground, though this, it should be noted, was only a marked acceleration of a trend apparent before 1914. The main beneficiaries were the United States and Japan in manufactures, and Latin America, Asia and the British Dominions in primary commodities (Pollard, 1981). Their supply capability had been boosted by war, as were their trade potentials, whereas Europe's were severely impaired. For many countries in Europe trade had been reduced to insignificant levels by the end of the war, with an overall loss of more than half. Protracted recovery, especially in the first half of the 1920s, meant that Europe could do little to regain lost ground. Consequently, despite fairly sustained recovery in the latter half of the decade Europe only just managed to surpass the prewar trade peak. Her shares of world trade therefore declined considerably, from 59 to 48 per cent of world exports, and from 64 to 56 per cent of world imports over the period 1913–28 (Table 4.3). The main beneficiary was North America, but all continents gained shares in this period, while Japan's trade performance was spectacular (Table 4.1).

The aggregate figures do, of course, conceal a wide dispersion of performance within Europe. Western Europe tended to do better on balance than Central and Eastern Europe including Russia, especially in the first half of the decade. But as Table 4.4 demonstrates, the inclusion of Russia drags down the European performance considerably compared with 1913 owing to that country's virtual withdrawal from international trade after the war. Even so, Central and Eastern Europe excluding Russia falls well short of its prewar trade volume in 1925, whereas Western Europe had more or less regained its former position. Subsequently, Central and Eastern Europe excluding Russia made greater

Table 4.3 World trade: regional shares (percentage)

	1913		*1928*		*1937*	
	Exports	*Imports*	*Exports*	*Imports*	*Exports*	*Imports*
UK and Ireland	13.1	15.2	11.5	15.8	10.6	17.8
North-west Europe[1]	33.4	36.5	25.1	27.9	25.8	27.8
Other Europe	12.4	12.4	11.4	12.5	10.6	10.2
North America	14.8	11.5	19.8	15.2	17.1	13.9
Oceania	2.5	2.4	2.9	2.6	3.5	2.8
Latin America	8.3	7.0	9.8	7.6	10.2	7.2
Africa	3.7	3.6	4.0	4.6	5.3	6.2
Asia	11.8	10.4	15.5	13.8	16.9	14.1

Note:
1. North-west Europe includes Finland, Sweden, Norway, Denmark, Germany, Belgium, The Netherlands, France, Switzerland and Austria.

Source: P. R. Yates (1959), pp. 32–3.

Table 4.4 Percentage changes in the quantum of trade by region (1913 = 100)

	Imports		*Exports*		*Total trade*	
	1925 as % of 1913	*1928 as % of 1913*	*1925 as % of 1913*	*1928 as % of 1913*	*1925 as % of 1913*	*1928 as % of 1913*
Eastern and Central Europe:						
excl. Russia	92.8	116.0	75.6	104.0	84.1	110.0
incl. Russia	83.7	105.0	66.7	90.0	75.1	98.0
Rest of Europe	101.3	113.0	98.1	109.0	100.3	112.0
Europe:						
excl. Russia	98.7	114.0	90.4	107.0	95.1	111.0
incl. Russia	95.4	111.0	85.9	102.0	90.6	107.0
North America	139.9	161.0	137.8	160.0	138.5	160.0
South America	102.6	124.0	102.6	129.0	102.9	126.0
Africa	113.7	140.0	103.2	125.0	108.1	132.0
Asia	130.1	144.0	157.1	154.0	143.7	149.0
Oceania	130.1	135.0	133.3	138.0	132.0	137.0
World	107.8	124.0	107.1	122.0	107.4	123.0

Sources: League of Nations (1928) and (1931).

headway, so that by the end of the decade the discrepancy between East and West was fairly small relative to the prewar datum period.

With reference to individual countries, it is possible, in so far as the data allow, to classify countries by their trade performance relative to their GDP through 1913–29 as follows:

1. *Absolute trade decline*: UK, Germany, Austria. All three have a very weak output record and exports fail to regain former peaks. The first two account for a large part of Western Europe's poor track record in trade in the period.
2. *Slow trade growth at less than GDP*: Belgium, Italy and Switzerland. The Swiss case is unusual given the significant rise in total output over the period.
3. *Fast trade growth above GDP*: France, Denmark, Finland, Norway, The Netherlands and Sweden. They all have fast trade and output growth. Apart from France they are the only European countries to gain shares in world trade.
4. *Mixed performance*: Hungary, Poland, Czechoslovakia, Romania, Yugoslavia, Bulgaria, Albania. Generally strong trade performance

Table 4.5 Percentage share in value of world exports

	1885	*1913*	*1929*	*1938*
Austria	4.4	3.0	0.9	1.7
Belgium–Luxembourg	3.7	3.9	2.7	3.2
Denmark	0.6	0.9	1.3	1.5
France	9.6	7.2	6.0	3.9
Germany	11.0	13.1	9.8	10.0
Ireland	—	—	0.7	0.5
Italy	3.0	2.6	2.4	2.5
Netherlands	1.9	2.2	2.4	2.5
Norway	0.4	0.6	0.6	0.8
Sweden	1.1	1.2	1.5	2.1
Switzerland	2.1	1.4	1.2	1.3
UK	16.7	13.9	10.8	10.2
Western Europe	54.4	50.0	40.5	40.4
USA	11.2	12.9	15.8	13.6
Canada	1.3	2.3	3.5	3.7
North America	12.5	15.2	19.2	17.3
Third countries	33.1	34.7	40.3	42.3

Source: A. Maddison (1962), p. 161.

in the later 1920s but data limitations and territorial changes make precise comparison with 1913 very difficult.

Most European countries lost market share in world trade over the period 1913–29. The biggest losers were the UK and Germany whose shares of world exports fell from 13.9 to 10.8 per cent and from 13.1 to 9.8 per cent respectively (Table 4.5). France, Belgium-Luxembourg and Austria were also significant losers. Only a few of the smaller countries, mostly neutrals, managed to gain market share in world trade – for example, Sweden, Denmark, Norway and The Netherlands (Tables 4.5 and 4.6). For Western Europe as a whole the loss in world market share was quite dramatic, nearly 10 percentage points from 50 to 40.5 per cent, though it should be noted that Western Europe was losing market share before 1914. Much of the loss can be attributed to the larger countries (Table 4.5).

Taking the whole of Europe it is clear that the major loss of market share was borne by the Western sector (Table 4.3). This of course is consistent with the fact that it was the large countries which were the chief sufferers. The rest of Europe excluding Russia experienced only a marginal share loss in exports, but not in imports, with relative strength in primary product exports and weakness in manufacturing exports

Table 4.6 Europe's shares in world trade (percentages based on current values)

	1913	*1928*
UK	13.6	10.7
Germany	12.5	8.8
France	6.5	6.2
Italy, Belgium–Luxembourg, Netherlands, Switzerland, Sweden	11.0	9.9
Denmark, Norway, Finland	1.9	2.4
Rest of Europe	7.1	7.5
Total Europe	52.6	45.5
USA	12.5	15.4
Rest of world[1]	34.9	39.1

Note:

1. Rest of Europe includes Ireland, Austria, Czeckoslovakia, Hungary, Poland, Romania, Yugoslavia, Bulgaria, Greece, Spain and Portugal.

Source: I. Svennilson (1954), p. 300.

Table 4.7 Exports and imports of primary products: regional shares in world total (percentage)

	1913		*1928*		*1937*	
	Exports	*Imports*	*Exports*	*Imports*	*Exports*	*Imports*
UK and Ireland	6.2	19.0	4.8	19.9	4.8	22.9
North-west Europe[1]	25.2	43.1	14.5	34.2	15.6	33.7
Other Europe	14.7	12.3	16.0	10.5	13.7	8.5
North America	17.3	11.3	20.0	16.7	15.5	15.8
Oceania	3.7	0.9	4.6	1.1	5.5	1.1
Latin America	12.6	4.3	15.8	4.1	16.4	3.9
Africa	5.6	2.2	6.4	2.3	8.3	2.8
Asia	14.7	6.9	17.9	11.2	20.2	11.3

Note:
1. North-west Europe includes Finland, Sweden, Norway, Denmark, Germany, Belgium, The Netherlands, France, Switzerland and Austria.

Source: P. L. Yates (1959), pp. 47, 51.

Table 4.8 Exports and imports of manufactures: regional shares in world total (percentage)

	1913		*1928*		*1937*	
	Exports	*Imports*	*Exports*	*Imports*	*Exports*	*Imports*
UK and Ireland	25.3	8.2	21.8	9.1	19.5	8.8
North-west Europe[1]	47.9	24.4	40.9	17.5	41.8	17.5
Other Europe	8.3	15.4	4.6	15.7	5.8	13.3
North America	10.6	12.1	19.2	12.8	19.7	10.6
Oceania	0.1	5.0	0.2	5.1	0.4	5.7
Latin America	0.7	11.9	0.6	13.5	0.5	12.9
Africa	0.4	6.1	0.4	8.3	0.5	12.3
Asia	6.7	16.9	12.3	18.0	11.8	18.9

Note:
1. North-west Europe includes Finland, Sweden, Norway, Denmark, Germany, Belgium, The Netherlands, France, Switzerland and Austria

Source: P. L. Yates (1959), pp. 49–50.

(Tables 4.7 and 4.8). The relative stability of market share in the case of the latter region may, however, be misleading given the greater number of independent trading units following the break-up of the Austro-Hungarian Empire.

Impediments to European trade recovery before 1925

The poor showing of Europe in international trade in the 1920s, and particularly in the first half of the decade, is not altogether surprising given the great wartime losses and the slow recovery in incomes thereafter. For many countries trade had almost ceased to exist by the end of the war since siege conditions and blockade, together with a network of trade restrictions designed to block imports and restrict exports, had all but cut off normal intercourse. Moreover, during the course of the war the supply capabilities of many European countries were severely damaged, particularly in agricultural products, so that few surpluses remained for export. In addition, severe shortages of shipping space and foreign exchange meant that import needs had to be curtailed. Inevitably, therefore, trading connections were severed which provided the opportunity for former trading partners to develop alternative sources of supply to replace European exports.

The problem after the war was not simply that former markets had been lost, but that Europe as a whole was in no fit state to recapture lost markets. For several years many European countries were desperately short of food, raw materials, capital equipment and foreign exchange which hampered the process of reconstruction and trade recovery. Unlike the situation following the Second World War, relief supplies and assistance from the United States were too little and too late, so that Europe was thrown upon her own limited resources to manage as best she could. This inevitably delayed the recovery in output and the re-entry into international markets. It is significant that it was those countries or regions with a low recovery potential that performed badly in trade terms – Germany, the UK, Belgium, Austria and Eastern Europe. By 1925 output in most cases had barely reached the prewar level, while export volumes were well below the 1913 standard (Table 4.2).

Slow recovery in production not only limited trading potential but it also affected the structure and competitiveness of production which had longer-term implications for the future trade performance of the countries concerned. These aspects will be taken up in later sections.

Limited supply capability was the most important influence on the configuration of Europe's trade in the first half of the 1920s. The reconstruction process was impeded by a whole series of adverse factors; these included the disfiguration of Europe through the peace treaty settlements which created several independent but weak states, the burden of reparations and war debts, rampant inflation throughout most of Europe, volatile exchanges and political insecurity. In fact after the war there was scarcely a year in which the revival of Europe was not checked by some untoward event: the slump in trade and economic activity in the Anglo-Saxon countries in 1920–21, the massive inflations in Germany, Hungary, Poland and Austria in 1922–23, the occupation of the Ruhr in 1923, stabilisation crises in Poland and Germany in 1924, the slump in Belgium and French currencies in 1925 together with deflationary stabilisation measures in Britain and Scandinavia, and the British coal dispute of 1926.

Financial and currency problems were the most severe and pervasive impediments to the restoration of equilibrium in this period. Apart from the UK, budgetary deficits were the norm as governments sought to ease postwar political and social tensions by high spending at a time when tax revenues were far from buoyant. Budgetary deficits helped to fuel inflation which, once started, was very difficult to stop. In such conditions it was very difficult to stabilise exchange rates which 'for seven years danced and jumped with spasmodic and tireless energy'. (Loveday, 1931, p. 31). Some currencies, for example those of Poland, Hungary and Germany, eventually collapsed under the strain. The process of currency stabilisation therefore proved to be a long-drawn-out affair, with countries adopting a new fixed exchange rate as and when they managed to regain control of their domestic financial systems. There was no coordinated plan of currency restoration, as devised in 1944, but a piecemeal resumption of fixed exchange rates when it best suited each country's individual needs. The result was a largely unworkable system of exchange rates, with some undervalued – the French and Belgian francs – and others overvalued – sterling, the Italian lira and the Swedish krona. Few countries managed to stabilise at an equilibrium rate of exchange.

Monetary and financial instability in the first half of the decade undoubtedly hindered the recovery of European trade. The exchanges were often so volatile that normal trade transactions were rendered difficult and risky. This did little to encourage planning for the future since short-term considerations predominated. Currency stabilisation eased the situation but still left problems because of the haphazard and uncoordinated manner in which stabilisation was carried out.

The problem of trade recovery in East-Central Europe, leaving aside the special case of the USSR, was very much greater than that of the West. Despite a doubling of the number of trading partners as a result of the redrawing of the map of Europe, the volume of trade of those countries lying east of Germany and west of Russia was still only 75 per cent of the 1913 quantum by 1925.

The task of reconstruction in this region was of a quite different dimension from that in the West. Virtually all the countries were faced with a whole series of almost insuperable difficulties, but with incomes and resources very much inferior to those elsewhere in Europe. The list is almost endless: physical devastation, territorial divisions and economic disorganisation; financial chaos, including unbalanced budgets, inflation and currency instability; balance of payments problems, unemployment, rapidly rising populations, land reforms, political instability and weak administrations; structural backwardness, illiteracy and shortages of almost everything. In most cases it was not simply a question of getting back to normal as quickly as possible, but rather one of trying to stave off economic disintegration.

It should be explained, however, that the war was not the only factor responsible for the desperate plight of the eastern sector. The structural characteristics of the countries in the East were for the most part inimical to modern economic growth. With the exception of Czechoslovakia, the most advanced industrially and closer to the West than to her eastern neighbours, together with a few pockets of modern development elsewhere, notably in Hungary and Western Poland, modern industrial development was conspicuous by its absence. Most of the countries were overwhelmingly dependent on agriculture which in the case of the Balkans absorbed more than three-quarters of the population. Population pressures were often acute – rates of increase were more than twice the Western rate – while in several cases levels of illiteracy were high. Population pressures coupled with inefficient, semi-feudalistic agrarian systems with low yields meant that there was a large surplus population on the land. The result was very low incomes and limited savings for investment outwith the agrarian sector. The commodity composition of trade also reflects the backward structure of the countries in this region. Except for Czechoslovakia, the bulk of exports consisted of primary products, mainly agrarian, while finished or semi-finished products constituted a large share of imports (Aldcroft, 1988).

With the best will in the world, therefore, these countries, with their 'gigantic backlog of backwardness' (Spulber, 1966, p. 75) would have been hard pressed to advance their development. Unfortunately they received little in the way of help following the First World War. If anything, the peace treaty settlements put further obstacles in the way of progress. Economic considerations were almost entirely ignored when defining the territorial boundaries of the newly created or reconstituted states. The new territorial arrangements made little economic sense and they merely served to impede economic recovery. Several new states emerged from the wreckage of the former large economic unit of the Austro-Hungarian Empire. But the economic potential inherited by the successor states bore no relation to their inheritance of land and people. The new states acquired various fragments of territory at different stages of development and comprised assorted ethnic minorities, which required welding together into viable and cohesive political and economic units. This was an almost impossible task given the clash of ethnic groups and the break-up of former economic connections. Patterns of communication and trading links were severed, industrial centres were divided from their sources of raw materials and their markets, and former trade routes were hastily barricaded by tariffs and prohibitions. Not only had the new states to deal with the ordinary problems of reconstruction but they literally had to create new administrations and national economies out of the motley collection of territories which they inherited. They were left to accomplish this task almost unaided at a time when resources were desperately short, with financial and administrative systems far from commensurate with the needs in hand, and at a time when political and social stability left much to be desired (Condliffe, 1941).

The task was too great to accomplish by normal methods in the time span available. As Berend and Ranki (1969, p.171) explain:

> Even in normal conditions, a considerable period of time, in fact an entire historical era, would have been required to complete the adjustment to new conditions, the integration into a unified economic whole, the opening up of new development possibilities and the attainment of a steady and sustained rate of economic growth. But history did not allow the problem to be presented in this fashion. The needs of the new order became apparent at a moment when the problems of transition from a war to a peace economy were being added to the already difficult problems faced by an economy crippled by war, and all clamouring for immediate attention. The simultaneous appearance on the scene of all these problems brought about complete economic chaos, almost inextricable confusion, and a state of utter hopelessness.

Time was one thing that was not on their side and so abnormal or drastic expedients were invoked to deal with the situation. Inflation, currency depreciation and trade control were the chief measures used to secure some relief. Many of the wartime exchange controls and restrictions on imports and exports were retained for some years after the war, gradually to be replaced by stiffer tariff protection than that prevailing before the war. Most of the countries, except Poland, had appreciably higher tariff levels by the mid-1920s, especially on industrial products, a reflection of what was to become a more sustained drive to economic autarchy in later years. Tariffs also covered a wider range of products than previously. The new Hungarian tariff, for example, averaged 31.1 per cent of imports as against 18.9 per cent under the former tariff, while the new Czech tariff structure of 1925–26 was almost double that of the old Austro-Hungarian and represented 36.4 per cent of the total value of imports (Gordon, 1941; League of Nations, 1927; Liepmann, 1938).

Rather more drastic was the resort to inflation and currency depreciation as a way of solving, albeit temporarily, budgetary difficulties and the low capacity problem. Apart from Czechoslovakia, which stabilised its currency early on and avoided excessive inflation, the rest of East-Central Europe went in for inflationary financing and currency depreciation. The results were far from encouraging. Inflation and currency depreciation did give an initial boost to economic activity and exports, but once inflation got out of hand, as in Hungary and Poland, it probably did more harm than good. Forced industrialisation gave rise to inefficient undertakings and excess capacity, with development being reflected more in terms of capacity creation than in increased output. Moreover, as in the case of Austria and Germany, when stabilisation and financial control were finally achieved a reaction set in and economic activity was checked. Thus both Hungary and Poland considerably expanded their industrial capacity when inflation was at its worst, but by the middle of the decade industrial output was still well down on prewar levels.

The political and social conditions of the time may have left little room for alternative policy options, but the measures resorted to in the early 1920s simply gave an artificial boost to economic activity with few lasting benefits. Inflation, currency depreciation and trade protection could do little to solve the fundamental structural problems of the region. By 1925 industrial activity in the region as a whole remained well below that of 1913, in some cases appreciably so. Poland fell short by 37 per cent, Hungary by 23 per cent and Romania by 8 per cent. The production of raw materials and foodstuffs fared somewhat better but trade volumes did not respond correspondingly because of increasing domestic needs. By contrast, Czechoslovakia, which had inherited valuable industrial interests from the old Empire and had reformed her financial and currency systems promptly, experienced quite rapid development, with manufacturing output over one-third higher than in 1913.

The fragile equilibrium of the later 1920s

Through to 1925 the trade of Europe had lagged behind the recovery in output and had still not regained the prewar level. The shortfall was due principally to the slow recovery in the East and stagnation in the major economies of the West. However, by the middle of the decade economic and political conditions were much more stable than they had been in the early 1920s. The Locarno Pact of 1925, the revised reparation settlement of the previous year, and the negotiated agreements regarding Allied war debts, did much to boost international confidence and reduce political tensions and suspicions of war. Most of the great inflations had run their course and Britain's return to the gold standard in April 1925 paved the way for the completion of currency stabilisation elsewhere. Primary commodity prices had firmed considerably after the disastrous drop following the postwar boom. Above all, reconstruction and recovery in Europe were nearing completion and 'real progress began to take the place of a painful struggle to regain a plateau of prosperity which had been lost' (Loveday, 1931, p. 47). If there were still signs of tension and weakness in the international economy these were all but forgotten as the world looked forward to a period of sustained prosperity.

The boom in world activity in the later 1920s was led by the United States. But the expansion in industrial and primary output world-wide was more rapid and pervasive than in the period through to 1925. In the years 1925–29 world industrial production rose by more than 20 per cent, a slightly larger absolute increase than in the 12 years through to 1925. Total production of primary products rose by more than 10 per cent, or 2.6 per cent per annum as against 1.4 per cent in the years 1913–25. The pace was set by raw materials, with a 27 per cent increase, whereas food products only recorded a fairly modest rise of 6 per cent. At the same time the volume of international trade rose by nearly 21 per cent (Aldcroft, 1977).

Most regions of the world shared in the prosperity and there was more uniformity in rates of advance than in the first half of the decade. Progress in Europe as a whole matched that of the United States, and in primary production it was distinctly better. Europe regained a little of the ground she had lost earlier, while Eastern Europe did better than countries to the west and north. The trade of Europe expanded faster than production and exceeded world trade growth by a small margin. East-Central Europe fared better in this period than Western Europe (Table 4.4; Drabek, 1985; Lampe and Jackson, 1982). Thus by the end of the period Europe's trade had surpassed the 1913 peak but only by a small margin.

The relative improvement in Europe's performance in the later 1920s prompted the observation by the author of the League of Nation's study into the world depression that the prewar equilibrium between Europe and the rest of the world had been more or less restored (Ohlin, 1931). In retrospect this view now seems rather wide of the mark. If there was an equilibrium it was more apparent than real. Below the surface there were plenty of signs of maladjustment, notably large areas of underemployed resources in certain sectors especially agriculture and heavy industries, the failure of some of the larger countries, for example Germany and the UK, to achieve a proper recovery, the rise in primary inventories and price weakness, the dependence of many countries on the inflow of foreign capital, and the patched up nature of the international currency system. Such factors rendered the equilibrium a fragile one, leaving Europe very exposed to external shocks.

Perhaps the most serious problem was the weakness of the two major countries, Britain and Germany, neither of which was strong enough to play a leading role in European or world development. Both had a very poor growth record in the 1920s, with trade volumes still well down on prewar by the end of the decade. The British problem was essentially one of reduced competitiveness as a result of an antiquated industrial structure and an overvalued exchange rate following the return to gold. But Germany's difficulties were both more complex and more serious. The aftermath of inflation and the continued reparations burden left scars on society which were manifest in the political and economic tensions present in Weimar Germany (Balderston, 1982; James, 1986; McNeil, 1986). It was the most unstable of the western democracies. It could not reconcile the clash of opposing interest groups, some of which predated the war, partly because of its failure to deliver on the economic front (James, 1986; Maier, 1981; Weisbrod, 1979). As Abraham (1981) notes, the Weimar system simply disguised old conflicts, but it was never fully accepted by the majority of the economic and political leaders of the dominant social classes.

Thus the stability of the middle Weimar years was more apparent than real and the system remained vulnerable to internal collapse. The regime 'was not grounded in any broad legitimacy, and it therefore proved vulnerable to economic and political strains that might cause any of the various participants to withdraw from the compact.' (Abraham, 1981, p. 8). Moreover, because of its inherent economic weakness, it was dependent on external support – mainly American capital – which left it as exposed as Eastern Europe once this support was withdrawn.

Failing a lead from the two powers which had been influential before 1914, there was no one to fill the political and economic vacuum left by the collapse of the Austro-Hungarian Empire. France was not strong enough, nor had the inclination, to exercise a hegemonic role. Consequently East-Central Europe, excluding Russia, remained a collection of weak states heavily dependent on foreign markets and external aid. This dependency might not have been so bad had the countries in the region been able to adapt their economic structures sufficiently to make them viable, but for the most part they could not. There was a modest shift from agriculture and some reorientation of the export product mix, for example towards tobacco in Bulgaria, forest products in Yugoslavia and petroleum in Romania. Nevertheless, agriculture still remained overwhelmingly predominant as did primary products in the export trade (Drabek, 1985; Lampe, 1986; Lampe and Jackson, 1982). The very low level of efficiency in agriculture meant that it could not act as a major source of accumulation, while reliance on this sector as a source of foreign exchange earnings was very precarious given the increasingly restricted nature of the market for foodstuffs in the west and the volatility of primary product prices. Moreover, the new states in Europe tended to be more trade sensitive than previously because of the loss of the large internal market of the Austro-Hungarian Empire, which therefore left them more exposed to the vagaries of the international trade cycle. Finally, because of the low level of domestic accumulation and the scarcity of foreign exchange, increasing reliance was placed on capital imports. These did make some contribution to development in the later 1920s but the dangers of such dependency soon became all too apparent. The servicing of the external debt was an ever-increasing burden on the balance of payments since capital borrowing costs could not be requited fully by export earnings. Thus in time a considerable proportion of merchandise export receipts were absorbed by external debt financing – 48 per cent in the case of Hungary, 36 per cent for Yugoslavia and Romania and 27 per cent for Poland (Nötel, 1986). In short, even had there not been a severe international depression and financial crisis in the early 1930s, East European countries would have found their position increasingly untenable, a situation not unlike that in Latin America in the 1980s, or for that matter in Latin America in the 1920s (Schuker, 1988).

There were many more elements of instability in Europe and the international economy in the later 1920s but it is not the purpose of this essay to unravel the causes of the world depression of the 1930s. What we have tried to demonstrate is that Europe could not reintegrate properly into the international economy in the 1920s because of inherent weaknesses and lack of leadership. It was struggling to recapture some of its former strength in the latter part of the decade but there was little prospect of it regaining its prewar role. It had lost this position not simply because the war and its aftermath had shattered its potential and allowed other countries outwith Europe to overtake it, but also because structural defects and inner tensions prevented it from grasping new opportunities which arose in the decade following the war. This becomes clear when we look at some of the structural features of Europe's trade in this period.

Shifts in the direction of trade

The declining importance of Europe in international trade after the war was mainly an intra-European phenomenon with the major countries accounting for the bulk of the losses in trade shares. From Table 4.9 it can be seen that inter-European trade as a percentage of world imports fell from 40 to 29.2 per cent between 1913 and 1928, whereas there was a rise of over five percentage points in the trade among non-European countries. At the same time trade between Europe and non-European countries also increased in importance. In other words, Europe was trading proportionately less with itself and more with the outside world. Rising tariff levels, especially on finished goods, were partly responsible for the relative decline in the intra-European share of world trade (Delle Donne, 1928; Liepmann, 1938).

The disintegration of the European component in world trade was largely a function of the decline in intercourse between the major industrial countries – the UK, Germany and France – together with the withdrawal of the Soviet Union from the international scene. The latter had accounted for about 4 per cent of world trade in 1913, but by the later 1920s its share was less than 1.5 per cent. Among the three major

Table 4.9 Percentage distribution of world trade in imports

	1913	*1928*	*1938*
World trade	100.0	100.0	100.0
Inter-European trade	40.0	29.2	29.1
Imports to Europe from non-European countries	21.5	24.7	26.6
Imports to non-European countries from Europe	15.2	17.2	17.5
Trade among non-European countries	23.3	28.9	26.8

Source: W. S. Woytinsky and E. S. Woytinsky (1955), pp. 71, 80.

countries the volume of trade fell by over one-quarter in the same period, while trade between the Big Three and Italy, Belgium, The Netherlands, Switzerland and Sweden also declined. By contrast, there was a modest rise in the trade conducted with smaller countries (Svennilson, 1954).

In contrast to the experience of the major powers, many of the smaller countries tended to improve their relative position in European trade (Tables 4.10 and 4.11). They not only did an increasing amount of business with each other but some of them also strengthened their links with Germany, the UK and France. The main exceptions were Belgium and Italy, whose experience was closer to that of the larger European countries.

Some of these directional shifts in European trade occurred among countries with a degree of political affinity or sympathy. Thus trade among the Scandinavian states increased as did British trade with these countries. Germany strengthened her interests in the Balkans and with other Germanic countries and also with Spain and Portugal. France shifted her attention to dependencies in North Africa, as did Britain

Table 4.10 Europe's exports (percentages based on current values)

	Exports of individual countries as % of total European exports		*Exports from individual countries to Europe as % of their total exports*	
	1913	*1928*	*1913*	*1928*
1. UK	26.1	23.6	30.1	31.6
2. Germany	24.7	19.3	66.3	69.9
3. France	13.6	13.7	66.6	62.5
Total 1 to 3	64.4	56.6	51.7	52.2
4. Italy	4.9	5.1	58.7	57.4
5. Belgium–Luxembourg	7.0	5.8	79.2	69.9
6. Netherlands	5.0	5.3	65.2	74.3
7. Switzerland	2.7	2.7	69.3	69.2
8. Sweden	2.3	2.9	83.6	74.9
Total 4 to 8	21.9	21.8	70.6	68.6
9. Rest of Europe[1]	13.7	21.6	79.5	85.6
Total Europe	100.0	100.0	59.6	63.0

Note:
1. Rest of Europe includes Denmark, Norway, Finland, Ireland, Austria, Czeckoslovakia, Hungary, Poland, Romania, Yugoslavia, Bulgaria, Greece, Spain and Portugal.

Source: I. Svennilson (1954), p. 171.

Table 4.11 Europe's imports (percentages based on current values)

	Imports of individual countries as % of total European imports		*Imports of individual countries from Europe as % of their total imports*	
	1913	*1928*	*1913*	*1928*
1. UK	26.9	27.6	37.5	38.9
2. Germany	21.2	17.8	40.7	47.1
3. France	13.3	11.2	46.5	42.7
Total 1 to 3	61.4	56.6	40.6	42.2
4. Italy	5.8	6.1	58.2	47.0
5. Belgium–Luxembourg	7.2	4.7	58.6	65.2
6. Netherlands	6.8	5.7	47.0	61.4
7. Switzerland	3.0	2.7	29.1	72.5
8. Sweden	1.9	2.5	81.5	74.0
Total 4 to 8	24.7	21.7	59.3	61.0
9. Rest of Europe[1]	13.9	21.7	70.3	75.9
Total Europe	100.0	100.0	49.4	53.6

Note:
1. Rest of Europe includes Denmark, Norway, Finland, Ireland, Austria, Czeckoslovakia, Hungary, Poland, Romania, Yugoslavia, Bulgaria, Greece, Spain and Portugal.

Source: I. Svennilson (1954), p. 173.

towards its empire. Spain, Italy and Portugal, on the other hand, tended to loosen their traditional links with Latin America.

Outwith the European nexus, the main changes occurred in the North American market. Almost without exception European countries increased their trade activity with the United States, in some cases substantially so. Despite stiff tariff protection the American market was a lucrative one for European exports in the 1920s, and it was of course also an important source of supply, especially in the early 1920s when Europe was so short of food and raw materials. In part the strengthening American connections were at the expense of other non-European countries.

Finally, one should mention the case of Britain since the European content of its trade was low by continental standards. It constituted around one-third of Britain's trade, or about half of the continental average. Unfortunately, lower dependence on European markets did not insulate Britain in the postwar period since she faced even worse losses in non-European markets, particularly the Asian and dominion markets (Foreman-Peck, 1983). In fact, Britain lost trade share in all main markets during the period but none more so than in those of Asia and the Dominions. In 1913 around one-half of Japanese imports of manufactures were British, but by 1929 the proportion had fallen by one-quarter with the United States being the main beneficiary. In the case of the Dominions – Australia, New Zealand and South Africa – the share for imported manufactures fell from three-quarters to three-fifths. Again the United States was the main competitor. The other major loss was in the Indian market where Britain had supplied 80 per cent of imported manufactures (mainly textiles) in 1913 but only 57 per cent by 1929. The main source of trouble in this case was the growth of Indian textile production and to a lesser extent Japanese competition. The losses borne by British exports in 1929 as against 1913 (see Table 4.12) were almost entirely due to the sacrifice of market share in Britain's major markets which were only partly offset by expanding world demand (Maizels, 1963).

Table 4.12 Shares of the world market for manufactures (percentage)

	1899	*1913*	*1929*
UK	33.2	30.2	23.0
Germany	22.4	26.6	21.0
France	14.4	12.1	11.1
Belgium–Luxembourg	5.5	5.0	5.5
Italy	3.6	3.3	3.8
Switzerland	4.0	3.1	2.8
Sweden	0.9	1.4	1.8
Western Europe total	84.0	81.7	69.0
USA	11.7	13.0	21.0
Canada	0.4	0.6	3.6
Japan	1.5	2.3	4.0
India	2.4	2.4	2.4
Total	100.0	100.0	100.0

Source: A. Maizels (1963), p. 129.

Commodity composition of trade and competitiveness

In both primary products and manufactures Europe lost market shares in international trade during the postwar period (Tables 4.7 and 4.8; Yates, 1959). The losses were considerably greater in the case of manufactures, and particularly serious for the high-income industrial countries of the West, which had dominated world trade in manufactures before the war.

As far as the trade in raw materials and agricultural products is concerned, it was Western Europe including the UK which bore the brunt of the market loss. Much of it could be accounted for by the relative stagnation in the demand for cereal products, the increasing self-sufficiency of Western Europe in non-tropical products and increasing tariff protection on farm products. Western Europe no longer provided a ready market for the surplus food of other countries as was the case before 1914. The other main feature was the contraction in the coal trade, especially relevant to Britain, due to the sharp slowing down in the world demand for coal. By contrast, Eastern Europe managed to improve slightly its market share in world exports of primary products as a result of some adaptation of its export product structure in the course of the decade (see above).

Much more striking was the large decline in Europe's share of world trade in manufactures, from over 80 per cent in 1913 to less than 70 per cent by the end of the 1920s, after which it remained remarkably stable through the next decade (Table 4.8 and 4.12). The decline in import shares was, however, much less dramatic. For some countries, the UK and France in particular, this represented a speeding up of a trend apparent before 1914, but for most European countries it was the beginning of a new trend. The fact also that Eastern Europe saw its already minuscule share of 8.3 per cent (1913) of world exports in manufactures almost halve, confirms the view that this region was relatively unsuccessful in shifting its export structure away from primary products. Most of the gains in world trade in manufactures were made by the United States and Japan.

If we examine the commodity structure of European manufacturing exports then it becomes clear that one of the main problems was the lack of adjustment to changes in patterns of world demand for manufactured goods. Svennilson (1954) has argued that Europe's ability to compete in world markets was closely connected with its ability to adjust its production structure to a rapidly shifting demand situation. Although the war may well have helped to delay this adjustment process, it is apparent that many European countries were handicapped before hostilities had commenced because of their heavy commitment to ex-growth sectors and the rigidity of their industrial structures. As Table 4.13 demonstrates, the UK, France, Italy, Belgium and Switzerland had a very large proportion of their trade in contracting sectors in world trade, and a low share in the expanding ones. Germany and Sweden were more favourably placed, while the United States was in the best position of all. It is significant

Table 4.13 Exports of manufactures from selected countries (percentage shares of three major commodity groups)

	Expanding groups Machinery and transport equipment		*Stable groups Metals and Chemicals*		*Contracting groups Textiles and miscellaneous manufactures*	
	1913	*1928*	*1913*	*1928*	*1913*	*1928*
UK	15.9	19.5	21.6	19.2	62.5	61.3
Germany	16.9	19.4	33.6	35.6	49.5	45.0
France	10.0	12.1	15.6	21.7	74.4	66.2
Italy	7.6	9.8	8.4	7.6	84.0	82.6
Belgium	9.3	8.3	29.9	35.4	60.8	56.3
Switzerland	11.8	16.9	11.3	16.8	76.9	66.3
Sweden	18.8	33.4	35.9	25.2	45.3	41.4
USA	23.8	44.3	38.9	24.9	37.3	30.8
Total 8 countries	15.8	23.2	26.6	24.9	57.6	51.9

Source: I. Svennilson (1954), p. 295.

moreover, that the two countries (Sweden and the United States) most favourably placed in terms of export commodity structures in 1913, were also the ones which responded most rapidly to the changes in world demand after that date by altering still further their export structures in the direction of expanding sectors. Thus by the end of the decade the United States had 44 per cent of its exports in the machinery and transport equipment groups, and Sweden one-third. But for most other European countries the changes in the export product mix were fairly marginal and in some cases anyway they were a product of declines in the importance of textiles rather than a genuine attempt to expand in the dynamic sectors of world trade. In fact, in the case of the UK and Germany, machinery exports actually fell in volume during the period.

The inflexibility of the export product structure takes on an added significance if we consider the effects of both import substitution and changes in competitive shares. The failure to modernise the production structure meant that European countries faced two adverse influences simultaneously: an inability to compete in expanding sectors in the high income markets, and the effects of import substitution in contracting sectors in the lesser developed countries. Thus the heaviest setbacks after the war occurred in the expanding commodity groups of machinery and transport equipment, and only in a few protected markets was Europe able to maintain its relative position. In the contracting sectors, textiles were the main problem area, especially for Britain and Switzerland since these goods bulked large in total exports in 1913. They were severely hit by import substitution in Asia and Latin America, and also from Japanese competition (see Table 4.14).

Overall the biggest losses through import substitution and competitive market shares occurred in the larger countries – the UK, Germany and France. Britain was by far the worst sufferer in both respects because of her heavy dependence on textiles and other basic sectors vulnerable to import substitution, but also because of general inefficiency in manufacturing and the impact of a high exchange rate after 1925. Britain in fact lost trade share in all main markets and in all major commodity groups. Germany also suffered quite heavily from import substitution and competitive handicaps; she experienced losses in most major markets except non-industrial countries, and in most commodity groups, though with some relative strength in the expanding sectors to Western Europe and non-industrial countries. French losses were mainly confined to import substitution since she displayed relative strength in trade with Western Europe and non-industrial countries in both expanding and stable sectors (Maizels, 1963).

As far as the smaller countries are concerned (Belgium, Italy, The Netherlands, Sweden and Switzerland), the effects of import substitu-

Table 4.14 Intra-trade of the industrial countries in manufactures (percentage changes)

	Intra-European		*Intra-North American*	*Inter-Continental*		*Total*
	UK – continental	*Intra-continental*		*Europe – North America*	*Japan – Europe and North America*	
1899–1913	32	105	238	68	125	172
1913–1929	–13	22	189	34	42	26

Source: A. Maizels (1963), p. 92.

tion were quite serious, but there was some compensation from overall relative strength in competitive shares. The record in the latter respect was somewhat mixed, however. Sweden did particularly well in the main markets and commodity groups as a result of her dynamic product structure. Switzerland, by contrast, experienced market losses, while Belgium and Italy managed a slight improvement of their shares in manufacturing trade (Maizels, 1963).

Conclusions

The main conclusions may now be summarised as follows:

1. World trade was generally less buoyant in the interwar years than it had been in the half-century or so before 1914. Trade growth fell below that of GDP. Much of the slowdown can be attributed to the relative decline of Europe whose trade–income ratio fell sharply in the 1920s.
2. The main trade share losses were borne by the larger countries, the UK, Germany and France, and the USSR.
3. Trade among some of the smaller western countries, especially the Scandinavian, showed signs of relative strength.
4. Intra-European trade declined in relative importance as European countries shifted the direction of their trading links towards North America and other non-European countries.
5. Not all the relative trade losses were due solely to the income and trade destruction effects of war and its aftermath. Even before the war there were signs of trade weakening in Europe due to import substitution, declining competitiveness and the increasing inflexibility of economic structures. However, these trends were sharply accelerated by the wartime dislocation.
6. Trade losses through import substitution were of considerable importance for some of the larger countries, notably the UK and Germany.
7. The inflexibility of economic structures, both in Eastern and Western Europe, meant that many countries did not adapt rapidly enough to changing patterns of world demand following the war. Many European countries therefore lost out to more dynamic non-European countries with the result that they were unable to take advantage of the expanding sectors of world trade.
8. The European trade situation was not helped by the unstable economic conditions of the period, especially in the first half of the 1920s. Even in the latter part of the decade, when trade and eco-

nomic activity were more buoyant, the underlying economic situation was unsound. In particular, the weakness of the major trading nations, the failure of international economic cooperation, especially on currency and tariff issues, and the increasing reliance of many European countries on inflows of foreign capital, made for a very fragile equilibrium.

References

Abraham, P. (1981), *The Collapse of the Weimar Republic: Political and Economic Crises*, Princeton, NJ: Princeton University Press.

Aldcroft, D. H. (1977), *From Versailles to Wall Street, 1919–1929*, London: Allen Lane.

Aldcroft, D. H. (1988), 'Eastern Europe in an age of turbulance, 1919–1950', *Economic History Review*, **41**.

Arndt, H. W. (1944), *The Economic Lessons of the Nineteen-Thirties*, London: Oxford University Press.

Balderston, T. (1982), 'The origins of economic instability in Germany, 1924–1930: market forces versus economic policy', *Vierteljahrschrift für Sozial-und Wirtschafts-geschichte*, **69**.

Baldwin, R. E. (1958), 'The commodity composition of trade: selected industrial countries, 1900–1954', *Review of Economics and Statistics*, **40**.

Berend, I. T and Ranki, G. (1969), 'Economic problems of the Danube region after the break-up of the Austro-Hungarian Monarchy', *Journal of Contemporary History*, **4**.

Berend, I. T. and Ranki, G. (1974), *Economic Development in East Central Europe in the 19th and 20th Centuries*, New York: Columbia University Press.

Bernstein, M. A. (1988), *The Great Depression: Delayed Recovery and Economic Change in America, 1929–1939*, Cambridge: Cambridge University Press.

Buchanan, N. S. and Lutz, F. A. (1974), *Rebuilding the World Economy: America's Role in Foreign Trade and Investment*, New York: Twentieth Century Fund.

Cairncross, A. K. and Faaland, J. (1952), 'Long-term trends in Europe's trade', *Economic Journal*, **62**.

Capie, F. (1983), *Depression and Protectionism: Britain between the Wars*, London: Allen and Unwin

Condliffe, J. B. (1941), *The Reconstruction of World Trade: a Survey of International Economic Relations*, London: Allen and Unwin.

Corner, D. C. (1956), 'Exports and the British trade cycle: 1929', *The Manchester School,* 24.

Delle Donne, O. (1928), *European Tariff Policies since the War*, New York: Adelphi Company.

Deutsch, K. W. and Eckstein, A. (1961), 'National industrialisation and the diminishing share of the international economic sector, 1890–1959', *World Politics,* 13.

Drabek, Z. (1985), 'Foreign trade performance and policy', in M. C. Kaser and E. A. Radice (eds), *The Economic History of Eastern Europe, 1919–1975.* Vol. 1, *Economic Structure and Performance between the Two Wars*, Oxford: Oxford University Press.

Foreman-Peck, J. (1983), *A History of the World Economy: International Economic Relations since 1850*, Brighton: Wheatsheaf Books.

Friedman, P. (1974), *The Impact of Trade Destruction on National Incomes: a Study of Europe 1924–38*, Gainsville, FL: University of Florida Press.

Gordon, M. S. (1941), *Barriers to World Trade: a Study of Recent Commercial Policy*, New York: Macmillan.

Grassman, S. (1980), 'Long-term trends in openess of national economies', *Oxford Economic Papers,* 32.

Hilgerdt, F. (1945), *Industrialization and Foreign Trade*, Geneva: League of Nations.

Hirschman, A. O. (1943), 'The commodity structure of world trade', *Quarterly Journal of Economics,* 57.

James, H. (1986), *The German Slump: Politics and Economics, 1924–1936*, Oxford: Oxford University Press.

Kindleberger, C. P. (1956), *The Terms of Trade: a European Case Study*, London: Chapman and Hall.

Lampe, J. R. (1986), *The Bulgarian Economy in the Twentieth Century*, London: Croom Helm.

Lampe, J. R. and Jackson M. R. (1982), *Balkan Economic History, 1550–1950*, Bloomington, IN: Indiana University Press.

League of Nations (1927), *Tariff Level Indices*, Geneva: League of Nations.

League of Nations (1928), *Memorandum on Production and Trade 1913 and 1923–26*, Geneva: League of Nations.

League of Nations (1931), *Memorandum on Production and Trade 1925 to 1929–30*, Geneva: League of Nations.

League of Nations (1942), *Commercial Policy in the Interwar Period*, Geneva: League of Nations.

League of Nations (1943), *Quantitative Trade Controls: their Causes and Nature*, Geneva: League of Nations.

League of Nations (1944), *International Currency Experience: Lessons of the Interwar Period*, Geneva: League of Nations.
League of Nations (1945), *Commercial Policy in the Postwar World*, Geneva: League of Nations.
League of Nations (1946), *The Course and Control of Inflation: a Review of Monetary Experience in Europe after World War I*, Geneva: League of Nations.
Lewis, W. A. (1949), *Economic Survey, 1919–1939*, London: Allen and Unwin.
Lewis, W. A. (1952), 'World production, prices and trade, 1870–1960', *The Manchester School*, 20.
Liepmann, H. (1938), *Tariff Levels and the Economic Unity of Europe*, London: Allen and Unwin.
Linder, S. B. (1961), *An Essay on Trade and Transformation*, New York: Wiley.
Loveday, A. (1931), *Britain and World Trade*, London: Longmans Green.
Maddison, A. (1962), 'Growth and fluctuation in the world economy, 1870–1960', *Banca Nazionale del Lavoro Quarterly Review*, 15.
Maddison, A. (1982), *Phases of Capitalist Development*, Oxford: Oxford University Press.
Maddison, A. (1991), *Dynamic Forces in Capitalist Development*, Oxford: Oxford University Press.
Maddison, A. (1995), *Monitoring the World Economy 1820–1992*, Paris: OECD.
Maier, C. S. (1975), *Recasting Bourgeois Europe: Stabilization in France, Germany and Italy in the Decade after World War I*, Princeton, NJ: Princeton University Press.
Maier, C. S. (1981), 'The two postwar eras and the conditions for stability in twentieth century Western Europe', *American Historical Review*, 86.
Maizels, A. (1963), *Industrial Growth and World Trade*, Cambridge: Cambridge University Press.
McNeil, W. C. (1986), *American Money and the Weimar Republic: Economics and Politics on the Eve of the Great Depression*, New York: Columbia University Press.
Nötel, R. (1986), 'International credit and finance', in M. C. Kaser and E. A. Radice (eds), *The Economic History of Eastern Europe, 1919–1975*, Vol. II, *Interwar Policy, the War and Reconstruction*, Oxford: Oxford University Press.
Ohlin, B. (1931), *The Course and Phases of the World Depression*, Geneva: League of Nations.
Pollard, S. (1981), *Peaceful Conquest: The Industrialization of Europe 1760–1970*, Oxford: Oxford University Press.

Rappard, W. E. (1938), *Postwar Efforts for Freer Trade*, Geneva: Geneva Research Centre.

Schuker, S. A. (1988), *American 'Reparations' to Germany, 1919–33: Implications for the Third-World Debt Crisis*, Princeton, NJ: Princeton Studies in International Finance.

Silverman, D. P. (1982), *Reconstructing Europe after the Great War*, Cambridge, MA: Harvard University Press.

Spulber, N. (1966), *The State and Economic Development in Eastern Europe*, New York: Random House.

Svennilson, I. (1954), *Growth and Stagnation in the European Economy*, Geneva: Economic Commission for Europe (UN).

Triffin, R. (1968), *Our International Monetary System: Yesterday, Today and Tomorrow*, New York: Random House.

Tyszynski, H. (1951), 'World trade in manufactured commodities, 1899–1950', *The Manchester School,* **19**.

United Nations (1949), *International Capital Movements during the Interwar Period*, New York: United Nations.

Weisbrod, B. (1979), 'Economic power and political stability reconsidered: heavy industry in Weimar Germany', *Social History,* **4**.

Woytinsky, W. S. and Woytinsky, E. S. (1955), *World Commerce and Governments: Trends and Outlook*, New York: Twentieth Century Fund.

Yates, P. L. (1959), *Forty Years of Foreign Trade*, London: Allen and Unwin.

Yeager, L.B. (1966), *International Monetary Relations: Theory, History and Policy*, New York: Harper and Row.

CHAPTER FIVE

International Lending, Debtor Countries and the Great Depression

Though debt delinquency and default were by no means unknown in the nineteenth century, especially among Latin American countries, most of the international lending in this period was serviced satisfactorily primarily because a large part of it found its way into areas of high growth potential, for example North America and the British Dominions. Twentieth-century experience has been a much less happy one. Apart from the losses incurred in the First World War, especially those by France as a consequence of the Bolshevik repudiation of Tsarist debts, the two major bursts of commercial lending in the 1920s and 1970s/early 1980s were both disasters. The first ended in delinquency and default, while the second gave rise to a global debt crisis which threatened to rock the Western financial world. Ironically, the more recent debt crisis was very much a rerun of that of the 1920s.

The pattern of postwar lending and borrowing

The First World War had a marked effect on the pattern and character of international lending and foreign investments. For one thing it created a whole series of new international debts in the form of reparations and Allied war loans. Secondly, Western Europe's status as a creditor was considerably weakened. Most creditor countries lost, or were forced to sell, part of their foreign holdings of securities, while Germany became a net debtor as a result of the peace treaty provisions. Thirdly, the United States emerged as the world's strongest creditor country, the more so if one includes inter-governmental debts owed to the United States by the Allied countries (Lewis, 1938, pp. 447, 450).

During the 1920s international lending was resumed on a scale comparable to that before 1914 and by the end of the decade the total volume of foreign-owned assets was considerably larger than before the war. During this period the United States replaced Western Europe as the major capital supplier. Between 1919 and 1929 her long-term investments abroad rose by nearly $9 billion and accounted for some two-thirds of global new investment. This raised America's stake to about $15.4 billion or nearly one-third of the world total, while her net long-term position, after allowing for the purchase of US securities by foreigners, rose to over $9.5 billion (Lewis, 1938, pp. 447, 450). No other country approached the American scale of lending. Britain resumed lending on a diminished scale shortly after the war but the total disbursed was less than half that of the United States. By the end of the 1920s Britain had just about managed to recover her prewar position, though her foreign assets now accounted for less than 40 per cent of the world total. France, by contrast, failed to recoup her large wartime losses despite substantial foreign lending in the latter half of the decade. Hence her share of the global total fell to less than 8 per cent. These three countries accounted for over three-quarters of all foreign investments in 1929. The other much smaller creditors were The Netherlands, Sweden, Switzerland and Czechoslovakia (Buchanan and Lutz, 1947, p. 156; Feinstein and Watson, 1995, pp. 100, 116).

The main borrowing regions were Europe, Latin America and the British Dominions. Within Europe Germany was by far the largest debtor, incurring a long-term debt of some $7.5 billion by the end of the 1920s, a large part of which was owed to the United States. This was a striking contrast to the position before 1914 when Germany, along with Britain and France, had been a major creditor country. The flow of American capital to Germany was largely responsible for the significant rise in the European share of American overseas investment, from 13.4 to 31.4 per cent between 1913 and 1930. Investments in other European countries combined were less than those to Germany, the major debtors being Austria, Italy, Hungary, Poland, Romania and Greece. South America and the British Empire accounted for the major part of the remaining new investment in fairly equal proportions. Much of the investment in the former was of US origin, with Argentina by far the largest borrower followed by Bolivia, Brazil, Chile, Columbia, Cuba, Mexico, Peru and Uruguay. London was the main source for imperial borrowing except for Canada which was served primarily by the United States. Australia, New Zealand and Canada had the distinction of having the highest per capita external debt in the world (Copeland, 1934, p. 15; Schedwin, 1970, pp. 2–3, 68–75).

The volatility of capital movements

The pattern and trend of capital movements during the postwar years was highly erratic with large swings in amplitude in certain years. In the immediate postwar period virtually the only country in a position to service the world's capital and foreign exchange needs was the United States. The UK resumed foreign lending soon after the war but was in no position to carry the burden alone. Most of the other former creditors were out of commission for one reason or another and, in fact, were capital importers in the immediate postwar years.

With a large favourable trade balance America therefore became the automatic source of finance in the years following the Armistice. In 1919 and 1920 her net outward capital movements totalled nearly $7 billion, much of which found its way into Europe whose needs were most pressing. France alone recorded net capital imports of some $2.3 billion in these two years much of it for reconstruction purposes, while Sweden imported $384 million. The flow of funds was disbursed in a somewhat haphazard fashion rather than in relation to specific needs. A considerable part of it – possibly $3 billion – consisted of inter-governmental credits of one form or another (sometimes under the auspices of the League of Nations), while much of the remainder was accounted for by short-term capital transactions on private account, often speculative funds attracted to Germany and other European countries with depreciated currencies or the repatriation of short-term balances abroad as in the case of The Netherlands, Sweden and Switzerland. These movements made an important contribution to financing Germany's import surplus in the form of much needed foodstuffs and raw materials (Holtfrerich, 1986, pp. 8, 27). Long-term privately floated capital issues were fairly rare in these uncertain years.

International lending was curtailed sharply once the postwar boom broke. The United States cut back its aid programme to Europe very abruptly, while the deterioration of the current account balance checked the outflow of private funds. The unstable political and economic conditions in Europe, especially the currency turmoils, deterred would-be private investors. Thus the net movement of capital from America had dwindled to a mere trickle by 1923 (Table 5.1). The resumption of lending by the UK and France only partly offset the massive fall in American capital so that the aggregate net capital movements from the creditor countries declined by 60 per cent between 1920 and 1923.

The setback in overseas lending occurred at a most inopportune time for debtor countries and it was a foretaste of what was to come later in the decade. Reconstruction in Europe was still far from complete and many countries, especially in Central and Eastern Europe, were desperately short of resources. The sudden drying-up of government aid and credits hit hard, since private investors were reluctant to commit funds to these countries. Under pressure they were forced to let their exchanges fall further, thereby exacerbating the inflationary potential, in an effort to balance external accounts and ease the process of reconstruction (Aldcroft and Morewood, 1995, ch. 2). Moreover, the sharp drop in commodity prices and export earnings imposed a heavy burden

Table 5.1 Net inward (+) or outward (–) capital movements, 1919–38 (measured by estimated deficits or surpluses on account of goods services and gold ($m))

	USA	*UK*	*France*	*Other creditors*	*Total*
1919	–3 990	—	+1 420	+145	–2 425
1920	–2 912	–881	+935	+354	–2 504
1921	–878	—	–394	–18	–1 290
1922	–376	–682	–268	–9	–1 335
1923	–162	–700	–187	+36	–1 013
1924	–731	–380	–535	–91	–1 737
1925	–784	–261	–450	–138	–1 633
1926	–352	+126	–483	–154	–863
1927	–829	–385	–504	–252	–1 970
1928	–1 250	–569	–236	–186	–2 241
1929	–628	–574	+20	–340	–1 522
1930	–380	–112	+257	–128	–363
1931	–330	+313	+791	+665	+1 439
1932	–116	+179	+917	+151	+1 131
1933	–280	—	+39	–65	–306
1934	+837	+35	+172	–164	+880
1935	+1 876	–158	–941	–435	+342
1936	+1 365	+90	–1 182	+131	+404
1937	+1 302	+277	–166	+137	+1 550
1938	+690	+269	+207	+35	+1 201

Source: United Nations (1949), p. 10.

on debtor countries everywhere, especially those which had incurred large debts at inflated price levels. It created a severe transfer problem for many primary producers who found difficulty in acquiring sufficient dollars to service their debts. This in turn encouraged them to raise output in an effort to maximise earnings, but this merely served to aggravate the downward pressure on prices (Lary, 1943, p. 146).

Fortunately things took a turn for the better in 1924. Foreign lending on a large scale was resumed in that year, encouraged by the improvement in political and economic conditions, especially in Europe where significant progress had been made with currency stabilisation and the control of inflation. During the next few years many countries obtained capital from the main creditor countries, though there was a heavy concentration in certain regions. American investment flowed mainly to

Europe, especially Germany, Latin America and Canada, while Britain focused on the Dominions and Asia. Europe and Latin America took up almost 60 per cent of the net capital issues on foreign account in the United States and Britain between 1924 and 1929 (League of Nations, 1931, p. 367). Apart from 1926, when there was a dip in capital exports, the net capital outflow from the major creditors more than doubled from 1923 to a peak of $2 241 million in 1928. Thereafter overseas lending diminished sharply; by 1930 it had almost dried up and in the following year the creditor countries had become significant net capital importers on balance (Table 5.1; North, 1962, p. 43).

International lending and global equilibrium

How significant was international lending in relation to the stability of the international economy in the later 1920s and its subsequent collapse? The pros and cons of foreign lending have frequently been debated, though with differing conclusions as to its impact. The argument here is that foreign lending did play a crucial role in the global economy of the 1920s in the sense that it created an illusion of soundness and stability which did not really exist (Ellsworth, 1964, p. 405). So long as the flow of funds from creditors to debtors continued the cracks in the international economic system remained concealed. Yet ironically, the flow of funds also served to widen the cracks so that once the flow was cut off the system was undermined. Dunning (1970, p. 20) read the situation correctly when he wrote that 'a climate of investment so radically different from that of prewar days, combined with substantial short-term capital movements, powerfully contributed to the world economic collapse of 1931 and its aftermath'.

On the other hand, theory would postulate that inter-country capital flows serve as an equilibrating device. A neo-classical factor flow model can be invoked in support of this contention. One such model, the regional convergence model, may be extended to a global situation wherein capital flows from rich to poor countries and labour resources flow in the reverse direction so that factor returns are equalised under conditions of perfect factor mobility. This is presumably what Beenstock (1983, pp. 82–5, 119) has in mind when he refers to poor nations' (LDCs) indebtedness as an equilibrium phenomenon. In this context any initial rise in the marginal productivity of capital as a result, say, of industrialisation in the LDCs leads to a temporary disequilibrium in world capital markets, because the marginal productivity of capital in the latter rises relative to that in the developed countries (DCs). Therefore capital will move from the DCs to the LDCs in order to restore equilibrium. It follows therefore that the LDCs must run current account deficits to match their capital account surpluses which reflect their import of capital goods from the DCs. In other words, the capital account drives the current account rather than the reverse, and this should be seen as a concomitant part of the process of industrialisation rather than an indication that poor nations are borrowing more than is good for them.

On the basis of this analysis one should have little cause to worry about debtor nation insolvency. However, the model does entail some heroic assumptions. First, it assumes perfectly ordered markets and free factor flows in which distortion and misallocations rarely arise. Secondly, it presupposes that borrowers ensure that capital imports are channelled into exchange earning activities (either import substitution, export promotion, or both), rather than into current consumption, so that debts can be serviced satisfactorily. Otherwise borrowing nations move deeper into debt. Thirdly, it reckons without the emergence of large destabilising shocks, for example, a sudden cutback in lending, a sharp fall in commodity prices or the presence of large destabilising short-term capital movements.

In the 1920s none of these conditions held. Capital misallocation was a common occurrence and borrowing was often used to finance consumption or prestigious projects rather than employed in productive exchange-earning investment. Consequently, few countries were able to gain entry to the virtuous circle whereby borrowing was self-financing, as in the case of the Pacific Basin region after the Second World War or many of the borrowing countries of the nineteenth century. More commonly, the majority of borrowers in the 1920s ran deeper into debt and renewed borrowings were required simply to service old debts. As a result, debt servicing costs rose and, ultimately, they exceeded the inflow of new funds. In this situation borrowers became highly vulnerable to sudden shocks such as the cessation of capital flows, the collapse in commodity prices and the volatility of short-term capital movements, all of which transpired at the end of the decade.

The experience of borrowing countries

There is ample evidence that debtor countries overborrowed in the 1920s and that the proceeds were not always used wisely: that is, imported capital was used to finance current consumption, retire previous debts or to finance prestige projects rather than being invested in foreign exchange generating activities. This is true of Germany, Eastern Europe, Latin America and the British Dominions.

The situation in Germany is well known. German business and banks had become very dependent on external funds during the 1920s and any curtailment was bound to be a cause of concern (James, 1986, pp. 136–7). Though the misappropriation of funds is sometimes exaggerated Schuker's (1988, p. 123) conclusion still holds good:

> The Reich was singularly vulnerable to the reverse flow of capital. It had overborrowed in the 1920s and squandered much of the proceeds on public or private consumption, and it had persistently failed in the early years to adjust tax, budgetary, labor, and trade policies to take account of reparations requirements added to a growing commercial debt.

Fleisig (1976, p. 35) reckons that Germany was severely affected by the 1929 downturn in American portfolio lending to Europe which amounted to some 10 per cent or more of the country's domestic net capital formation.

During the latter half of the decade most of the debtor countries of Eastern Europe and the Balkans relied heavily on capital imports to plug the gap in their external accounts. Of the total flow of funds, both long and short term, into Hungary, Poland, Bulgaria and Yugoslavia between 1924 and 1928, one-half went to cover an import surplus of goods and services, while most of the remainder was earmarked for servicing foreign debts. By 1929 capital inflows were barely sufficient to cover interest and dividends on existing debts (Nötel, 1974, pp. 84–5, 1984, pp. 182–3). Only a small proportion of the loans was used to increase productive capacity (Ellis, 1941, p. 74; Political and Economic Planning, 1945, p. 110). By the end of the decade the financial position of much of Europe was becoming critical. The increasing burden of Europe's payments on account of private loans, war debts and reparations together with the suction of funds back to New York as a result of the stock market boom, served to intensify Europe's dollar shortage and threatened the collapse of the international financial system (Costigliola, 1976, p. 499).

In the case of Latin America, few countries were as fortunate as Venezuela, where valuable oil wells managed with great efficiency enabled the country to retire the whole of its external debt by 1930 (Royal Institute of International Affairs, 1937a, p. 277, 1937b, p. 182). In many cases capital imports were used to retire previous debts, to cover domestic deficits or to prevent default on exiting loans. The Bolivian government, for example, relied on American loans to cover its domestic deficits, while some of the proceeds were used to retire previous debts in Britain and France (Harris, 1944, p. 264). A large part of the debt contracted by Argentina was used for unproductive purposes, in that it gave rise to little additional exchange earnings, and the success in obtaining funds abroad allowed the country to maintain persistent budgetary deficits (Peters, 1934). Similarly, much of Columbia's borrowing was dissipated in public works projects of a somewhat dubious nature. Between 1924 and 1928 Columbia borrowed some $153 million, a large part of which went into constructing an expensive railway project between two valleys, the commercial justification for which was limited as Sir Arthur Salter (1933, p. 105) explained:

> There was no commercial justification for it, since both valleys had their own outlet to the sea. A very expensive tunnel through the top of the mountain range was begun and then abandoned; and while the Federal authorities were driving a tunnel through the mountains the local authorities were making a costly road over them. I have had a vivid account from one who was in Columbia at the time of the way in which the offers of competing lenders resulted in the public authorities incurring greater and greater obligations for these extravagant ventures.

The position was much the same in the British Dominions where public authorities were the major borrowers. In the case of Australia public foreign borrowing did little to promote exchange earnings since two-thirds of the proceeds went to cover the deficit in the balance of payments (Gilbert, 1973, p. 104). Salter (1933, p. 106) was very dubious about the utility of public borrowing; with particular reference to the years 1926–28 he wrote: 'with the exception of loans recommended by the League of Nations and the Central Banks, the *bulk* of the foreign loans in these years to public authorities in debtor countries would better not have been made'.

Responsibility of the creditors

Of course the creditor countries must share some of the blame for the increasing vulnerability of the debtor nations in the later 1920s. As Salter (1933, p. 101) recognised, both lending and borrowing could be 'reckless, extravagant and wasteful'. Inadequate control over the volume of foreign lending and the uses to which it was put, together with the failure to ensure that debts would be self-liquidating, consituted the initial lapse in responsibility. The second was the sharp curtailment of lending at the end the decade when debtors had piled up heavy obligations, the servicing of which would have proved onerous even at the best of times. In the case of Latin America, for example, the United States and Great Britain had accumulated by the end of the decade a total stock of investment claims equal to four times the combined value of the continent's exports (Jorgensen and Sachs, 1989, p. 53).

Arguably a smaller and more stable flow of investments would probably have been better. But, instead, borrowers were encouraged by the more unscrupulous investment houses to live beyond their means. The attractions for the lenders were considerable since many countries were avid to secure capital for infrastructure investments and the returns offered were far better than those at home. Nominal rates varied between 6 and 9 per cent, but the low price of bond issues and other charges often raised the effective rates to 12 per cent or more (Political and Economic Planning, 1945, p. 110). Thus, overborrowing could easily arise through creditors pressing funds on their clients with little regard for their ability to repay. Palyi (1972, p. 207) quotes the case of the Bolivian government which was said to have pledged 80 per cent of its country's tax revenues for the service of just one loan, with no questions asked as to how the Bolivian state would manage on the remaining 20 per cent. While not all foreign lending was a product of ruthless and greedy international bankers inducing impoverished and unwilling debtors to run further into debt, there is evidence that, with the lure of high profits, the creditors could easily overlook the pecuniary welfare of the recipient countries. The United States was most at fault in this respect. There was little control over foreign lending (Hogan, 1977) and competition for business among the banking organisations coupled with the share-pushing activities of the issue houses ensured that the borrowers were rarely left in peace. According to Lary (1943, p. 96):

> Enticed by the prospect of commissions much higher than those available on domestic issues and faced with the necessity for a continuous flow of new securities to keep large staffs of bond salesmen employed, American investment bankers had their agents 'sitting on the doorsteps' of prospective borrowers, as one observer put it, offering them money and many times persuading them to borrow more than they actually needed.

Even Great Britain, whose long experience in the field of international lending might have ensured more prudent behaviour, can be criticised for the rather lenient attitude to the excesses committed by some of her European and imperial clients (Royal Institute of International Affairs, 1937a, p. 165).

Uncontrolled lending inevitably led, as in the 1970s and early 1980s, to unwise and wasteful borrowing and it should have been obvious by the later 1920s that many countries were finding difficulties in meeting their obligations. In any case, the fact that much of the lending, especially to public authorities, consisted of fixed interest securities at relatively high interest rates, was bound to cause difficulties once the international economic climate deteriorated. Yet by and large the creditor countries gave little thought to the ultimate question of the repayment of debts, nor even for that matter to the servicing of the growing debt burden. Lending to repay rather than ensuring the means of repayment became the order of the day. In turn, the debtor nations became adjusted to a situation whereby new borrowing provided the wherewithal to service old debts (Smith, 1934, p. 430; Timoshenko, 1933, pp. 86–7). 'Neither in lending nor in borrowing countries was it generally appreciated that debtors could only repay the service charges on their debts by means of an export surplus of goods and services' (Royal Institute of International Affairs, 1937a, p. 289).

The point of no return

It would be misleading of course to imply that all foreign lending was used unproductively, but in general borrowing countries failed to utilise capital imports in a manner which permitted full servicing of their debts. To complicate matters the volume of foreign short-term funds was larger than before the war and these were not self-liquidating in terms of foreign exchange. For example, funds used to finance the holding of agricultural stocks in South America generated little foreign exchange so that borrowers could not readily amortise their debts. The same applies to the substantial short-term funds located in Central and Eastern Europe some of which were used for long-term purposes, and the consequences of which were 'to transfer abroad the effective ownership of some countries' international monetary reserves' (Williams, 1963, p. 94). It was the unstable and volatile nature of these funds which was to prove so troublesome in the financial crisis of the summer of 1931.

But before that point was reached the writing was already on the wall for many debtor countries. Debt service burdens were growing steadily larger in the 1920s (Table 5.2) and capital imports were barely covering these costs. By the late 1920s Latin America was paying some $660 million abroad annually on its debts, nearly three times its then current capital inflow (United Nations, 1955, p. 15). On long-term account the debtors of the US and UK were paying $686 million in 1928 (in interest, dividends and amortisation payments) more than they received in new loans and investments, and by the following year this burden had nearly doubled (Royal Institute of International Affairs, 1937a, p. 284). The crossover point between repayments and receipts probably occurred late in 1928 or early in 1929 in the case of American lending and from then onwards the major creditor was draining liquidity from the borrowing regions, that is, new lending fell short of servicing costs; in the case of Britain on the other hand, interest and amortisation costs

Table 5.2 Debt servicing as a percentage of export earnings

Country	*1926*	*1928/29*	*1931/32*
Argentina	10.0	10.4	27.6
Australia	—	28.0	—
Bolivia	7.3	7.8	50.0
Brazil	13.1	16.7	40.4
Bulgaria	—	12.3	22.0
Chile	5.5	9.2	102.6
Columbia	2.7	11.9	21.8
Greece	—	32.0	44.0
Hungary	—	17.9	48.0
Peru	2.6	7.4	21.4
Poland	—	11.3	27.0
Romania	—	14.6	36.0
Yugoslavia	—	18.1	36.0

Sources: Drabeck (1985), p. 425; Nötel (1986), p. 223; Mazower (1991), pp. 112, 202; Jorgensen and Sachs (1989), p. 58; Cardoso and Dornbusch (1989), p. 119.

exceeded new lending throughout the interwar period (Eichengreen and Portes, 1986, p. 604; Fleisig, 1975, pp. 12–13).

The increasing burden of servicing costs in terms of export earnings is shown for a selection of countries in Table 5.2. The ratios rose sharply after 1928/29 as a result of the large fall in commodity prices. At the same time there was a significant decline in capital inflows between 1928 and 1930 (Table 5.3). Germany recorded a fall of 50 per cent, Hungary 58 per cent, Poland 45 per cent, Finland 70 per cent, Australia 48 per cent, India 45 per cent and Italy 27 per cent. In the cases of Argentina, Yugoslavia and Japan large capital inflows were transformed into losses. The areas most severely affected were Latin America, Central and Eastern Europe, Australia and the Far East.

It has been argued that movements in the volume of long-term lending were sufficiently large and unstable as to impart a major deflationary impact on the international economy in the late 1920s and early 1930s (Fleisig, 1975, pp. 5–6, 17–18, 54–5). More specifically, it was the sharp curtailment of US lending, the rising flow of funds to New York to take advantage of the last leg of the stock market boom, together with the concomitant tightening of monetary policy in America in the 15 months or so prior to the stock market crash of October 1929, that were of crucial significance for the world economy. These events

Table 5.3 Net capital movements of selected debtor countries, 1929–32 ($m)

Country	*1927*	*1928*	*1929*	*1930*	*1931*	*1932*
Argentina	+61	+131	–10	+287	–89	+10
Australia	+187	+209	+250	+40	–50	–31
Finland	–2	+40	+12	–5	–24	–18
Germany	+1 037	+967	+482	+129	–540	–103
Italy	+28	+133	+97	+47	–50	–23
Japan	+50	+80	–9	–128	–11	–44
New Zealand	+8	–9	+52	+52	+2	–12
South Africa	+26	+46	+65	+32	+19	–76
Bulgaria	+4	+7	+21	+1	+5	+1
Greece	—	—	+45	+34	+37	+12
Hungary	+89	+91	+38	+22	+37	+4
India	+120	+67	+37	+92	–86	–25
Poland	+82	+124	+68	+3	–1	–4
Turkey	+22	+11	+50	–6	+3	–3
Yugoslavia	+23	+27	–13	+35	+3	+7

Source: United Nations (1949), pp. 11–12.

led to a tightening of credit conditions and a check to investment and activity in capital importing countries which reduced the demand for primary commodities and so prices declined. This in turn led to a decline in the incomes of primary producing countries which reduced their demand for the industrial products of the metropolitan core countries.

The thesis is a persuasive one, though it is sometimes difficult to unravel the precise timing of the sequence of events. Certainly there is some evidence that there was a tailing off in investment and economic activity in countries heavily dependent on imported capital. In the case of Central and Eastern Europe the reduced volume of lending caused some check to economic activity (Williams, 1963, p. 98), though Temin (1971) has argued that it was the decline in domestic inventory investment that was crucial in the case of Germany (see also Balderston, 1993, p. 401). Outside Europe, it has been suggested that as early as 1928 the decline in American lending was inflicting a balance of payments constraint on many primary producing countries and that this had an adverse effect on Britain's traded services with low income economies (Corner, 1956; Solomou, 1996, p. 95). This was soon followed by a weakening in the European demand for primary commodities which, in conjunction with rising stock levels in some commodities, was sufficient to cause a significant decline in primary prices and incomes (Fleisig, 1972). As a result the export revenues of Asia, Africa, South America, Oceania and Canada declined by some 25 per cent on average in 1930 (Fleisig, 1975, p. 47).

It was through the balance of payments mechanism that the impact first made itself felt in many of the primary producing debtor countries since many had come to depend upon a continued flow of lending to meet their debt service costs. Thus when capital imports declined the only way of meeting their obligations initially was to draw upon their limited reserves of gold and foreign exchange. The collapse of foreign borrowing by the Australian state governments, for example, led to a substantial liquidation of overseas reserves in 1929–30 (Gilbert, 1973, pp. 104–5; Walker, 1933, p. 14). Latin America was affected severely by the sharp contraction of American lending and the region suffered substantial gold losses in 1929. Germany and many East European countries also faced a similar situation while several countries in Asia and Africa were experiencing strains in their external balances (Aldcroft and Morewood, 1995, pp. 60–61; Fleisig, 1972, pp. 156–7; Phelps, 1938, pp. 53–4, 116). In brief, long-term lending declined, short-term loans were being called in or not being renewed and the reserves of the debtor countries began to seep away in the backwash (League of Nations, 1943, p. 23).

The initial shock to the system might have been accommodated, at least for a time, had it not been for the subsequent turn of events. Debtor countries could meet temporary difficulties by drawing upon their reserves, but this process of adjustment could not go on indefinitely in the face of a prolonged strain following the collapse of primary product prices and the decline in American import demand after the downturn in economic activity in the summer of 1929. Many primary producers therefore faced a severe and prolonged deterioration in their terms of trade and in their trade balances as export earnings fell faster than import values, while external interest obligations, which were fixed in terms of gold, rose sharply as a proportion of export receipts (Table 5.2; Raupach, 1972, p. 240; Smith, 1934, p. 447). Attempts to make up the deficiency in international income by releasing stocks of commodities on to the world market only made matters worse by aggravating the fall in prices. Thus, with dwindling reserves and an inability to borrow further, debtor countries of the periphery were forced to take drastic measures to staunch the outflow of funds. The way out of the impasse was sought eventually through a combination of measures including deflation, devaluation, exchange control and debt default.

Inevitably the burden of external adjustment fell with a vengeance on the domestic economy, especially in countries which adopted deflationary measures to suppress internal demand (Bandera, 1964, p. 132). Consequently, several countries sought to ease the pressure on their domestic economies by abandoning gold and devaluing at an early date. They included Australia, New Zealand, Argentina, Bolivia, Brazil, Paraguay and Uruguay, all of which depreciated their currencies in relation to gold in 1929–30. This was the first crack in the restored gold standard system and it imposed a greater burden for those countries still on gold and hence intensified the deflationary spiral. The initial deflation was quickly transmitted through the links forged by the fixed exchange rates of the gold exchange standard. Once started the deflationary process became cumulative and ultimately ended in the complete collapse of the gold standard (Campa, 1990, p. 678; Cassel, 1936, p. 62; League of Nations, 1937, table 1 appendix).

The process was aggravated by the short-term liquidity crisis in Europe in 1931. The curtailment of capital flows in 1928–29 was the initial shock to the stability of the international economic system which set the stage for the disturbances which culminated in the international financial crisis of the summer of 1931 (United Nations, 1949, pp. 66–7). The problem arose from the very large volume of short-term credits on capital account in the European banking system which were vulnerable to any crisis such as the failure of a major bank. The collapse of the Credit-Anstalt rocked the whole economic structure of the Continent and alerted creditors to the inherent dangers in countries dependent on short-term credits from abroad and the implications this might have for currency convertibility, especially in those countries which had experienced serious inflation in the previous decade (Balderston, 1994, p. 64; Eichengreen and Portes, 1987, pp. 25–7; Schubert, 1991, p. 4). It led to pressure on many continental banks and resulted in the large-scale withdrawal of short-term funds and loss of reserves from Germany and Eastern Europe in the summer of 1931 until brought to a halt by the imposition of exchange control (Ellis, 1941, p. 74; James, 1984, p. 84, 1986, p. 398; Ranki, 1985, p. 71; Saint-Etienne, 1984, p. 17). The gold and foreign exchange reserves of 18 European debtor countries fell by nearly one-half between 1928 and 1931 and most of this loss occurred in 1930–31 (League of Nations, 1944, pp. 40–41). The consequences of the crisis for Eastern Europe have been well told by Nötel (1986, p. 227):

> The financial crisis of mid-1931, superimposed upon the protracted export crisis in both commodities and manufactures, transformed the haunting spectre of the collapse of national currencies, within a few months or weeks, into an immediately threatening and practi-

> cally unescapable reality for most east European countries. The sudden shift from continuing, even if irregular, capital imports to fast-spreading capital withdrawal and flight – with the balance-of-payments position already weakened by the sharp and long-lasting fall in export receipts and the rising or at least maintained debt service – in all countries threatened to exhaust, or actually exhausted, the rapidly shrinking proceeds and reserves of foreign exchange.

The final consequences of the crisis are well known. The continental panic had repercussions in Britain whose short-term liquidity position gave rise to concern and eventually Britain was forced to suspend the gold standard in September. In quick succession countries adopted defensive measures including the abandonment of gold and devaluation, import controls, exchange control and debt default. The majority of borrowing countries defaulted on their debt payments or negotiated moratoria. In the case of Latin America all but Argentina, Haiti and the Dominican Republic suspended debt servicing. For two years or more currencies remained in a state of turmoil and the prospects for international lending remained bleak.

However dramatic the events of the summer of 1931 may seem, it is important to put them into proper perspective. The short-term liquidity flows of this period were in no way the initiator of the great depression. They were merely the icing on the cake: 'they served rather to deliver the economic coup de grace' (Fleisig 1975, p. 103). The main deflationary force was the collapse in long-term lending, and the size and volatility of short-term capital movements, especially within European financial centres, was partly a consequence of that event. The problem in 1931 was not so much the scale of the short-term movements or their negative implications for the real economy, but the fact that it was not possible to muster sufficient short-term liquidity to stem the crisis of confidence as it swept from one centre to another in turn. This failure can be attributed to several factors: justifiable fears of exchange losses through depreciation, exchange control and the possible collapse of financial institiutions; political motives such as Germany's refusal of financial assistance from France in July 1931 because it was made conditional on dropping the proposed union with Austria; and the absence of a country willing to act as a lendor of last resort.

Conclusion

While the short-term liquidity crisis of 1931 culminated in the final disintegration of the postwar international economic system, it is easy to read too much into the tumultuous events of that summer. For most debtor nations the crucial turning point occurred much earlier when creditor countries began to cut back on their lending. It is not always fully appreciated that by the late 1920s most of the main debtors were already overstretched and that capital movements, far from working as a global equilibrating device, were producing a destabilising situation. Thus, once capital imports ceased to shore up their external accounts the situation became critical and many debtors were left in a very vulnerable position. But the pressure was compounded by the simultaneous collapse in commodity prices, the declining import capacity of the creditors and the large volatile movements of short-term capital. This convergence of adverse forces was more than sufficient to undermine the postwar international economic system.

References

Aldcroft, D. H. and Morewood, S. (1995), *Economic Change in Eastern Europe since 1918*, Aldershot: Edward Elgar.

Balderston, T. (1993), *The Origins and Course of the German Economic Crisis, November 1923 to May 1932*, Berlin: Haude and Spener.

Balderston, T. (1994), 'The banks and the gold standard in the German financial crisis of 1931', *Financial History,* **1**.

Bandera, V. N. (1964), *Foreign Capital as an Instrument of National Economic Policy: a Study Based on the Experience of East European Countries between the Two World Wars*, The Hague: Nijhoff.

Beenstock, M. (1983), *The World Economy in Transition*, London: Allen and Unwin.

Buchanan, N. S. and Lutz, F. A. (1947), *Rebuilding the World Economy*, New York: Twentieth Century Fund.

Campa, J. M. (1990), 'Exchange rates and economic recovery in the 1930s: an extension to Latin America', *Journal of Economic History,* **50**.

Cardoso, E. A. and Dornbusch, R. (1989), 'Brazilian debt crisis: past and present', in B. Eichengreen and P. Lindert (eds.), *The International Debt Crisis in Historical Perspective*, Cambridge, MA: MIT Press.

Cassel, G. (1936), *The Downfall of the Gold Standard*, London: Oxford University Press.

Copeland, D. B. (1934), *Australia in the World Crisis 1929–1933*, Cambridge: Cambridge University Press.

Corner, D. C. (1956), 'Exports and the British trade cycle: 1929', *The Manchester School,* **26**.

Costigliola, F. (1976), 'The United States and the reconstruction of Germany in the 1920s', *Business History Review*, **50**.

Drabek, Z. (1985), 'Foreign trade performance and policy', in M. C. Kaser and E. A. Radice (eds), *The Economic History of Eastern Europe, 1919–1975*, Vol. I, *Economic Structure and Performance between the Wars*, Oxford: Oxford University Press.

Dunning, J. H. (1970), *Studies in International Investment*, London: Allen and Unwin.

Eichengreen, B. and Portes, R. (1986), 'Debt and default in the 1930s: causes and consequences', *European Economic Review*, 30.

Eichengreen , B. and Portes, R. (1987), 'The anatomy of financial crises', in R. Portes and A. K. Swoboda (eds), *Threats to International Financial Stability*, Cambridge: Cambridge University Press.

Ellis, H. S. (1941), *Exchange Control in Central Europe*, Cambridge, MA: Harvard University Press.

Ellsworth, P. T. (1964), *The International Economy*, third edition, New York: Macmillan.

Feinstein, C. H. and Watson, K. (1995), 'Private international capital flows in Europe in the inter-war period', in C. H. Feinstein (ed.), *Banking, Currency, and Finance in Europe between the Wars*, Oxford: Oxford University Press.

Fleisig, H. W. (1972), 'The United States and the non-European periphery during the early years of the great depression', in H. van der Wee (ed.), *The Great Depression Revisited. Essays on the Economics of the Thirties*, The Hague: Martinus Nijhoff.

Fleisig, H. W. (1975), *Long-Term Capital Flows and the Great Depression: the Role of the United States, 1927–1933*, New York: Arno Press.

Fleisig, H. W. (1976), 'War-related debts and the great depression', *American Economic Review, Papers and Proceedings*, 66.

Gilbert, R. S. (1973), *The Australian Loan Council in Federal Fiscal Adjustments, 1890–1965*, Canberra: Australian National University Press.

Harris, S. E. (1944), *Economic Problems of Latin America*, New York: McGraw-Hill.

Hogan, M. J. (1977), *Informal Entente: the Private Structure of Cooperation in Anglo-American Diplomacy, 1918–1928*, Columbia, MO: University of Missouri Press.

Holtfrerich, C.-L. (1986), 'U. S. capital exports to Germany 1919–1923 compared to 1924–1929', *Explorations in Economic History*, 23.

James, H. (1984), 'The causes of the German banking crisis of 1931', *Economic History Review*, 37.

James, H. (1986), *The German Slump: Politics and Economics 1924–1936*, Oxford: Clarendon Press.

Jorgensen, E. and Sachs, J. (1989), 'Default and renegotiation of Latin

American bonds in the interwar period', in B. Eichengreen and P. Lindert (eds), *The International Debt Crisis in Historical Perspective*, Cambridge, MA: MIT Press.

Kooker, J. (1976), 'French financial diplomacy: the interwar years', in B. M. Rowland (ed.) *Balance of Power or Hegemony; the Interwar Monetary System*, New York: New York University Press.

Lary, H. B. (1943), *The United States in the World Economy*, Washington, DC: Government Printing Office.

League of Nations (1931), *The Course and Phases of the World Economic Depression*, Geneva: League of Nations.

League of Nations (1937), *Money and Banking 1936/37*, Vol. I. *Monetary Review 1937*, Geneva: League of Nations.

League of Nations (1943), *The Transition from War to Peace Economy: Report of the Delegation on Economic Depressions*, Part I, Geneva: League of Nations.

League of Nations (1944), *International Currency Experience: Lessons of the Interwar Period*, Geneva: League of Nations.

Lewis, C. (1938), *America's Stake in International Investments*, Washington, DC: Brookings Institution.

Mazower, M. (1991), *Greece and the Interwar Economic Crisis*, Oxford: Oxford University Press.

North, D. C. (1962), 'International capital movements in historical perspective', in R. F. Mikesell (ed.), *U. S. Private and Government Investment Abroad*, Eugene, OR: University of Oregon Books.

Nötel, R. (1974), 'International capital movements and finance in Eastern Europe, 1919–1949', *Vierteljahrschrift für Sozial-und Wirtschaftsgeschichte*, 61.

Nötel, R. (1984), 'Money, banking and industry in interwar Austria and Hungary', *Journal of European Economic History*, 13.

Nötel, R. (1986), 'International credit and finance', in M. C. Kaser and E. A. Radice (eds), *The Economic History of Eastern Europe 1919–1975*, Vol. II, *Interwar Policy, the War and Reconstruction*, Oxford: Oxford University Press.

Palyi, M. (1972), *The Twilight of Gold 1914–1936: Myths and Realities*, Chicago: Henry Regnery.

Peters, H. E. (1934), *The Foreign Debt of the Argentine Republic*, Baltimore: Johns Hopkins Press.

Phelps, V. L. (1938), *The International Economic Position of Argentina*, Philadelphia, University of Pennsylvania Press.

Political and Economic Planning (1945), *Economic Development in S. E. Europe*, London: Political and Economic Planning.

Ranki, G. (1985), 'Problems of Southern European economic development (1918–38)', in G. Arrighi (ed.), *Semiperipheral Development:*

the Politics of Southern Europe in the Twentieth Century, Beverly Hills, CA: Sage Publications.

Raupach, H. (1972), 'The impact of the great depression on Eastern Europe', in H. van der Wee (ed.), *The Great Depression Revisited. Essays on the Economics of the Thirties*, The Hague: Martinus Nijhoff.

Royal Institute of International Affairs (1937a), *The Problem of International Investment*, Oxford: Oxford University Press.

Royal Institute of International Affairs (1937b), *The Republics of South America*, Oxford: Oxford University Press.

Saint-Etienne, C. (1984), *The Great Depression, 1929–1938: Lessons for the 1980s*, Stanford, CA: Hoover Institution Press.

Salter, A. (1933), *Recovery: the Second Effort*, London: Bell.

Schedwin, C. B. (1970), *Australia and the Great Depression: a Study of the Economic Development and Policy in the 1920s and 1930s*, Sydney: Sydney University Press.

Schubert, A. (1991), *The Credit-Anstalt Crisis of 1931*, Cambridge: Cambridge University Press.

Schuker, S. A. (1988), *American Reparations to Germany 1919–33: Implications for the Third World Debt Crisis*, Princeton, NJ: Princeton University Press.

Smith, L. (1934), 'Suspension of the gold standard in raw material exporting countries', *American Economic Review*, 24.

Solomou, S. (1996), *Themes in Macroeconomic History: the UK Economy, 1919–1939*, Cambridge: Cambridge University Press.

Temin, P. (1971), 'The beginning of the depression in Germany', *Economic History Review*, 24.

Timoshenko, V. P. (1933), *World Agriculture and the Depression*, Ann Arbor, MI: University of Michigan Business Studies.

United Nations (1949), *International Capital Movements during the Inter-War Period*, New York: United Nations.

United Nations (1955), *Foreign Capital in Latin America*, New York: United Nations.

Walker, E. R. (1933), *Australia in the World Depression*, London: P. S. King.

Williams, D. (1963), 'The 1931 financial crisis', *Yorkshire Bulletin of Economic and Social Research*, 15.

CHAPTER SIX

Europe in Depression

In the first half of 1929 there was little indication that the world was poised on the threshold of one of the worst slumps in history. Though there were signs of a slackening of activity and prices in some countries in Europe and along the periphery, partly as a result of the cutback in American long-term lending after the middle of 1928, the international economy by and large was still in a reasonably healthy state. The world's largest economy was enjoying an unprecedented stock market boom and many Americans were of the opinion that prosperity was here to stay. Such hopes were soon dashed. By the end of the year the rosy scenario had changed dramatically. The American economy had peaked in the summer of 1929, the stock market plunged ominously in October and economic indices the world over were on a nasty downward slide. During the next three years things went from bad to worse; output, incomes, trade and prices all fell to undreamed of levels and unemployment soared. Few countries escaped the economic holocaust. The year 1932 saw a bottoming out of the depression with signs of revival in some countries, but it was not until the following year that recovery became more general (League of Nations, 1933, pp. 16–17). The subsequent upswing from the trough, though reasonably strong, saw a wide diversity of experience among countries some of which failed to achieve a full cyclical recovery by the end of the decade.

Dimensions of the Crisis

Some idea of the magnitude of the depression and the diversity of its incidence can be gained from the data in Tables 6.1 and 6.2, which show the fluctuations in GDP and industrial production over the cycle 1929–37/38 for all countries for which information is available. The figures are best used for interpreting the broad dimensions of change since not all the estimates are equally reliable. Virtually all countries suffered declines in output and industrial production during the early 1930s, the major exception being the USSR which by that time had isolated herself from the ravages of the capitalist system. There output moved forward smartly under the impetus of the first Five Year Plan, providing a sharp contrast to what was happening elsewhere in Europe and the rest of the free world. Outside the United States, the most

Table 6.1 Fluctuations in GDP/GNP and exports, 1929–37/38

	Gross domestic product			*Export volume*		
	1929–32/33	*1932/3–37/38*	*1929–37/38*	*1929–32*	*1932–37*	*1929–37*
Exchange control						
Austria	–22.5	25.8	–2.5	–43.9	35.3	–24.1
Bulgaria	–7.1	63.3	51.8	—	—	—
Czechoslovakia	–12.9	13.1	–1.5	—	—	—
Germany	–23.5	63.7	25.2	–40.5	15.2	–31.5
Greece	36.7	25.4	71.4	—	—	—
Hungary	–3.7	18.0	13.6	—	—	—
Italy	–5.5(a)	21.7	15.0	–42.1	3.9	–39.8
Romania	–5.2	22.7	16.3	—	—	—
Spain	–5.3(a)	–9.4(b)	–14.2(c)	—	—	—
Yugoslavia	–9.4	24.5	12.7	—	—	—
Gold bloc						
Belgium	–7.1	9.8	2.0	–31.4	51.4	3.8
France	–14.7	13.5	–3.1	–41.5	–2.3	–42.9
Netherlands	–7.6	14.2	5.5	–33.4	31.8	–12.2
Switzerland	–8.0	14.4	5.2	–50.1	39.4	–30.4
Poland	–20.7	40.8	14.9	—	—	—

Table 6.1 concluded

	Gross domestic product			*Export volume*		
	1929–32/33	*1932/3–37/38*	*1929–37/38*	*1929–32*	*1932–37*	*1929–37*
Sterling bloc						
Australia	–5.8	27.5	20.1	31.8	1.1	33.2
Denmark	4.3	16.9	21.9	20.1	–10.6	7.3
Finland	–4.0	46.9	41.1	—	—	—
Ireland	–4.3	2.4	–2.0	—	—	—
Norway	–1.0(a)	32.5	31.2	2.6	36.1	39.6
Portugal	13.3	14.4	29.7	—	—	—
Sweden	–4.3	31.4	25.8	–37.0	60.8	1.3
UK	–5.1	24.7	18.4	–37.6	28.8	–19.7
Other countries						
Japan	–6.5(a)	47.0	37.4	1.3	145.7	149.1
USA	–28.5	38.1	–1.3	–48.6	54.4	–20.5
Canada	–29.5	41.5	–0.3	–32.0	53.7	4.4
USSR	20.5	40.7	69.6	—	—	—

Notes:
(a) 1929–31; (b) 1931–40; (c) 1929–40
Italy was originally in the gold bloc but imposed exchange control in May 1934 and devalued October 1936.
Greece and Turkey, along with Bulgaria, Hungary, Romania and Yugoslavia, formed part of the Reichsmark bloc.
Japan devalued early and the United States late.

Sources: Bairoch (1976), p. 295; Maddison (1991), pp. 316–18, (1995), pp. 148–50; Nunes, Mata and Valério (1989), pp. 293–95; Spulber (1966), p. 58; Prados de la Escosura (1993); Hjerppe (1996), p. 93.

Table 6.2 Fluctuations in industrial/manufacturing production, 1929–37/38

	1929–32	*1932–37/38*	*1929–37/38*
Exchange control			
Austria	–34.3	53.9	1.0
Bulgaria	8.9	25.6	36.9
Czechoslovakia	–39.8	60.0	–3.7
Germany	–40.8	122.2	31.6
Greece	0.9	60.0	61.5
Hungary	–19.8	64.2	31.7
Italy	–22.7	48.5	14.8
Romania	–18.2	63.4	33.6
Spain	–15.7	–19.7[1]	–32.3[2]
Yugoslavia	–17.1	63.8	35.7
Gold bloc			
Belgium	–27.1	42.3	3.7
France	–25.6	20.0	–10.7
Luxembourg	–32.0	40.2	–4.7
Netherlands	–9.8	35.1	22.0
Poland	–38.6	99.6	22.5
Switzerland	–20.8	29.8	2.8
Sterling bloc			
Australia	—	—	—
Denmark	–5.6	47.1	38.9
Finland	–15.0	89.4	60.9
Ireland	–9.0	54.0	40.3
Norway	–18.2[3]	58.7[4]	29.9
Portugal	33.0	9.8	46.0
Sweden	–10.8	72.4	53.8
UK	–11.4	52.9	35.4
Other countries			
Japan	–3.3[3]	100.0[4]	93.3
USA	–44.7	86.8	3.3
Canada	–32.3	68.3	14.0
World	–29.3	80.6	27.7

Notes:
1. 1933–40; 2. 1929–40; 3. 1929–31; 4. 1931–37.

Sources: OEEC (1960), p. 9; League of Nations (1936), table 107; United Nations (1949b), table 36; Berend and Ranki (1974), pp. 298–300; Mitchell (1975), p. 357; Freris (1986), p. 90; David (1996); Lains and Reis (1991); Prados de la Escosura (1993); Hjerppe (1996), p. 128; Pryor (1973), p. 203.

serious declines in economic activity occurred in Austria, Germany, France, Belgium, Poland and Czechoslovakia. In the case of Britain, Sweden, Denmark, Bulgaria, Greece and Portugal the impact was milder, though few countries apart from Greece, Portugal and Denmark actually managed to record a positive movement in GDP. Other indicators of economic activity tell a similar story; commodity prices, share prices, exports and imports all fell sharply, while unemployment rose to alarming levels. Wholesale prices and share prices fell by one-half or more, while the value of European trade declined from $58 billion in 1928 to $20.8 billion in 1935, and even by 1938 it had only recovered to 41.5 per cent of its former peak. Socially perhaps the worst aspect of the crisis was the high levels of unemployment, since at least for those in work there was some compensation in so far as prices tended to fall faster than wages and salaries. In this respect Germany had one of the worst records; between 1929 and the end of 1930 unemployment more than doubled to 4.5 million, two years later it had crept up to 6 million. Britain's peak figure was in excess of 3 million, or over one-fifth of the insured labour force. For Europe as a whole it is difficult to estimate the precise total of unemployment because of statistical under-recording and the presence of underemployment, but at a guess it was probably not far short of 20 million (for details see Eichengreen and Hatton, 1988). During the course of the depression many firms, banks, financial and commercial institutions went out of business altogether. In 1931, the year of the famous Credit-Anstalt crash, 17 000 enterprises closed down in Germany.

Bald statistics fail to do justice to the dramatic events of the depression and its social repercussions, but they do provide some indication of the scale of the cataclysm. Nor is it easy as Landes (1969, p. 372) has observed, to give a coherent analysis of the crisis 'that does justice to the rush of disasters, tumbling one upon the other; or to give a narrative account that illuminates the confusion of events'. In any case, it is doubtful whether a blow-by-blow account would serve any useful purpose in a chapter of this sort.

Was the depression unique?

Contrary to the opinion of some writers (Solomou, 1996, pp. 86–8), the war did not destroy the basic framework of prewar cycles. It can be argued that, apart from its unusual severity, the depression of the early 1930s was no exception to the long-run historical sequence of cyclical activity and hence requires nothing more in the way of explanation than a general theory of the business cycle. After all, it did occur at a logical sequence in time on the basis of past business cycle history and some of its characteristics had been repeated in previous downturns. The war did not break the previous cyclical pattern of business cycle periodicity. In 1914 most industrial countries were about to move into recession but the outbreak of hostilities disturbed the pattern and instead produced a distorted or muted continuation of the upswing culminating in the speculative boom of 1919–20. A sharp reaction in 1920–21 was then followed, with minor interruptions, by another major upswing through to a peak at the end of the decade. Thus the nineteenth-century Juglar pattern of cycles averaging seven to eight years in duration was maintained and a depression could have been expected around 1929–30. Moreover, one should also note that the amplitude of the 1929–32 slump was less severe in some countries, for example the UK, Sweden and Switzerland, than that following the postwar boom, while its duration had been matched in some crises in the nineteenth century, though perhaps not simultaneously with the same intensity. Even the world-wide scope of the depression was not especially unique; the immediate postwar depression fell not far short in this respect, while international recessions were not unknown in the nineteenth century.

Therefore, should we regard the 1929–32 downturn as unique or just another phase in the business cycle sequence? On balance, given the combination of duration, intensity and world-wide scope the crisis may be seen as something of a special case worthy of particular attention. Moreover, if we ignore the relatively minor recession of 1937–38 it can be regarded as the grand culmination of trade cycle history, for after the Second World War the growth cycle became the established norm, at least until the 1970s. However, this does not mean that the downturn can be explained specifically in terms of unique causation. For instance, it would be difficult to argue that the First World War and its aftermath was the chief causal factor in the crisis. Certainly the war created maladjustments and elements of instability within the world economy which thereby made it more vulnerable to shocks of one sort or another, but the turning point cannot be attributed directly to the war itself. Indeed, though the war imparted a severe shock to the economic mechanism, it did not, as already noted, upset the former cyclical periodicity. It distorted the economic system in several ways and rendered it more unstable, while it probably also aggravated the amplitude of subsequent cyclical movements, but it did little, if anything, to destroy the traditional pattern of cyclical activity.

Origins of the slump

The origins of the world-wide slump are usually located in the United States. It is quite possible, however, that several European countries would have experienced at least a moderate recession in the early 1930s even had conditions not deteriorated so badly in America. But events in the United States, together with that country's strong influence over the world economy, determined to a large extent the timing, the severity and the duration of the depression throughout the world. Though some of the possible means of transmission effects relating to gold stocks, trade flows and rules of the gold standard game have been disputed (Fremdling, 1985), the fact remains that the United States administered three powerful shocks to the world economic system at a time when it was least able to withstand them. The initial shock came with the cutback in foreign lending in 1928–29; the second with the peaking of the American boom in the summer of 1929; and the third comprised the imposition of tighter import control by the Smoot-Hawley Tariff of 1930.

The first of these had serious implications for debtor nations. Many countries, both in Central and Eastern Europe, Latin America and elsewhere, were in a precarious financial position in the latter half of the 1920s. They had borrowed freely and accumulated massive obligations which for the most part were not self-liquidating. These fulfilled their purpose in the short-term but inevitably they aggravated the debt burden and concealed the basic disequilibrium between creditors and debtors. The process could not continue indefinitely and any adverse reaction on the part of the creditors was bound to throw the burden of adjustment on to the debtors (see Chapter 5).

The initial reaction came from France whose foreign lending (much of it short term) was curtailed sharply in 1927–28 and eliminated altogether in 1929. But in sheer magnitude it was dwarfed by the collapse of US lending from the summer of 1928, prompted by the domestic boom and the action of the Federal Reserve to check it by raising interest rates, both of which attracted funds into the home market. Capital issues on foreign account fell by over 50 per cent between the first and second halves of 1928; there was a slight revival in the first half of 1929 but this was followed by a further sharp drop, giving a total of $790 million for 1929 compared with $1 336 million in 1927. Altogether the net outward capital flow (both short and long term) from the major creditors fell from $2 214 million in 1928 to $1 414 million in 1929 and to as little as $363 million in 1930 (North, 1962, p. 40; United Nations, 1949a).

This dramatic curtailment in foreign lending exercised a powerful deflationary impact on the world economy and was sufficient to undermine the fragile stability of many countries (Fleisig, 1975, pp. 5–6, 54–5). The position of many debtor countries deteriorated sharply between 1928 and 1929 as capital inflows declined. Net capital imports into Germany, the largest borrower, fell from $967 million in 1928 to $482 million in 1929 and $129 million in 1930. Schuker (1988, p. 123) stresses the precarious position of that country which, he says, 'was singularly vulnerable to the reverse flow of capital', since it had overborrowed in the 1920s and squandered much of the proceeds on public and private consumption. Similarly, capital inflows into Bulgaria, Hungary, Poland and Yugoslavia were virtually wiped out in this period, declining from $246 to $8.1 million between 1928 and 1930 (Aldcroft and Morewood, 1995, p. 56). Other borrowers in Latin America, the British Dominions and along the periphery also experienced similar setbacks. The cessation of lending affected these countries directly in that it led to a curtailment of domestic investment and economic activity. However, it was in the balance of payments that the impact was first felt since most debtor countries depended on capital imports to close the gap in their external accounts. Hence once capital imports ceased to flow the only way of adjusting their balance of payments was to draw upon their limited reserves of gold and foreign exchange to cushion the impact. When these were exhausted more drastic measures were required, including domestic deflation, trade restrictions, exchange control and debt default.

The initial shock to the system might possibly have been overcome had it not been for the subsequent course of events. For a time debtor countries could meet temporary difficulties by drawing on their reserves and taking measures to ease the strain on their external accounts. But this type of adjustment could not cope with prolonged strain following a permanent reduction in lending at a time when primary product prices were falling. Nor could it cope with further pressures, namely the breaking of the American boom. The reasons for the reversal in US activity have been the subject of much debate, but it seems very likely that it was partly a reaction to the over-hectic expansion of the 1920s leading to temporary saturation of markets, especially in consumer durables and residential construction (Romer, 1990, 1993). Restraint on the growth of real incomes and consumer spending due to the skewed distribution of income gains in the boom also dampened business prospects (Holt, 1977). A tightening of interest rates to curb excessive stock market speculation had a similar effect, though monetary factors probably played a relatively minor role in the initial breaking of the boom. However, once the downswing was underway it was aggravated and prolonged by the severe monetary contraction initiated by the Federal Reserve System (Calomiris 1993; Friedman and Schwartz 1963;

Hamilton 1987; Temin 1976). The rapidity of the American slide into depression was further assisted by the collapse of business confidence following the stock market collapse of October 1929.

The American downturn was accompanied by a further reduction in foreign lending and by a sharp contraction in imports, especially following the tariff legislation of 1930, the consequences of which were a severely reduced flow of dollars to Europe and the rest of the world (Meltzer, 1976, p. 460). The process of attrition in the debtor primary producing countries was completed as commodity prices fell dramatically (by 50 per cent or more through the course of the depression). These countries faced severe deterioration in their trade balances as export values fell faster than import values, while external interest obligations, which were fixed in terms of gold, rose sharply as a proportion of export receipts. Attempts to make up the deficiency by releasing stocks of commodities on to the market only made matters worse since it aggravated the fall in prices. Thus with dwindling reserves and an inability to borrow further, debtor countries in Europe and overseas were forced to take drastic measures to staunch the loss of funds. The way out of the impasse was sought through deflation, devaluation, default on debts and restrictive measures to protect external accounts, though not necessarily in that order.

Initially deflationary forces were quickly transmitted through the links forged by the fixed exchange rate mechanism of the gold standard (Bernanke and James, 1991; Choudhri and Kochin, 1980; Friedman and Schwartz, 1963). As Temin (1993, p. 92) notes, 'The single best predictor of how severe the Depression was in different countries is how long they stayed on gold. The gold standard was a Midas touch that paralysed the world economy'. But if policymakers became boxed in by the constraints of the restored gold standard (Cooper, 1992; Hamilton, 1988) some countries recognised that deflation could never be more than a temporary expedient, since to meet external obligations would have required politically intolerable levels of internal compression. Consequently the easiest solution was to jettison the straitjacket of the gold standard which Australia, New Zealand and several Latin American countries did at an early stage (1929–30). This then imposed a greater burden on the countries still on gold and hence intensified the deflationary spiral automatically as well as through deliberate government action. Industrialised countries in Europe felt the impact directly from America and indirectly via the periphery as demand for their industrial goods declined, while in turn declining demand for raw materials and foodstuffs on the part of the industrialised countries fed back to the periphery. Once started therefore, the deflationary process became cumulative and eventually it led to a general collapse of the gold standard and the adoption of a wide range of restrictive measures to protect domestic economies.

Though the role of the United States is seen as crucial in determining the world-wide slide into recession, it should be noted that the sequence of events in that country came at a bad time as far as the international economy was concerned. For one thing cyclical forces were reaching their peak in a number of countries, notably Britain, Germany and Poland, in the later 1920s and in some cases independently of the United States. Britain for example experienced sagging demand for her exports to primary producers a year or so before the turning point in American activity. At the same time, the incomes of primary producers in Eastern Europe and elsewhere were being squeezed as a result of the weakness in many commodity prices stemming from oversupply problems in some cases. Secondly, the cyclical developments of the period must be set against the background of an unstable international economy arising partly from the legacies left by war. Thus the cyclical downturn came at a time when many countries were still struggling with postwar distortions to their economies which left them inherently unstable. Though Europe, along with the rest of the world, had enjoyed rising prosperity in the later 1920s, the international economy remained fragile and vulnerable to shocks. Structural or sectoral deflationary tendencies were common in both industrialised and primary producing countries and these were reflected in excess capacity problems and external account imbalances arising from reparations and war debts, tariff protection and the distortions produced by the ill-conceived currency stabilisation process during the 1920s. The structure of banking and financial institutions was particularly precarious in some countries, especially in the United States and in Central and Eastern Europe. The position was also exacerbated by the transformation of economic power relationships due to the war and the lack of strong and enlightened leadership on the part of the new creditor powers which might have helped to stabilise the international economic system (Aldcroft, 1991, pp. 43–54).

These disequilibrating forces may not have been crucial to the initial downturn but they were sufficient to ensure that the system exploded once the initial shocks had been imparted, thereby producing a depression of unusual severity. The structural weaknesses in particular came to the fore in 1930–31 when financial crisis led to a wave of bank failures in both the United States and Central Europe, culminating in the spectacular crash of the Credit-Anstalt in May 1931, the repercussions of which spread throughout the continent and contributed to forcing Britain off the gold standard in September 1931 (Bernanke, 1983).

The financial panic of 1931 effectively signalled the end of the old regime. As the panic spread from one centre to another, hurried measures of national economic defence were taken and these eventually resulted in further damage to economic activity. During the next two years many countries abandoned the gold standard and proceeded to shield their domestic economies with a battery of protective restrictions including tariffs, import quotas and licensing, exchange controls and clearing agreements. This spelt the end of the prewar system of multilateral trade and payments and the free movement of resources across national boundaries. Instead nationalistic economic policies and managed currencies became the order of the day. The finishing touch to the previous system came with the breakdown of the World Economic Conference of 1933 which effectively put paid to any general attempts at international action in the economic field for the rest of the interwar period.

The diversity of recovery experience

The beginnings of recovery can be detected in some countries late in 1932, but it was not until the following year that it took firm hold on a wider front. Even then the process was by no means rapid and universal. Some countries, notably France and Czechoslovakia, continued to experience further declines in economic activity, while in the United States the pace of revival was slow and faltering initially due partly to the late departure from gold (Temin and Wigmore, 1990). During the next two years the momentum strengthened so that by the middle of the decade many countries were reporting at least modest gains in activity compared with the previous cyclical peak of 1929. Recovery was temporarily interrupted in 1937–38 when several countries experienced a mild recession, but this was soon reversed because of the influence of rearmament for war.

What is most noticeable is the great diversity of experience among countries in the 1930s. It can be seen from the data in Tables 6.1 and 6.2 that some countries made very little or no headway through the cycle, 1929–37. These included Austria, Czechoslovakia, France, Belgium, Spain, Switzerland and Ireland. Others such as Bulgaria, Germany, Finland, Norway, Portugal, Sweden and the UK recorded substantial progress. The two most successful countries were Germany and the USSR but under regimes which imposed severe social costs. Generally speaking, those countries which left the gold standard and devalued did better than the countries where retention of the gold standard until the mid-1930s led to domestic deflation to compensate for overvalued exchange rates. Leaving gold and devaluing removed constraints on both the domestic and external fronts. International competitiveness improved, investment opportunities became more attractive, while the macro-policy stance, both monetary and fiscal, could be relaxed. The performance of exchange control countries was somewhat mixed. Some did very well, especially Germany, Greece and Bulgaria, whereas Austria, Czechoslovakia and Spain experienced stagnating conditions punctuated by years of feeble recovery. Much depended upon the extent of the overvaluation of the official exchange rates under exchange control and the use which was made of special rates for exporters, as well as the benefits arising from trade links with Germany.

By April 1935, when the first defection (Belgium) from the gold bloc took place, about half the countries in Europe had depreciated their currencies in relation to gold. As Table 6.3 shows, most of the departures from gold occurred at or shortly after Britain's abandonment of gold in September 1931. About half the devaluing countries also instituted exchange control. Most of the remaining countries maintained their currencies at the same gold value as in 1929, often with the

Table 6.3 Currency depreciation in Europe, 1929–April 1935

	Percentage depreciation	*Date of depreciation in relation to gold*	*Date of exchange control*
Czechoslovakia	16	2/34	10/31
Austria	22	10/31	10/31
Yugoslavia	23	7/32	10/31
Belgium	28	4/35	—
Great Britain	41	9/31	—
Irish Free State	41	9/31	—
Estonia	42	6/33	11/31
Portugal	42	10/31	10/32
Spain	44	—[1]	5/31
Sweden	45	9/31	—
Norway	46	9/31	—
Finland	50	10/31	—
Denmark	52	9/31	11/31
Greece	57	4/32	9/31

Note:
1. Spain never formally returned to gold standard after the war.

Source: Bank for International Settlements (1935), p. 9.

assistance of exchange control. However, several countries, principally in Central and Eastern Europe, practised selective devaluation through the use of multiple exchange rates. The principal gold bloc countries (France, The Netherlands, Poland, Switzerland and Belgium until April 1935) eschewed exchange control and did not abandon gold until the middle of the decade.

Several writers (Campa, 1990; Cooper, 1992; Eichengreen, 1992a, 1992b; Eichengreen and Sachs, 1985; Kitson and Michie, 1994) have noted the advantages for those countries which released their 'golden fetters' early on. Countries which devalued early and by a large amount experienced the strongest recoveries: that is, Denmark, Norway, Sweden, Finland, Great Britain and Greece. It is noteworthy that the last-named country had the largest devaluation in Europe and the fastest rate of growth outside the USSR between 1932 and 1937 (Mazower, 1991a, pp. 225–6, 1991b, pp. 250–53). Much of this improvement could be attributed to import substitution through a combination of import restrictions, devaluation and exchange control. Overall, countries with depreciated currencies performed much better than gold bloc or exchange control countries. The former saw their industrial production rise on average by some 27 per cent between 1929 and 1936, whereas the gold bloc and exchange control countries experienced declines in activity (Eichengreen, 1992b, p. 351). Contemporary studies (Ellis 1939, 1941, p. 152; Harris, 1936, p. 103) concluded that exchange control countries tended to experience a worse trade and income performance than either gold or paper currency countries, but recent research suggests that it was the gold bloc group which fared the worst.

On the other hand, there were a number of notable exceptions to the general pattern. Germany and Bulgaria performed very strongly despite overvalued currencies under exchange control. The Baltic States also did quite well even though Latvia and Lithuania were late devaluers (Royal Institute of International Affairs, 1938, pp. 187–8; Simutis, 1942, pp. 70–71). On the other hand, substantial devaluations did not help Spain and Portugal a great deal. The latter had come through the depression quite well with positive gains in output and industrial production. But after 1932 the economy remained rather flat and subsequently felt the backwash of the Spanish Civil War. Thus industrial production charted an erratic course and actually fell slightly between 1932–36, before rising sharply in 1937 and then falling back again (Lains and Reis, 1991; Nunes, Mata and Valério, 1989). Spain is an interesting case since she had one of the worst records in the 1930s, much of the setback being due to the impact of the Civil War and its aftermath. It is sometimes argued that Spain avoided the depression because of its flexible exchange rate (Choudhri and Kochin, 1980, p. 569; Temin, 1993, p. 92). This is not strictly correct. Though Spain initially fared better than many countries due to her depreciating currency, the early 1930s still saw a considerable decline in industrial activity even though good weather favoured agricultural output (Lieberman, 1995, p. 18; Mitchell, 1975, p. 357; Payne, 1968, p. 48). At the trough in 1933 industrial production was one-fifth or more lower than in 1929 while trade volumes declined by a quarter (Prados de la Escosura, 1993; Ranki, 1985, p. 63). Once devaluation became widespread Spain lost the advantage of never having returned to gold. However, the depression was prolonged by the Civil War and the emergence of the Franco regime which erected an extensive system of bureaucratic controls that led to a seizing up of the economic system. Thus there was no real recovery in the 1930s and it was not until the 1950s that the 1929 levels of economic activity and income per head were finally regained (Lieberman 1995, p. 18; Payne, 1968, p. 57; Prados de la Escosura, 1993).

However, one should not exaggerate the benefits derived from devaluation. There was widespread exchange instability in 1932–34 following the general abandonment of the gold standard which only served to complicate the economic situation initially. Fluctuating exchange rates aggravated by speculative and non-economic capital movements, the prospects of competitive depreciation of currencies and restrictive measures of defence thrown up by this threat, together with renewed deflationary policy measures, banking crises and rigid exchange controls to protect weaker currencies, created a thoroughly unstable situation. These uncertainties were not only a serious impediment to early recovery, but they presented a constant threat of further deterioration. The League of Nations in their world report for 1932–33 (League of Nations, 1933, pp. 15, 221) were in no doubt that the most destructive element resulting from the breakdown of the gold standard was exchange instability which was seen as 'one of the principle causes of further economic deterioration in 1932 and figured prominently among the factors which limited and checked the revival of prices and productive activity in the third quarter of that year'. It was not until after 1933–34 that there was a slow approximation towards exchange rate stability as the majority of trading currencies gradually moved into a more stable relationship with sterling, the dollar and the franc (League of Nations, 1937b, pp. 15–16). Yet even by the spring of 1935 the Bank for International Settlements (1935, p. 5) could complain that the world still suffered 'without relief from the unrest and uncertainties caused by moving currencies' and that 'no fundamental, durable recovery can be hoped for unless and until a general stabilisation at least of the leading currencies has been brought about'. Secondly, while countries going off gold early secured temporary relief, the benefits reaped by the leaders soon evaporated as other countries followed suite. No doubt a coordinated programme of devaluation would have produced wider benefits than the sequential approach adopted at the time, but failing international action the second best solution was better than none at all. Thirdly, trade expansion was certainly not the engine of recovery in the 1930s even for those countries which devalued early. One or two countries, notably Finland and Norway, did quite well on the export front through the complete cycle, but for the most part exports failed to regain their previous cyclical peaks.

One reason for the desultory export performance was, of course, the restrictive policies taken to protect external accounts despite some modest relaxation later in the decade. Protection, import quotas, exchange control and the drying-up of international investment all helped to depress economic intercourse, even though they may have helped domestic recovery through import substitution. To an increasing extent also the trade of the major European countries gravitated towards 'economic blocs', within the orbit of the UK, France, Belgium, The Netherlands and Italy and their dependent territories, and Germany with South-Eastern Europe and Latin America. One feature of the latter was the increasing importance of bilateral clearing agreements which had been unknown in 1929. By 1937 they accounted for about 12 per cent of world trade, though in the case of Reichsmark bloc countries of Germany, Bulgaria, Greece, Turkey, Hungary, Romania and Yugoslavia the proportion of trade passing through clearing agreements exceeded 50 per cent (League of Nations, 1938 pp. 172–3, 1939, pp. 186–9).

Policy strategy

One common factor of the period was the increased role of government in economic matters. Given the severity of the depression it was almost inevitable that this would be the case, though governmental intervention had been increasing since the war. The methods varied widely, as did their impact, though rarely can policy factors be said to have been a significant force in the recovery process. Initially much government intervention tended to be a defensive response to crisis events. Public budgets were cut back, taxes were increased and varying degrees of restriction were imposed on trade, payments and capital movements. The latter were designed to insulate domestic economies from unfavourable external influences. In some cases, notably Germany and much of Eastern Europe, the 'planning' of foreign trade came to be widely accepted as a normal function of the state, and the weapons originally forged as an emergency defence of prices, production and currencies were not discarded but tended to be pressed into service as permanent elements of trade regulation, dovetailed into programmes of national economic development (Aldcroft, 1969).

Such policies tended to be income destructive overall and did little to assist the recovery of international trade (Friedman, 1974, 1978). More positive was the move to expansionary monetary policies in countries which abandoned gold and devalued; in some cases, for example Britain and Sweden, this was quite effective in stimulating activity in certain sectors such as residential construction. But direct action was generally limited and inadequate. It is true that, once the initial crisis had past, most countries eventually inaugurated public works and other relief programmes to relieve unemployment, though for the most part these were wholly inadequate given the scale of the task, and in time they came to be associated with rearmament plans. However, the role of the latter should not be underestimated. Most countries, including Holland and Switzerland, embarked on substantial defence spending from the middle of the 1930s and in many cases this contributed to maintaining the recovery momentum and moderating the impact of the American downturn of 1937–38 (Aldcroft and Morewood, 1995, pp. 78–9; Robertson, 1983; Thomas, 1983; Tipton and Aldrich, 1987, p. 182).

On the other hand, much of the interventionist policy was often concentrated on bolstering up and protecting producers in ex-growth industries rather than promoting development of newer growth sectors. General expansionary fiscal polices accompanied by deficit financing were notable for their absence. Fear of rekindling inflation (the memory of the early 1920s was still close at hand), adherence to the time-honoured principle of balanced budgets, coupled with a general ignorance of the role of state spending in a depression, inhibited governments from taking enlightened fiscal action. There were a few exceptions, notably the Scandinavian countries and of course the United States, though even here the measures left something to be desired.

Given the narrow scope of government policies in the 1930s it is not surprising that their impact in terms of recovery was fairly limited. With the exception of the special case of Germany, to a lesser extent Sweden and possibly one or two East European countries which attempted to foster industrialisation by autarkic planning measures, national economic development policies made only a limited contribution to recovery from depression. Even in Sweden, often seen as an exemplar of fiscal policy, the impact of budgetary policy can easily be exaggerated (Gustafsson, 1993, pp. 66–8). Yet at least policy was not positively detrimental to recovery as it was in those countries, notably Belgium,

France and Switzerland, which remained wedded to gold until the mid-1930s.

The gold bloc was a formal response to the imminent collapse of the World Monetary and Economic Conference (convened in London in June 1933), due to failure to agree on immediate measures in the currency field. On 3 July therefore, France Belgium, Italy, The Netherlands, Poland and Switzerland issued the following statement:

> The undersigned governments, convinced that the maintenance of their currencies is essential for the economic and financial recovery of the world and of credit and for the safe-guarding of social progress in their respective countries, confirm their intention to maintain the free functioning of the gold standard in their respective countries at the existing gold parities and within the framework of existing monetary laws. They ask their central banks to keep in close touch to give the maximum efficacy to this declaration.
>
> (Bank for International Settlements, 1934, p. 13)

In point of fact the gold bloc was to have very little significance in terms of actual cooperation between member countries, and inter-country financial assistance was conspicuous by its absence. Members were more concerned about husbanding resources for defence of their own currencies than coming to the rescue of their partners. In fact as Einzig (1937, p. 241) noted: 'What was established originally to develop into a monetary and economic union became eventually a small group of members who watched each other jealously, half hoping and half fearing that their fellow-members would be the first to devalue.'

More significantly, however, the deflationary policies pursued by the gold bloc members effectively precluded measures to stimulate recovery. Adherence to the former gold values made it difficult to adopt any sort of reflationary action to promote recovery, since in order to maintain the old parities in the face of depreciation elsewhere, deflationary policies were unavoidable because of the continued pressure on their balance of payments (Condliffe, 1941, p. 235). In the end such policies proved intolerable because of the disastrous effect on domestic economies and the gold bloc crumbled in 1935 and broke up entirely in September 1936, with France, The Netherlands and Switzerland the last to go as international pressures on their exchanges led to capital flight (League of Nations, 1937a, pp. 26–8).

Most of the gold bloc countries were affected very badly by the restrictive policies. Industrial production in these countries (excluding Italy) declined on average by 13.94 per cent between 1929 and 1936, whereas in the sterling bloc countries and other countries with devalued currencies it rose by some 27 per cent (Eichengreen, 1992b, p. 351). Switzerland suffered equally with the rest of the gold bloc. Negative rates of growth were recorded for most of the 1930s and only in 1933, 1937 and 1939 was there any worthwhile expansion. By the end of the decade output and production levels were little better than they had been at the previous cyclical peak in 1929 (David, 1995, pp. 115–18, 1996; Siegenthaler, 1976, p. 531). The export industries and the Swiss tourist trade were especially hard hit by the overvaluation of the currency, whereas industries producing for the domestic market fared somewhat better as a result of protection of the home market and the relatively high floor to real incomes through the depression (David, 1995, pp. 122–3). The Swiss banking system was also in a fragile state during the first half of the 1930s due largely to the heavy loan commitments to Germany and other Central European countries which became immobilised following the 1931 financial crisis and the accompanying payments moratoria and standstill agreements (Einzig, 1937, p. 41).

Thus one can argue that recovery eventually took place in most countries despite rather than because of domestic policy action which, if not actually harmful, was generally too little and too late to have much impact on the recovery effort. Again there are exceptions to the rule. One should not underestimate the indirect effects of cheap money and even tariff protection in, say, Britain nor should one belittle unduly the fiscal novelty in Sweden and other Scandinavian countries even though it fell short of the ideal. Moreover, one should bear in mind that by abandoning gold and devaluing there was greater scope for manoeuvre in domestic monetary policy in many countries and for raising the general price level in order to restore business profitability.

By and large it was real or spontaneous forces rather than induced (policy) factors that were instrumental in bringing about recovery. And to a large extent that recovery was based on home markets rather than exports. The outstanding example in this context is Britain where the demand for the products of the newer industries and the strong upsurge in building activity did much to get the recovery going. In this case it was the high floor to real incomes coupled with the gains from a favourable shift in the terms of trade that were instrumental in stimulating consumer spending. In part it also reflected a process of structural transformation which many Western European countries were experiencing to a greater or lesser degree in the interwar years, partly because of the impact of wartime changes on markets and new technological developments. Svennilson (1954) was correct to stress the severe structural transformation problems of this period which in the industrialised countries were characterised by a shift of resources from older staple industries to newer lines of endeavour, while in Eastern and Southern Europe it was largely a question of effecting a transformation from predominantly agrarian structures to economies based more firmly on manufacturing activities. In neither case was the transformation completed during the period under consideration.

Structural factors also explain why so few countries, apart from Germany, were able to eliminate unemployment during the 1930s. The continued presence of high unemployment does not necessarily denote an abortive recovery, however, since in several cases the cyclical indicators, measuring from peak to peak (1929–37), suggest otherwise. Much of the remaining unemployment at the peak of the cycle in the 1930s probably consisted of structural unemployment which is to be expected at a time of structural transition due to a mismatch of resources, limited mobility of labour, skill deficiencies and other factors. Such unemployment is not easily eradicated in the normal course of cyclical recovery since it requires, as Keynes recognised, specific long-term measures to deal with the underlying causes. Only the extreme exigencies of war, which gave a new lease of life to some of the ex-growth industries, would mop up the excess reserves of labour.

Europe in decline

The interwar period taken as a whole was for Europe one of chequered growth, crisis, political tension and latterly the threat of war. Some economic advance was made during the period but at a slower pace than before 1914. Not only was progress severely interrupted by war and the slump of 1929–32, but most countries faced important structural problems which were not resolved before war once again intervened. Recovery from the depression was slow and patchy and even by the end of the 1930s many economies were operating at less than full capacity.

But perhaps the most significant change was the decline in Europe's position in the world economy. The First World War had seriously weakened Europe and provided opportunities for other countries, notably the United States and Japan, to strengthen their economic power. Western Europe was no longer strong enough to dictate the pattern of world development as she had more or less done in the nineteenth century. America now assumed that role and with fateful consequences in the depression. Of even greater concern was the political disintegration of Europe and the loss of the former balance of power following the geographical fragmentation of the Continent as a consequence of the postwar peace settlements. It was the resulting political vacuum in East-Central Europe that paved the way for the Second World War.

References

Aldcroft, D. H. (1969), 'The development of the managed economy before 1939', *Journal of Contemporary History*, 4.

Aldcroft, D. H. (1991), 'Destabilising influences in the European Economy in the 1920s', in C. Holmes and A. Booth (eds), *Economy and Society: European Industrialisation and its Social Consequences. Essays Presented to Sidney Pollard*, Leicester: Leicester University Press.

Aldcroft, D. H. and Morewood, S. (1995), *Economic Change in Eastern Europe since 1918*, Aldershot: Edward Elgar.

Bairoch, P. (1976), 'Europe's gross national product: 1800–1975', *Journal of European Economic History*, 5.

Bank for International Settlements (1934), *Fourth Annual Report, 1 April 1933–31 March 1934*, Basle: Bank for International Settlements.

Bank for International Settlements (1935), *Fifth Annual Report, 1 April 1934–31 March 1935*, Basle: Bank for International Settlements.

Berend, I. T. and Ranki, G. (1974), *Economic Development in East Central Europe in the 19th and 20th Centuries*, New York: Columbia University Press.

Bernanke, B. S. (1983), 'Nonmonetary effects of the financial crisis in the propagation of the great depression', *American Economic Review*, 73.

Bernanke, B. and James, H. (1991), 'The gold standard, deflation and financial crises in the great depression: an international comparison', in R. G. Hubbard (ed.), *Financial Markets and Financial Crises*, Chicago, University of Chicago Press.

Calomiris, C. W. (1993), 'Financial factors in the great depression', *Journal of Economic Perspectives*, 7.

Campa, J. M. (1990), 'Exchange rates and economic recovery in the 1930s: an extension to Latin America', *Journal of Economic History*, 50.

Choudhri, E. V. and Kochin, L. A. (1980), 'The exchange rate and the international transmission of business cycle disturbances: some evidence from the great depression, *Journal of Money, Credit and Banking*, 12.

Condliffe, J. B. (1941), *The Reconstruction of World Trade: a Survey of International Economic Relations*, London: Allen and Unwin.

Cooper, R. N. (1992), 'Fettered to gold? Economic policy in the interwar period', *Journal of Economic Literature*, 30.

David, T. (1995), 'Un indice de la production industrielle de la Suisse durant l'entre-deux guerres', *Schweizerische Zeitschrift für Geschichte*, 45.

David, T. (1996), 'Indices de la production industrielle suisse', in H. Ritzmann (ed.), *Statistique historique de la Suisse*, Zurich: Charonos.
Eichengreen, B. (1992a), 'The origins and nature of the great slump revisited', *Economic History Review,* 45.
Eichengreen, B. (1992b), *Golden Fetters; the Gold Standard and the Great Depression, 1919–1939*, Oxford: Oxford University Press.
Eichengreen, B. and Hatton, T. J. (eds) (1988), *Interwar Unemployment in International Perspective*, Dordrecht: Kluwer Academic Publishers.
Eichengreen, B. and Sachs, J. (1985), 'Exchange rates and economic recovery in the 1930s', *Journal of Economic History*, 45.
Einzig, P. (1937), *World Finance 1935–37*, London: Kegan Paul, Trench, Trubner and Co.
Ellis, H. S. (1939), 'Exchange control in Austria and Hungary', *Journal of Economics*, 54.
Ellis, H. S. (1941), *Exchange Control in Central Europe*, Cambridge, MA: Harvard University Press.
Fleisig, H. W. (1975), *Long-Term Capital Flows and the Great Depression: the Role of the United States, 1927–1933*, New York: Arno Press.
Fremdling, G. M. (1985), 'Did the United States transmit the great depression to the rest of the world?', *American Economic Review*, 75.
Freris, A. F. (1986), *The Greek Economy in the Twentieth Century*, London: Croom Helm.
Friedman, P. (1974), *Impact of Trade Destruction on National Incomes: a Study of Europe, 1924–1938*, Gainesville, FL: University Presses of Florida.
Friedman, P. (1978), 'An econometric model of national income, commercial policy and the level of international trade: the open economies of Europe, 1924–1938', *Journal of Economic History,* 38.
Friedman, M. and Schwartz, A. (1963), *A Monetary History of the United States*, Chicago: University of Chicago Press.
Gustafsson, B. (1993), 'Unemployment and fiscal policy in Sweden during the 1930s: myths and realities', in W. R. Garside (ed.), *Capitalism in Crisis: International Responses to the Great Depression*, London: Pinter Publishers.
Hamilton, J. D. (1987), 'Monetary factors in the great depression', *Journal of Monetary Economics,* 19.
Hamilton, J. D. (1988), 'The role of the international gold standard in propagating the great depression', *Contemporary Policy Issues*, 6.
Harris, S. E. (1936), *Exchange Depreciation: its Theory and its History 1931–35, with some Consideration of Related Domestic Policies*, Cambridge, MA: Harvard University Press.

Hjerppe, R. (1996), *Finland's Historical National Accounts 1860–1914: Calculation Methods and Statistical Tables*, Jyväskylä: Kari-Pekka Kivirauma.
Holt, C. F. (1977), 'Who benefited from the prosperity of the twenties?' *Explorations in Economic History*, **14**.
James, H. (1992), 'Financial flows across frontiers during the interwar depression', *Economic History Review*, **45**.
Kitson, M. and Michie, J. (1994), 'Depression and recovery: lessons from the interwar period', in J. Michie and J. Grieve Smith (eds), *Unemployment in Europe*, London: Academic Press.
Lains, P. and Reis, J. (1991), 'Portuguese economic growth, 1833–1985: some doubts', *Journal of European Economic History*, **20**.
Landes, D. S. (1969), *The Unbound Prometheus: Technological Change and Industrial Development in Western Europe from 1750 to the Present*, Cambridge: Cambridge University Press.
League of Nations (1933), *World Economic Survey 1932–33*, Geneva: League of Nations.
League of Nations (1936), *Statistical Yearbook 1935/36*, Geneva: League of Nations.
League of Nations (1937a), *Money and Banking 1936/37*, Geneva: League of Nations.
League of Nations (1937b), *World Economic Survey 1936/37*, Geneva: League of Nations.
League of Nations (1938), *World Economic Survey 1937/38*, Geneva: League of Nations.
League of Nations (1939), *World Economic Survey 1938/39*, Geneva: League of Nations.
Lieberman, S. (1995), *Growth and Crisis in the Spanish Economy: 1940–93*, London: Routledge.
Maddison, A. (1991), *Dynamic Forces in Capitalist Development*, Oxford: Oxford University Press.
Maddison, A. (1995), *Monitoring the World Economy 1820–1992*, Paris: OECD.
Mazower, M. (1991a), 'Banking and economic development in interwar Greece', in H. James, H. Lindgren and A. Teichova (eds), *The Role of Banks in the Interwar Economy*, Cambridge: Cambridge University Press.
Mazower, M. (1991b), *Greece and the Interwar Economic Crisis*, Oxford: Oxford University Press.
Meltzer, A. H. (1976), 'Monetary and other explanations of the start of the great depression', *Journal of Monetary Economics*, **2**.
Mitchell, B. R. (1975), *European Historical Statistics 1750–1970*, London: Macmillan.

North, D. C. (1962), 'International capital movements in historical perspective', in R. F. Mikesell (ed.), *U.S. Private and Government Investment Abroad*, Eugene, OR: University of Oregon Books.

Nunes, A. B., Mata, E. and Valério, N. (1989), 'Portuguese economic growth 1833–1985', *Journal of European Economic History*, 18.

OEEC (1960), *Industrial Statistics 1900–1959*, Paris: OEEC.

Payne, S. G. (1968), *Franco's Spain*, London: Routledge and Kegan Paul.

Prados de la Escosura, L. (1993), 'Spain's gross domestic product, 1850–1990', Madrid: Ministerio de Economía y Hacienda.

Pryor, Z. P. (1973), 'Czechoslovak economic development in the interwar period', in V. S. Mamatey and R. Luza (eds), *A History of the Czechoslovak Republic 1918–1948*, Princeton, NJ: Princeton University Press.

Ranki, G. (1985), 'Problems of southern European economic development (1918–38)', in G. Arrighi (ed.), *Semiperipheral Development: the Politics of Southern Europe in the Twentieth Century*, Beverly Hills, CA: Sage Publications.

Robertson, A. J. (1983), 'British rearmament and industrial growth, 1935–1939', *Research in Economic History*, 8.

Romer, C. D. (1990), 'The great crash and the onset of the great depression', *Quarterly Journal of Economics*, 105.

Romer, C. D. (1993), 'The nation in depression', *Journal of Economic Perspectives*, 7.

Royal Institute of International Affairs (1938), *The Baltic States: a Survey of the Political and Economic Structure and the Foreign Relations of Estonia, Latvia, and Lithuania*, Oxford, Oxford University Press.

Schuker, S. (1988), *American 'Reparations' to Germany: Implications for the Third World Debt Crisis*, Princeton, NJ: Princeton University Press.

Siegenthaler, H. (1976), 'Switzerland 1920–1970', in C. Cipolla (ed.), *The Fontana Economic History of Europe: Contemporary Economies*, Part II, London: Collins.

Simutis, A. (1942), *The Economic Reconstruction of Lithuania after 1918*, New York: Columbia University Press.

Spulber, N. (1966), *The State and Economic Development in Eastern Europe*, New York: Random House.

Solomou, S. (1996), *Themes in Macroeconomic History: the UK Economy, 1919–1939*, Cambridge: Cambridge University Press.

Svennilson, I. (1954), *Growth and Stagnation in the European Economy*, Geneva: United Nations.

Temin, P. (1976), *Did Monetary Factors Cause the Great Depression?* New York, Norton.

Temin, P. (1993), 'Transmission of the Great Depression', *Journal of Economic Perspectives*, 7.

Temin, P. and Wigmore, B. (1990), 'The end of one big deflation', *Explorations in Economic History*, 27.

Thomas, M. (1983), 'Rearmament and Economic Recovery in the late 1930s', *Economic History Review*, 36.

Tipton, F. B. and Aldrich, R. (1987), *An Economic and Social History of Europe, 1890–1939*, Basingstoke: Macmillan.

United Nations (1949a), *International Capital Movements during the Interwar Period*, New York: United Nations.

United Nations (1949b), *Statistical Yearbook 1948*, New York: United Nations.

CHAPTER SEVEN

Coping with Depression in Eastern Europe

Economic background to depression

Throughout the interwar years the new and reconstituted states of Eastern Europe (Czechoslovakia, Hungary, Poland, Yugoslavia, Romania and Bulgaria) faced a constant struggle for survival, politically as well as economically. Weak states, barely fit for nationhood, internally rent by nationality conflicts and divided one against the other, they became pawns in the renewed struggle among the major powers for the hegemony of Europe (Momtchiloff, 1944, p. 84; Newman, 1968, pp. 11–13, 27, 201; Ranki, 1983, pp. 33–4). Apart from Czechoslovakia, which inherited an economic structure more closely resembling that of the West having gained the lion's share of the industrial capacity of the former Austro-Hungarian Empire (*The Economist*, 1938a, pp. 544–5), all the states in the region remained heavily dependent on agriculture for a living. Between one-half and three-quarters of the occupied population was engaged in agriculture (even higher in Albania) which generated one-half or more of national income (Dovring, 1965; Hocevar, 1987, p. 565; Polonsky, 1975, p. 164; Royal Institute of International Affairs, 1940, p. 86). More to the point, despite varying degrees of land reform in the postwar period, agriculture remained extremely backward by any standard, with yields a fraction of those of western countries (Moore, 1945, pp. 35, 51; Warriner, 1939, p. 9). The result was low incomes, limited domestic purchasing power, and very limited agrarian accumulation, all of which inhibited structural diversification towards industry (Teichova, 1989, pp. 903–4). Rapid population growth exacerbated pressure on the land leading to widespread underemployment and surplus labour (Moore, 1945, pp. 63, 71).

The backward state of Eastern Europe can be seen from a glance at Table 7.1, which shows some of the salient economic features of the countries in the region. The Balkan countries were, in every respect, the poorest nations, only surpassed by Albania, while Czechoslovakia stands out as being much closer to the West than any of the other countries. Poland and Hungary occupy an intermediate position. What is especially noticeable, with one or two exceptions, is the high proportion of the population engaged in agriculture, the rapid rate of population

Table 7.1 Economic characteristics of Eastern Europe in the interwar years

	1	*2*	*3*	*4*	*5*	*6*	*7*	*8*
Bulgaria	84	1.34	36.5	96.1	70.9	68	300	110
Czechoslovakia	37	0.71	4.1	28.0	30.9	176	450	200
Hungary	53	0.76	9.3	71.3	40.4	112	340	150
Poland	65	1.44	24.6	76.6	40.4	104	400	130
Romania	79	1.27	42.0	99.1	73.9	70–75	290	80
Yugoslavia	79	1.45	48.0	91.9	69.7	81	300	100
Great Britain	6	0.49	—	—	—	—	—	—
France	36	—	5.5	—	—	236	580	280
Germany	26	—	—	—	—	337	790	290
USA	—	—	4.3	—	—	521	1 730	580

Key:
1. Percentage of active population engaged in primary sector, *circa* 1930.
2. Percentage annual growth rate of population during the interwar period.
3. Illiteracy percentage of those aged 10 or over in 1929.
4. Primary products and semi-manufactures as a percentage of total exports, 1929–38.
5. Finished goods as a percentage of total imports, 1929–38
6. Net national income per head of population in 1938 US dollars.
7. Value of net output per worker in industry and handicrafts in 1938 US dollars (Czechoslovakia 1937, USA 1936).
8. Value of net output per worker in agriculture in 1938 US dollars.

Sources: Deldlycke, Gelders and Limbor (1968); Kaser and Radice (1985), pp. 358–9, 532; Polonsky (1975), pp. 172, 178.

growth, and the skewed structure of foreign trade. Such characteristics epitomised the 'gigantic backlog of backwardness', to use Spulber's phrase (Spulber, 1966, p. 75), that faced the East European countries in this period, and which required a major structural transformation of their economies at a time when world events conspired to overwhelm them. Wartime hostilities and the aftermath had left a legacy of problems – destitution and starvation, reconstruction, territorial changes, inflation, currency instability, ethnic and social tensions – which would take many years to solve, if at all (Aldcroft, 1988, p. 595). The new and reconstituted states which emerged as a result of the postwar peace settlement were scarcely designed to facilitate economic progress since the new geographical configurations destroyed many of the former prewar economic relationships. Consequently, economic performance was very chequered in the first half of the 1920s since the countries in question were grappling with the tasks of territorial and ethnic assimilation, as well as with a host of other problems in the wake of postwar reconstruction. It was not until the latter half of the decade that a measure of stability and progress was achieved, but this was based on rather insecure foundations as subsequent events were soon to demonstrate.

Prosperity in the latter half of the 1920s – and ultimately the means of breaking the structural bottleneck in the longer term – was very much dependent on three factors: a favourable market environment for agrarian products; trade expansion; and capital imports. Each in turn was also a source of weakness. First, agriculture, despite its inefficiency, was the main foreign exchange earner with dependence on a narrow range of crops. Market conditions, however, became increasingly less favourable in the later 1920s as western countries sought to protect their home markets and prices weakened, especially in cereals where stocks were piling up rapidly (Royal Institute of International Affairs, 1937, p. 287). Secondly, the loss of the large internal market of the Austro-Hungarian Empire meant that the new states were more trade-dependent than previously, and therefore more trade-sensitive and vulnerable to the vagaries of the international business cycle. Thirdly, because of low domestic accumulation, increasing reliance was placed on capital imports. Foreign capital may have made a positive contribution to development but it also had its drawbacks (Lethbridge, 1985, p. 557; Nötel, 1986, p. 287). Inflows of capital were less than self-liquidating partly because of the unproductive way in which some of the foreign capital was used (Political and Economic Planning, 1945, p. 110). The consequence was that servicing the foreign debt absorbed a steadily increasing proportion of export earnings. By the end of the decade most East European countries had incurred unmanageable debt levels and were forced to continue borrowing in order to service past loans (Aldcroft, 1991, p. 53). In 1928 outpayments on account of capital services were 40 per cent of net capital inflows in the case of Hungary and 28 per cent for Poland, while, apart from Czechoslovakia, debt service payments constituted one-quarter or more of the value of export receipts (Aldcroft, 1977, p. 254; Political and Economic Planning, 1945, p. 110; United Nations, 1949b, p. 59).

Impact of the crisis

Arguably, therefore, Eastern Europe was already facing an untenable situation even before the start of the international slump of the early 1930s (Bandera, 1964, p. 115; Lee, 1969, p. 141). The crisis itself shattered the region's fragile prosperity and eliminated any hope of its reintegration into the international economy. In aggregate terms, East-Central Europe, and especially those countries closely associated with the German economy, suffered more severely from the great depression than many western countries (Maddison, 1973, p. 20–21). The most important manifestations of that event as far as the region was concerned were the massive fall in primary product prices, the collapse of international lending and the shrinkage in international trade. Each of these had very serious implications not only for the economies in general, but in particular for their balance of payments, budgets and debt burdens.

The price collapse had multiple implications. Agrarian prices, especially for cereals, fell by one-half or more, faster than import prices of industrial products, so that all countries except Czechoslovakia suffered a significant deterioration in their terms of trade. The decline was accentuated in the early stages as farmers attempted to compensate for the price decline by increasing output and raising the quantities exported. This policy met with only limited success, however, as external market conditions deteriorated rapidly after 1930 and export volumes declined. Thus, through a combination of price and quantity factors export receipts dropped sharply. In the case of Romania they fell by no less than 73 per cent and on average they had shrunk to around 40 per cent of the 1929 level by 1932/33. This massive drop in export earnings entailed a serious loss of international purchasing power and a rising debt burden relative to exchange earnings. Since most international debts remained fixed in foreign currency terms the debt servicing power of exports fell by between one-half and two-thirds in the case of Hungary and the Balkan countries (Nötel, 1986, pp. 217–19). Though Czechoslovakia's export earnings also fell heavily because of the collapse of former markets, her much stronger international position meant that external debt servicing was not a major problem.

The price changes had equally momentous repercussions on the domestic front. Agrarian incomes declined by up to one-half in Poland and the Balkans and by as much as two-thirds in Hungary. The situation was aggravated by the unfavourable gap between agrarian and industrial prices. Whereas the former fell by 50–60 per cent, the price of goods purchased by the peasants rarely fell by more than 30 per cent (Seton-Watson, 1946, p. 82). At times the gap became so great that food producers had to give up nearly double the prewar amount of grain and cattle to secure the same amount of manufactured articles (Hertz, 1947, p. 194). As incomes declined debt burdens increased as a proportion of income and by 1932 many peasants were on the verge of bankruptcy. In Yugoslavia, for example, more than one-third of rural households were heavily in debt – and many more were far too poor even to obtain credit – and the sum of their indebtedness was equal to 80 to 90 per cent of their total cash incomes (Rothschild, 1974, p. 271). The situation was even worse in Hungary where debt as a proportion of agrarian income rose from 78 to 133 per cent between 1928 and 1933 (Berend and Ranki, 1974a, p. 245). Together with the heavy burden of taxation the peasants' lot became intolerable: many sold their land simply to survive.

The diminished incomes of the farming community also had a serious fiscal impact. The main tax base of the State was seriously eroded at a time when the demand for relief payments became ever greater because of the distress caused by the depression. This forced governments to curtail expenditure wherever possible and therefore left little scope for the implementation of more expansive policies to combat the depression. Schönfeld (1975, pp. 197–8) notes how little room for manoeuvre there was for governments to experiment with novel fiscal policies: 'Der finanzielle Spielraum der Regierungen die Depression durch öffentliche Aufträge und Subventionen zu bekämpfen, wurde immer geringer.' [The scope for governments to combat depression by public works and financial incentives became ever more limited.]

It was the breakdown of the international financial mechanism in 1930/31 that finally undermined the solvency of Eastern Europe. Long-term foreign lending, already faltering in 1928/29, had virtually dried up by 1931, gold and foreign exchange reserves had drained away, and short-term credits were hastily withdrawn in the panic flight of capital in 1931 (United Nations, 1949b, p. 10). The cessation of foreign lending not only led to a curtailment of investment and activity in debtor countries, but it also had a more immediate impact through the balance of payments. Most of the debtor countries had depended heavily on capital imports in the later 1920s to close the gap in their balance of payments. Thus of the total flow of funds (both long and short term) into Hungary, Poland, Bulgaria and Yugoslavia between 1924 and 1928, five-tenths went to cover an import surplus of goods and services, four-tenths to meet interest and dividend payments on outstanding foreign debts, and one-tenth for the purchase of gold. In 1929 capital inflows barely covered interest and dividend payments and thereafter they dwindled to insignificant amounts. For the whole of the crisis period, 1929 to 1933, they covered less than one-half of interest and dividend payments, which meant that the former import surplus on goods and services had to be converted into a positive balance (Nötel, 1974, pp. 84–5; 1984, pp. 192–3).

The collapse of export receipts, together with the cessation of capital inflows and the subsequent panic withdrawal of funds in the 1931 financial crisis, effectively rendered Eastern Europe insolvent. Creditors were unwilling to commit funds to countries for fear of the likelihood of currency depreciation, the imposition of exchange control or even debt default, all of which materialised in due course.

It was little consolation that the industrial sector suffered less acutely from the crisis since for most countries in the region industry accounted for a small share of economic activity. Experience varied more widely than in the case of agriculture, depending in part on the structure of individual economies. The light sector of manufacturing appears to have been the worst hit and it was this branch that predominated in the region as a whole (Zauberman, 1976, p. 598). Yet for the Balkan countries industrial over-production was scarcely a major problem given the insignificant weighting of this sector in total economic activity, and in any case reduced domestic consumption was partly offset by increasing protection and therefore import substitution. Thus, production declined only moderately in Romania, thanks also to a large increase in oil output, while Bulgaria appears to have managed a significant advance in manufacturing output during the depression years. Czechoslovakia was one of the worst sufferers in this respect because of her advanced industrial sector, while the mixed agrarian–industrial countries of Poland and Hungary were affected to a lesser extent. Nevertheless, except in the case of Czechoslovakia, it was the agrarian sector which largely determined the scale and severity of the crisis (Aldcroft, 1980, pp. 100–11).

The contours of policy action

There was no lack of policy response to meet the exigencies of the crisis of the 1930s, but it is difficult to detect any clearly defined and coordinated strategy designed to combat the depression. The majority of policy measures, at least in the early part of the 1930s, were *ad hoc* defensive ones, often inconsistent and contradictory, and more likely to depress than to lift the level of economic activity. That the approach was orthodox and defensive is not altogether surprising when one recalls the very difficult circumstances of the time. The problem initially was not so much one of generating recovery, rather it was one of sheer economic salvation. Drastic measures were therefore required to shore up tottering economies and these were not long in coming: they included severe deflationary policies together with a battery of restrictions typical of siege economies which were designed to deal primarily with the external account. Among these were temporary closure of banking institutions, rigorous exchange control, limitation on debt payments, and the imposition of trade restrictions such as import quotas and higher tariffs. Moreover, given the speed and intensity of the crisis, the strong defensive measures taken by many of the major economic powers, and the limited theoretical guidance and practical experience on how to deal with a major economic crisis, it is difficult to conceive of a viable alternative open to the Eastern European economies. Desperate problems called forth desperate remedies. Only when conditions began to improve by the mid-1930s did they turn their attention to more constructive policies.

The policy response was not, however, quite so indeterminate as one might suspect from the more immediate reaction to the crisis. There were several more fundamental factors which helped to shape the course of policy over the medium term. One was the almost pathological fear present in most of the countries of the region of repeating the inflationary episode of the 1920s, which above all else was associated with currency depreciation and budgetary deficits. Hence the strong emphasis on financial rectitude, which meant balanced budgets and currency stabilisation at all costs (League of Nations, 1938, para. 8; 1944, p. 167).

Second, in keeping with this approach, and to maintain international confidence in the hope that foreign lending would be resumed, the debtor nations were reluctant initially to repudiate or default on their foreign debts. A corollary of this was an equal reluctance to depreciate their currencies since this would entail a rise in the nominal value of debts and service costs in domestic currency (Bandera, 1964, p. 119).

A third important factor shaping the course of policy was the growing force of nationalism. This had already been evident in the nostrification policy (the reduction or confiscation of alien property rights) of the 1920s which gathered force in the following decade (Pasvolsky, 1928, p. 75). It was associated with increasing state intervention and the ideology of autarky and self-determination which appeared to offer a more promising solution to the problems of the region than any attempt to regain re-entry into the international economy (Condliffe, 1941, p. 303). Liberal capitalism and bourgeois democracy had become discredited and this left the way open for right-wing autocratic governments to exploit nationalistic sentiments in both the economic and political spheres. Ultimately, as subsequent events were to demonstrate, this proved a high-cost exercise in both respects (Macartney and Palmer, 1962, pp. 285–8).

One final issue which became increasingly critical in the later 1930s was rearmament. Defence expenditure had always been a significant component in the budgets of these countries, but the increasing international tension in the later part of the period threw it into even greater prominence. Thus from the mid-1930s many of the sponsored or assisted industrial developments were geared in some way to the military needs of rearmament (Tomasevich, 1949, p. 179).

Within this framework of determining factors one can detect some subtle shift in policy direction during the course of the decade. Up to the mid-1930s policy tends to be highly orthodox and defensive, largely in an effort to avoid complete financial collapse and to provide relief for the most distressed sectors. Thereafter there is an element of relaxation both on the external and domestic fronts, aided by the recovery in international trade, the pressure of rearmament and the growing influence of Germany in the economies of the Danubian states. The change was reflected in some of the more ambitious policies to foster industrial development.

We now turn to a consideration of the relevance of various policy measures within the context of the following themes: external protection; macroeconomic policy; the relief of agriculture; and state intervention and the promotion of industry. The final section provides an overall assessment.

In defence of external accounts

'By 1935 Europe had descended to a historical nadir in trade and commercial policy' (Friedman, 1978, p. 158). Almost every conceivable form of trade restriction, barring blockade, was then in use to a greater or lesser degree. Soon after the start of the crisis all European countries attempted to defend their external position and to improve their trade balances by utilising various methods of controls. Most of them – the main exceptions were France, Sweden and Czechoslovakia – managed to improve their trade balances but at considerably lower levels of trade and income (Friedman, 1974, p. 413). Thus, though commercial policy achieved its immediate purpose, it was at the expense of economic activity since countries were unable to offset the contractionary effects of much reduced trade levels.

Eastern Europe was no exception in this respect. Indeed, external policy was pursued more vigorously than in many other countries. Tariff levels were raised sharply between 1929 and 1931 to be followed by an extensive system of import controls (Condliffe, 1941, p. 103; Pollard, 1981, p. 302). In the latter half of 1931 Bulgaria, Yugoslavia, Hungary and Czechoslovakia introduced exchange control, followed by Romania in May 1932. Only Poland remained free of exchange control until April 1936 (League of Nations, 1933, pp. 222–3; 1937, p. 11; 1942, p. 70).

Strong action was even more important in Eastern Europe than elsewhere. Trade balances had on average been unfavourable before 1929 and they were soon hit badly by falling export values and adverse trade terms. Rapidly dwindling capital imports reduced the ability to finance import surpluses and so imports had to be reduced at all costs. Protection of domestic agriculture and industry also became an important consideration in a world awash with products. Initially, however, there were even more pressing motives for the introduction of exchange control. One of the main factors was to stem the capital outflow in the financial panic of 1931. A second reason seems to have been the states' desire to collect foreign exchange to cover foreign debt services. Initially it was hoped to maintain debt servicing in order to demonstrate financial soundness. Additionally, Eastern European countries were reluctant to relinquish their old currency parities, associating devaluation with inflation and mindful, as we have noted, of the implications for debt service costs (League of Nations, 1943, pp. 9–11; 1944, pp. 162–7).

During the course of the 1930s the burden of foreign debt was considerably eased by one means or another. Partial or complete suspension of servicing was declared by all countries between 1931 and 1933. Subsequently the burden was reduced through negotiation with creditors, both as to capital sums and repayment terms, while devaluation in the major creditor countries – the United States and Britain – afforded a substantial measure of relief. Overall, the total outstanding debt of the six countries fell from $3.8 to $2.0 billion between 1931 and 1937, and by the latter date servicing costs as a proportion of exports had fallen to less than 10 per cent compared with 25 per cent or more at the earlier date (Condliffe, 1941, pp. 243–4; Nötel, 1974, pp. 89–91).

Rigorous exchange control achieved some of its immediate objectives. It staunched the capital flow and reversed the deterioration in trade balances. The overall trade balance of the six countries was converted from a deficit of $32.5 million in 1929 to a surplus of $107.8 million in 1930 and $141.9 million in 1931 (Nötel, 1974, p. 87). But the costs involved were not inconsiderable. Harris (1936, p. 103) noted that exchange control countries tended to suffer a worse trade position than gold or paper currency countries. In the case of Hungary, Ellis (1941, p. 152) could find little net gain apart from the obstacles placed in the way of capital flight. Exchange control tended to raise domestic prices and to make exporting more difficult in so far as the control helped to maintain fictitious currency parities. This then led to a lower level of trade and income than under conditions where the currency is allowed to find its equilibrium level (Heuser, 1939, p. 230; League of Nations, 1938, p. 49). By 1934 Eastern European currencies were overvalued in relation to the pound and the dollar by up to 60 per cent (Nötel, 1986, p. 229). Furthermore, exchange control countries tended to trade more among themselves and less with free exchange countries and at higher prices than those ruling in the free market (League of Nations, 1938, p. 37).

Several countries eventually relaxed the controls to a certain extent to counter the adverse effects. At the end of 1934 Bulgaria modified its exchange control system with considerable benefits to its trade performance in the following year (League of Nations, 1938, p. 41). In time most countries, apart from Poland, introduced a measure of devaluation, either overt or concealed. The latter took the form of an export bonus or premium whereby exporters received a larger amount of domestic currency for their exports than under the official rate. The premia varied over time and from country to country, but usually ranged between 20 and 50 per cent (Lampe and Jackson, 1982, pp. 464–5; League of Nations, 1944, p. 171; Ranki, 1983, p. 90; Royal Institute of International Affairs, 1936, pp. 85–9). Even so their currencies continued to remain overvalued in relation to those of free market countries (League of Nations, 1938, p. 5).

One important development arising out of the closer affinity among exchange control countries was the spread of clearing agreements. By 1937 around 12 per cent of world trade and more than 50 per cent of the trade of Hungary, Bulgaria, Romania, Yugoslavia, Greece and Turkey passed through clearing, while in the case of Germany it was as high as 80 per cent (League of Nations, 1935a, p. 15; 1942, pp. 70–72; 1944, pp. 182–3). Clearing agreements were one of the principal instruments for minimising the need for and maximising the acquisition of foreign exchange. They allowed the bilateral balancing of claims between exchange control countries thereby eliminating the need for foreign exchange. The chief drawback was that they enabled Germany to exert an increasing influence on the economies of south-east Europe (Hungary and the Balkans) since Germany was one of the few countries prepared to accept agrarian products and other commodities at favourable prices. Though trade with the whole of Eastern Europe rarely accounted for more than around 10 per cent of Germany's total foreign trade, Germany managed to secure a very firm foot-hold in the trade of south-eastern Europe, especially following the *Anschluss* with Austria in 1938. The extent of the penetration in Hungary and the Balkans can be seen from the trade shares indicated in Table 7.2.

There is still controversy as to what benefits south-east Europe derived from the system. The conventional argument is that Germany exploited the region to gain access to food and raw materials on advantageous terms, and piled up large import surpluses, the Reichsmark

Table 7.2 Germany's share of Eastern Europe's trade (%)[1]

	Exports to Germany				*Imports from Germany*			
	1929	*1932*	*1937*	*1938*	*1929*	*1932*	*1937*	*1938*
Hungary	11.7	15.2	24.0	40.0	20.0	22.5	25.9	40.9
Romania	27.4	12.5	22.3	26.5	24.1	23.6	28.9	40.0
Yugoslavia	8.5	11.3	21.7	42.0	15.6	17.7	32.4	39.4
Bulgaria	29.9	26.0	43.1	59.0	22.2	25.9	54.8	52.0
Poland	34.2[2]	16.2	14.5	24.1	26.9[2]	20.1	14.5	23.0
Czechoslovakia	22.1[2]	19.6	13.7	20.1	24.9[2]	22.9	15.5	19.1

Notes:
1. Figures for 1938 include Austria.
2. Figures refer to 1928.

Sources: Hiden (1977), p. 173; Kaiser (1980), pp. 325–6.

balances from which could only be used to purchase German goods, thereby indirectly financing a German rearmament programme at the expense of weaker countries. Such balances also rendered the client countries highly vulnerable to political and economic pressure when market conditions deteriorated as they did in the later 1930s. In return Germany exported large quantities of unwanted goods such as aspirins and cuckoo clocks to requite the balances (Berend and Ranki, 1969, p. 183; 1974a, ch. 11). Einzig (1938, p. 26) quotes the case of Yugoslavia buying enough aspirins from Germany to last her a decade or more in order to reduce her balances with Germany.

On the credit side one has to bear in mind that these countries had few other secure outlets for many of their products and that they did receive more than ephemeral goods in return. They secured a large part of their machinery imports from Germany (Basch, 1944, p. 179) and detailed trade statistics certainly show a variety of producer goods, including arms supplies, being purchased from Germany (Momtchiloff, 1944, p. 56, appendices 1–4). Though *The Economist* (1938b, pp. 262–7; 1939, pp. 537–8) had reservations about Germany's monopsonist power, the position was by no means an exploitive one. German purchases helped to raise export prices and incomes of the countries in question since normally they were made well above world prices (Bonnell, 1940, p. 131; Kaiser, 1980, p. 160), while Germany did not take advantage of her position to turn the terms of trade in her favour (Royal Institute of International Affairs, 1939, p. 119; see also Munting and Holderness, 1991, pp. 38–9). No doubt increasing dependence on the stronger economy delayed diversification and reintegration into the world economy as Basch (1944, p. 183) suggests, but this is perhaps a somewhat academic point given Germany's long-term plans for the region. On balance therefore, south-east Europe probably gained from its association with Germany. Rothschild (1974, p. 22) has little doubt on this score:

> Contrary to frequent allegations at the time and since, Germany did not flood East Central Europe with cuckoo clocks, aspirin and thermometers in exchange for grains, minerals, and timber; rather she supplied capital goods for industry, encouraged the diversification of vulnerable one-crop agriculture, and supplied a steady market at reasonable prices.

So far as trade shares are concerned the main impact was in the sharp increase in intercourse between members of the Reichsmark bloc countries, which raised their share of intra-European trade largely as a result of increased trade between the dependent countries and Germany. On the other hand, Eastern Europe's share in world trade declined between 1928 and the later 1930s, mainly due to a contraction in the region's trade in primary products. By contrast a small gain was recorded in their share of world exports of manufactures, though as with the rest of Europe that share remained well below the level recorded in 1913 (Aldcroft, 1989, p. 32; Yates, 1959, pp. 32–3, 47–50).

Macroeconomic stance

Even with the protection of their external accounts secured, there was very limited scope for imaginative fiscal and financial policies to counter the crisis. The financial position of Eastern Europe was far too weak to allow constructive government spending policies of a magnitude to produce worthwhile results, even assuming they had been disposed to contemplate such action in the first place (Royal Institute of International Affairs, 1936, p. 114). Public finance was in severe straits as revenue collapsed during the depression. The yields from indirect taxes and dues fell by at least one-third, those from direct taxes by more than one-half (Schönfeld, 1975, pp. 197–8). Governments were therefore primarily concerned with the task of offsetting recession-induced budget deficits by expenditure cuts and increased taxation wherever possible, than in devising ways of stimulating activity and employment by fiscal means. The orthodox goals of currency stabilisation and budgetary equilibrium were regarded as top priorities in order to re-establish confidence at home and abroad (Spigler, 1986, p. 141).

Thus in the first half of the 1930s at least monetary and fiscal policy tended to take on a distinctly deflationary tone. Poland provided the most extreme manifestation in this respect as a consequence of her determination to maintain the value of the zloty without resorting to exchange controls. Stringent credit control was implemented by the commercial banks while total budgetary expenditure was reduced by about one-third in the four years 1930 to 1934 (Gorecki, 1935, p. 109; Taylor, 1952, p. 43). The approach very much mirrored that of contemporary France, where the authorities were similarly forced to adjust the whole cost and price structure downwards to accommodate the overvalued currency (Smith, 1936, pp. 168–78; Zweig, 1944, pp. 54–6). The deflationary policy undoubtedly helped to intensify and prolong the depression in Poland and it was not until 1936 that a marked shift in direction occurred.

Hungary and the Balkan countries also followed the orthodox line with varying degrees of intensity. The belief in Hungary was that a rigid deflationary policy was necessary in order to secure foreign funds again, while the retrenchment policy adopted in Yugoslavia relied heavily on French advice (Polonsky, 1975, pp. 56–7; Royal Institute of International Affairs, 1936, p. 127). Only in the case of Czechoslovakia did government fiscal policy exert a small but positive impact to offset the decline in economic activity in the early 1930s (Pryor, 1979, pp. 236–7.)

Conventional budgetary practice did not of course prevent governments from taking measures such as public works and unemployment relief to ease the impact of the crisis, while at the same time trimming expenditure in other directions in an effort to balance their budgets. Moreover, towards the middle of the decade there were noticeable signs of relaxation. Yugoslavia was first off the mark in this respect in 1934/35 when cheaper money and reflationary government expenditure through public works loans signalled a decisive break with past orthodoxy (Royal Institute of International Affairs, 1936, p. 128). Soon after other countries, notably Hungary and Poland, relaxed their stance and announced major programmes of expenditure and investment. The slow improvement in economic conditions and state finances was partly responsible for this shift, but perhaps the major factor in the later 1930s was the ever-pressing needs of defence. Such requirements befitted the more interventionist and directive outlook of the autocratic regimes. As Hauner (1986, p. 50) notes:

> The rising military expenditures and investments thus constituted one of the most effective instruments of state interventionist policies, by means of which the majority of east European states sought after the depression to re-activate a whole range of economic sectors, particularly domestic savings, which in turn were to contribute to the strengthening of the defence potential.

Exigencies of war therefore became an increasingly important influence in the later 1930s, accounting for up to one-third of government spending in most countries. Judging by the Czech experience, government-induced rearmament expenditure was a significant stimulating force to the economy (Pryor, 1979, pp. 236–7). On the other hand, if one looks at budgetary structures in more detail one cannot fail to entertain doubts as to their relevance to economic and social needs. Defence and civil administration (including government pensions) absorbed one-half or more on average of government spending, and if one adds debt service this left about one-third or less of the public budgets for productive purposes. The latter share may be compared with the figure of 60 per cent for contemporary Sweden (Political and Economic Planning, 1945, pp. 118–19, 164). Little wonder therefore that infrastructure facilities were tending to lag behind economic development (Ehrlich, 1973, p. 22; 1985, p. 369). Berend (1974, p. 191) reckons that the infrastructure of Eastern Europe was more backward relative to the West in 1938 than it had been in 1913.

As for the tax system itself this was highly regressive despite some attempts at reform in the 1930s. Taxation systems tended to be designed more for official convenience than for equity and economic rationale. In Yugoslavia, for example, where indirect taxes constituted three-quarters of total revenues, the principles enshrined in state fiscal policy were those 'of charging its citizens as often as possible and as heavily as possible; taking the money where it could find it, and getting it from those who make the least outcry rather than according to the principle of the ability to pay' (Tomasevich, 1955, p. 688). Income and other direct taxes constituted on average less than one-third of total revenues, whereas indirect taxes (excise and sales taxes and customs dues) accounted for two-thirds or more. The most extreme case was Bulgaria where direct taxes provided no more than 12 per cent of revenues; the least regressive was Poland where income, industrial and property taxes brought in half the revenue (Political and Economic Planning, 1945, pp. 118–22; Spigler, 1986, p. 154).

Such regressive fiscal systems, very characteristic of backward countries, were bound to hit the low-income groups – primarily the peasants – hardest. In the case of the Balkan countries some 50 per cent of the total cash income of the peasantry went in taxes, an enormous burden considering their low incomes (Political and Economic Planning, 1945, p. 122; Tomasevich, 1955, p. 702). This heavy fiscal imposition undoubtedly acted as a strong disincentive to investment and improvement and was one of the major causes of backwardness and low incomes in the agrarian sector. Yet while the peasants were taxed to the hilt, other more prosperous groups, such as government officials and rent receivers, escaped fairly lightly. A glaring example was the case of owners of urban housing in Yugoslavia who incurred minimal tax liabilities on their rental income. This was one reason, together with subsidised interest rates, why so much capital formation (50 to 60 per cent) went into residential construction at the expense of investment elsewhere in the economy (Tomasevich, 1955, pp. 686–7). Yugoslavia was by no means unique in this respect, for tax anomalies were fairly widespread. The structure of taxation was ripe for reform and as one contemporary survey concluded: 'there are few spheres of public policy in which a constructive approach would yield speedier results' (Political and Economic Planning, 1945, p. 124).

The relief of agriculture

Given the size of the farm lobby and the severity of the agrarian crisis, it was a foregone conclusion that governments would be forced to intervene to ease the situation. The collapse in prices, the adverse shift in the farmers' terms of trade and the rising burden of debts left many in a state of destitution. Though farm output in physical terms was often well maintained, its real value was very much reduced. In Hungary for example, output was little changed between 1929 and 1934, but in real terms its value was almost halved (Zauberman, 1976, p. 598). Consequently at the depth of the crisis returns on farm capital were totally inadequate and often non-existent, and recovery was painfully slow (League of Nations, 1939a, p. 22). True, many smallholders consumed much of what they produced so that the real impact was less disastrous than the low returns on capital would seem to imply, but even the poorest peasant could scarcely live by bread alone. Clothing, shelter, repairs, farm implements and tools, fuel and many other supplies had to be paid for at a time when the farmer's terms of exchange had moved against him. For the larger commercial growers trading on the external market the prospects were no less bleak in a world glutted with food at a time when former customers were anxious to protect their own agrarian interests. Moreover, Eastern European exporters suffered an additional handicap in terms of price because of their low levels of efficiency compared with western producers and their overvalued official exchange rates.

Indeed, the poverty of agriculture had deeper roots than the immediate deterioration in the terms of trade. It was also the product of unyielding agrarian structures based on traditional ownership patterns and practices, exacerbated in some cases by a sheer shortage of decent land. A good case in point is that of Slovenia where widespread small-scale ownership, coupled with a shortage of fertile land, set limits to improvements in efficiency. Because of the adverse man–land ratio, investment in agriculture to raise productivity only really made sense if it could substitute for labour, but the rate at which the latter could be drawn off the land depended ultimately on the availability of alternative employment outside the agrarian sector. Non-agrarian employment, though increasing after 1933, was never sufficient to cope with the potential excess labour on the land, and so, in the absence of strong and positive measures to achieve resource reallocation, the most that could be accomplished were marginal improvements in agrarian practices such as seed selection, improved manuring practices, better livestock breeding and the like (Hocevar, 1965, pp. 131, 148–54, 166).

Various attempts were of course made to relieve the situation: the measures included protection, debt and taxation relief, subsidies and export premia, price support schemes, concessions on payment of rent arrears, marketing boards, and incentives to reduce costs, diversify and encourage technical improvement (League of Nations; 1939a, pp. 29, 93–4, 98–9; 1939b, pp. 15–17, 27–30). Yet for the most part the measures were too limited and incoherent to provide a long-term solution to the basic agrarian problems of the region. They may have helped to stave off complete disaster, but they did little to transform the agrarian structure. Consequently investment in agriculture stagnated, incomes remained low, relative efficiency declined further, and the surplus agrarian population remained as large as ever. Postwar land reforms of varying extent, based as they were primarily on tenurial rights rather than on economic logic, had done little to ensure the viability of many of the small peasant farms that subsequently emerged, so that underemployment remained a pressing problem throughout the period. In theory, a substantial part of the agrarian manpower, especially in the Balkans and Poland, could have been eliminated without loss of output since marginal productivity was zero or negative. In practice, however, this solution was a non-starter for the very simple reason that there was nowhere for the surplus labour to go (Zauberman, 1976, pp. 594–5). Yet without such a transformation there was little prospect of raising efficiency in this sector and as a consequence agriculture could not perform the role it had done in the West, as a source of accumulation and a market for industrial goods (Teichova, 1989, pp. 900–904). It was the inherent limitations of the agrarian sector coupled with the social and political pressures of millions of underemployed rural workers that prompted governments to turn their attention towards industrialisation as a way out of the impasse.

Most governments readily acknowledged the farm debt problem and took action to impose moratoria and to negotiate a general scaling down of indebtedness. For the Romanian peasant, the most heavily indebted in south-east Europe with smallholders of less than 10 hectares accounting for over 70 per cent of agrarian debt, a government moratorium on debt repayment was proclaimed in 1932, and two years later the principal was reduced by 50 per cent at a low rate of interest (Lampe and Jackson, 1982, p. 451; Seton-Watson, 1946, p. 83). Some 70 per cent of farm debtors benefited from these provisions which were accompanied by a large-scale programme of agricultural reconstruction (League of Nations, 1939b, pp. 15–16). Bulgaria in 1933 granted a five-year moratorium, rates of interest were reduced, while debts of small farms – less than 10 hectares – were halved (Berend, 1985, p. 178). Rather more extensive relief was provided in Yugoslavia between 1932 and 1936, with an initial moratorium, reduced taxation and the liquidation of the debts of many smallholders which benefited some 654 000 farms (Berend, 1985, p. 178). Similar debt relief policies were also passed in Poland and Hungary in addition to measures to ease the burden of paying tax arrears (League of Nations, 1939a, pp. 29, 98–9; 1939b, p. 16).

A second method of assistance was through the use of subsidies. These took various forms including direct production subsidies, administered prices and export incentives. They were most widely used in Czechoslovakia, the only importer of agrarian products in Eastern Europe. Here the state encouraged a policy of import substitution by a combination of strict control on imports and heavy subsidisation. By 1937 subsidies, negligible in 1929, amounted to 12.9 per cent of total agrarian production (Pryor and Pryor, 1975, p. 509). This gave such a boost to agricultural output that it led to severe over-production in wheat and so the policy had to be modified. Moreover, it gave a stimulus to a sector in which Czechoslovakia had a marked comparative disadvantage in terms of international trade (Pryor and Pryor, 1975, p. 531).

In other countries subsidies were mainly confined to exports, either directly or through the use of special export premia to offset the overvalued exchange rates. By the mid-1930s most countries had introduced export premia ranging between 20 and 50 per cent (Lampe and Jackson, 1982, pp. 465–6; Royal Institute of International Affairs, 1939, p. 145). Additional support for prices and exports came with the establishment of state purchasing and marketing boards which were set up for a variety of products, especially cereals, sugar and potatoes, in all countries. Some of these virtually monopolised the marketing of certain agrarian products, usually at guaranteed prices, and they became a useful instrument in the barter trade agreements concluded with Germany for the export of agrarian products. One of the most notable was the Czecho-Slovak Cereals Company, established in July 1934, with powers to buy all home-grown cereals at a fixed price for resale in the market and which conducted all transactions with foreign countries (League of Nations, 1939b, pp. 27–30). Romania and Poland also adopted price support measures, not without some degree of success (League of Nations, 1939a, pp. 93, 98). In so far as such policies tended to encourage crop production by virtue of the more favourable prices offered, it could be argued that they simply accentuated the over-production problem.

Assistance designed to effect cost reductions, technical improvements and product diversification were somewhat more limited. Here the Balkan countries, especially Bulgaria, took the lead by encouraging the shift away from cereals (already under way before the crisis) towards stock-breeding, industrial crops, dairy and poultry production, fruit farming and market gardening. The policy met with some degree of success (Lampe and Jackson, 1982, pp. 368–9; Royal Institute of International Affairs, 1939, p. 145). Technical improvements such as crop rotation, new strains of crops and stable feeding of livestock were also promoted. In Hungary the government also tried to secure reductions in the cost of standardised agricultural implements and machines (League of Nations, 1939b, p. 17). However, probably the major relief in this respect was in the cost of wage labour which in Poland fell by nearly two-thirds from 1927/30 to 1934/35 (League of Nations, 1939a, p. 99).

Such policies helped to alleviate the crisis and brought about a limited measure of improvement in the later 1930s as markets slowly improved. But agrarian incomes remained depressingly low, in some cases below prewar levels, as did agricultural practices, while the burden of taxation on agriculture remained a constant source of grievance. Agrarian interests felt that they were unduly penalised financially for the benefit of industry and rearmament, and that exports were being subsidised at the expense of domestic consumption (Basch, 1944, pp. 101–2; Hertz, 1947, pp. 102–3). On both counts they may well have been right, but in its traditional form peasant farming had by then reached the end of the road.

State intervention and the promotion of industry

During the 1930s there was a more concerted effort to push forward industrialisation than ever before. The depression, by exposing the poverty of the agrarian sector, acted as a catalyst in this respect, while the absence of capital inflows made it imperative that Eastern Europe harness its own resources for development. The prevailing political and economic ideology also prompted a shift in direction. With liberal capitalism now discredited the forces of nationalism and nostrification intensified and the emergence of autocratic forms of government facilitated the advance of more autarkic methods of control and state ownership and direction of industry, especially in sectors of strategic importance (Turnock, 1986, p. 59). It is doubtful, however, whether there was sufficient coherence in the exercise to warrant the term 'planning' to be used in any meaningful sense (Ranki and Tomaszewski, 1986, pp. 40–41).

Many of the measures employed to foster industry were not, of course, new. Subsidies, tax exemptions, tariffs, public works, for example, had all been used well before the 1930s, while state ownership of infrastructures such as railways, ports and forests had a long lineage. What was really different about the 1930s was the much greater intensity with which controls were used to encourage import substitution and promote industrial development and the much enlarged role of the state in industrial activities. The need to erect stringent controls to protect external accounts and currencies in the early 1930s also gave an added dimension to the drive for greater self-sufficiency. From 1935 onwards many of the projects for industrial expansion were closely associated with rearmament (Singleton and Carter, 1982, p. 61; Tomasevich, 1949, p. 179).

The extent of state ownership varied considerably among the different countries. It was extensive in Poland, least so in Czechoslovakia, with other countries falling in between (Spulber 1959, p. 268). State ownership in Poland was probably more extensive than in any other European country outside the USSR. Apart from the traditional infrastructure holdings, the Polish state, by the end of the 1930s, employed about one million people (excluding the armed forces) and owned around 100 industrial enterprises with over 1 000 establishments. The supply of military equipment was dominated by the state which also owned 80 per cent of the chemical industry, 40 per cent of the iron and steel, 50 per cent of the metallurgical industry, 20 per cent of the oil refineries, most of the main transport services, together with five state monopolies in alcohol, matches, tobacco, salt and a state lottery (Spulber, 1966, p. 35; Taylor, 1952, pp. 93–4). State industries and monopolies were also quite extensive in Yugoslavia where they accounted for some 15 per cent of the country's industrial investment in 1938, mainly in metals, chemicals and food processing. The figure rises to 22 per cent if cartels, which were placed under the control of the Ministry of Commerce and Industry in 1935, are included (Lampe and Jackson, 1982, p. 500). In the case of Bulgaria, where expansion of state activity was prompted by the need to make up tax shortfalls, state-owned enterprises numbered 169 by 1939 and accounted for 8 to 9 per cent of total industrial production, and 15 per cent if cooperatives are included (Lampe, 1986, pp. 100–110). On the other hand, the spread of state enterprise was rather less extensive in Hungary, accounting for only about 5 per cent of industrial investment in the late 1930s (Berend, 1974, p. 189). Romania was closer to the Polish model.

In conjunction with state enterprises, cartels became an integral part of government economic policy in all Eastern European countries. By the latter part of the decade they accounted for well over 40 per cent of Hungary's industrial production, 66 per cent of the Polish, most of the Czech and 23 per cent of Romanian (Berend and Ranki, 1974b, p. 141; Spulber, 1959, p. 276; Teichova, 1985, pp. 958–9, 1988, pp. 44–6). Cartels, many of which were international in scope, were essentially restrictive in nature. They reduced competition by controlling prices, allocating production quotas among members, and generally regulating the conditions of trade. They therefore stifled competitive forces and encouraged industrial concentration, especially in heavy industry. During the later 1930s Germany utilised the cartel system to increase its influence in south-eastern Europe (Teichova, 1989, pp. 960–61).

A third feature of the governments' industrial strategy was the launching of major investment programmes, usually associated with public works for the relief of unemployment and later with rearmament. Whether such policies can be regarded as evidence of an eschewal of classicist budgetary principles in the genuine interests of stimulating economic activity and employment, as Zauberman (1976, p. 600) implies, is a moot point in view of the obvious social and political pressures which activated the policymakers' stance at the time. Be that as it may, most countries embarked on substantial state-sponsored programmes during the course of the 1930s. Yugoslavia announced a large programme of public works in 1934/35. In 1936 Poland launched an ambitious six-year Defence Expansion Plan entailing the expenditure of 6 000 million zloty (later scaled down) on armament plants, military equipment and general defence. Prior to the war about half the original sum had been spent. Coterminous with this project was the plan to develop the Central Industrial District (the triangle bounded by Warsaw, Cracow and Lvov) as a major industrial region concentrating on the development of heavy industry and military equipment away from the country's frontiers (Hauner, 1986, pp. 101–2; Landau and Tomaszewski, 1985, pp. 118–19; Taylor, 1952, pp. 96–8). Two years later Hungary also announced a Five Year Plan of 1 000 million pengos with emphasis on public works and rearmament (Berend and Ranki, 1985, pp. 91–2; Royal Institute of International Affairs, 1939, p. 118).

In the case of Romania, the government, from the mid-1930s, offered two-year monopolies for the establishment of industries considered essential to the national interest, while it also contributed part of the capital cost of new arms factories with the guarantee of purchasing output at favourable prices (Royal Institute of International Affairs, 1939, pp. 129–30).

The overall results of the efforts to foster industrialisation were somewhat mixed, and certainly less impressive than the indices of manufacturing output growth through 1929 to 1938 would seem to indicate (see Table 7.3). The Balkan countries clearly achieved a much better performance than Poland, Hungary and Czechoslovakia, the last of which stagnated industrially in the 1930s. However, it should be borne in mind that the statistical data for industrial output are still far from robust for this period and consequently it is difficult to arrive at a very definitive conclusion. Jackson and Lampe (1983, pp. 408–9) give a rather more optimistic interpretation of the industrial record of the Balkan countries. They argue the case for relatively fast industrial growth in south-east Europe before the Second World War, with rates of growth of the following magnitudes for the years 1929 to 1938: Bulgaria 4.8 per cent, Romania 3.4 per cent and Yugoslavia 2.4 per cent. They are particularly impressed by some of the structural shifts away from artisan activities and towards modern factory production. In the case of Yugoslavia they argue that: 'Modern, mechanised production had ... become the predominant form of industrial activity by 1939 in a territory where little statistical significance had existed before the turn of the century' (Jackson and Lampe, 1983, p. 409). Moreover, in some cases, especially textiles and food processing, import substitution registered quite significant gains.

Table 7.3 Indices of manufacturing output, 1929–39 (1913 = 100)

	1929	*1938*	*% change*
Hungary	112	128	14.3
Poland	86	105	22.0
Romania	137	180	31.4
Yugoslavia	140	190	35.7
Bulgaria	179	245	36.9
Czechoslovakia	140	136	-2.9

Sources: Berend and Ranki (1974), pp. 299–300; United Nations (1949c), Table 36.

Nevertheless, industrial production only achieved a very modest increase in its share in these economies. Overall, the scale and scope, as well as the timing, of the industrial changes were too limited to effect any radical transformation of the economic structure. Moreover, the efficiency of industry still fell far short of that of the advanced countries of the West.

Thus the fundamental problems of the region remained basically unchanged. The total number of people employed in industry in 1937 in the Balkan countries, for example, was still very modest and the increase in the numbers so employed was nowhere near sufficient to absorb the increasing agrarian population. In the case of Yugoslavia, to take one example, the number of industrial workers rose by about half-a-million between 1929 and 1937, yet over the same period the total population increased by 1.8 million (Basch, 1944, p. 241).

Despite the declared emphasis on industry during this period, the share of total investment going into this sector was quite modest, averaging 15 to 30 per cent through 1929 to 1937 (Political and Economic Planning, 1945, p. 102). Moreover, in the latter part of the period a substantial part of this was defence oriented. Berend (1974, pp. 191–2) draws attention to the weakness of industrial investment and the lag in infrastructure investment which was noted earlier. In fact the larger part of new investment, at least in the Balkans, appears to have gone into housing (40–60 per cent), stimulated in part by favourable tax treatment of rental incomes (Political and Economic Planning, 1945, p. 102; Tomasevich, 1955, p. 687).

On balance, the efforts to foster industrial development were not an unqualified success. Industry certainly proved to be the most dynamic sector in the 1930s and in most cases its share in total activity increased, albeit marginally. Even so, by 1938 industry's share of national income was still only one-quarter or less in the Balkans, one-third or so in Hungary and Poland, compared with well over one-half in the highly industrialised countries of the West. Only Czechoslovakia, with just over half its national income derived from industry, could match the latter (Berend and Ranki, 1974a, pp. 307–8). Thus it was still the state of the harvest which determined the prosperity of most of Eastern Europe.

Several aspects of the state's industrial promotion policies can be called into question. State policy tended to foster unproductive and non-economic investments. This can be seen in the large proportion of investment that went into residential construction, the concentration on defence-related industrial activities in the latter part of the period, and the fact that some state enterprises were designed for tax revenue purposes. State control and direction also led to excessive bureaucratic interference and at times an unfriendly attitude towards private enterprise. Doreen Warriner (1940, p. 16) argued that it was the bureaucrat, not the capitalist or large landowner, who exploited the worker in the Balkans. It has also been suggested that the attempts to force industrial growth were at the expense of agriculture which remained short of capital and highly taxed (Hertz, 1947, pp. 102–3).

Second, the state's financial resources were limited: it could not replace the role of foreign capital when overseas loans dried up in the 1930s, while the nostrification policy designed to discourage foreign funds and ownership did not help matters. True foreign capital still remained a significant element in Eastern Europe throughout the period, but the less congenial climate tended to discourage new enterprise and skill formation from abroad.

Third, efforts to mobilise domestic resources were frequently offset by restrictive monetary and fiscal policies including higher taxation, while the structure of taxation tended to direct resources into less essential areas of activity, for example housing.

Fourth, the direction of investment even within industry itself was not conducive to rapid development. A large proportion of industrial investment went into textiles, food processing and light industries, where the growth potential was low, to the comparative neglect of modern dynamic sectors such as chemicals, the electrical trades, telecommunications and the motor industry (Berend, 1974, pp. 192–4). The motor vehicle, for example, did not replace the railways as a force of growth as it did in the West.

The emphasis on traditional sectors was the main reason the industrial structure remained remarkably static during the period. The major gains in employment shares occurred mainly in textiles, except in Poland and Czechoslovakia, with little advance in producer goods groups (Teichova, 1981, pp. 183–4). Thus in Yugoslavia the number of textile factories rose from 30 in 1929 to 363 in 1936. One of the reasons for this outcome was that import substitution was easiest in textiles given the low domestic purchasing power and the shortage of capital and skilled labour. Protection of the home market therefore favoured import substitution in the least cost activities. Despite the greater encouragement given to heavy industry later on in the period, markets for the products (outside government procurement) were limited by the depth of demand at home and the lack of comparative advantage on the international market. Cartelisation, by bolstering product prices, also circumscribed effective demand (Teichova, 1981, pp. 181–5).

Apart from the rather lop-sided industrial structure, Eastern Europe also retained its traditional dual structure, with many small-scale inefficient firms competing with a few modern large-scale enterprises. Small businesses remained as viable as ever, partly because of the weakness of big business, the abundance of labour and the predominance of those activities in which small-scale enterprise tended to flourish. Moreover, large-scale corporations failed to make much headway in modern production and management methods. Western-style mass-production methods were something of a rarity, and the typical large company was little more than a 'general store' which supplied a multiplicity of products in small batches to limited markets within a rigid protectionist framework.

The inconsistent logic of some of the industrial policies is well illustrated by the case of Czechoslovakia, a country with by far the largest industrial sector in the region. It was badly hit in international markets during the crisis and had a very slow and chequered recovery subsequently. In part this was due to the uncoordinated domestic and foreign trade policies which resulted in relative expansion in those sectors with a comparative disadvantage, especially agriculture where a strongly subsidised import substitution policy was pursued, and a loss of share in those industries in which Czechoslovakia enjoyed a comparative advantage. The Czechs failed to capitalise on their previous industrial gains in international markets with the result that exports and production in industries with a comparative advantage remained well below the 1929 levels throughout the 1930s, whereas those sectors at a comparative disadvantage managed to regain or exceed former peak levels of activity (Pryor, 1973, p. 201; Pryor and Pryor, 1975, pp. 509, 520).

The overall balance

It is easy to paint a gloomy picture of the economies of Eastern Europe in the 1930s. The detailed accounts of industrial development, infrastructure facilities and agriculture certainly point to some modest progress in certain sectors, but they do not alter the conventional picture of an absence of fundamental change in economic structures. Apart from Czechoslovakia, they remained low income agrarian-dependent economies whose economic and social structures were not conducive to rapid economic development. In the words of Berend and Ranki (1974a, p. 318): 'East-Central Europe became an area struggling with permanent crisis and fraught with inner contradictions in a tense, explosive atmosphere where everything called for change.'

Yet despite the unfavourable background, national incomes did expand and they even managed to exceed former peaks (1929) by a reasonable margin in most cases. The real problem, however, was that much of the increase was swamped out by rapid population growth – up to three times the average for Western and Northern Europe (League of Nations, 1941, p. 50). Consequently, through 1929 to 1938 income per capita fell slightly in Yugoslavia and Czechoslovakia, was almost static in Poland, rose very modestly in Hungary and Romania, and only in Bulgaria did it increase significantly overall. Taking the region as a whole, average per capita income probably advanced by no more than about 5 to 6 per cent if that, which was about half the European average (Bairoch, 1976, p. 297; Lethbridge, 1985, p. 538; Spulber, 1966, p. 58). This means that by the end of the 1930s the disparity in income levels between Western and Eastern Europe had widened since 1929 and probably also since 1914. In 1938 net national income per head in the Balkan countries was only one-fifth to one-quarter that of Germany, in Poland and Hungary barely one-third, and even in Czechoslovakia it was only just over one-half (Lethbridge, 1985, p. 532; see also United Nations, 1949a). In fact by every conceivable indicator Eastern Europe was less productive, less healthy and less literate than Western Europe.

Could do better no doubt. It was a potentially rich region stocked with a poor people in which the maldistribution of income was the central feature and where development had been stunted by the vicissitudes of war and the unfavourable economic climate which followed. The immediate policy reaction to the crisis of the early 1930s was predictable, given its severity and global dimensions, together with the ardent desire to avoid complete economic and financial collapse. But the strategy could be no more than a holding operation at a much reduced level of economic activity. On the other hand, when the slow improvement in economic conditions allowed some relaxation in the orthodox policy stance, the inconsistencies and incoherence of government strategies became more apparent. Tax systems were inefficient and inequitable, budgetary expenditures were largely unproductive, infrastructures were neglected, rearmament came to dominate industrial activity, while agriculture and the associated population problem were not accorded any special priority. It was the neglect of the latter in particular which effectively stifled what forces of change were present.

References

Aldcroft, D. H. (1977), *From Versailles to Wall Street 1919–1929*, Harmondsworth: Penguin Books.

Aldcroft, D. H. (1980), *The European Economy, 1914–1980*, London: Croom Helm.

Aldcroft, D. H. (1988), 'Eastern Europe in an age of turbulence, 1919–1950', *Economic History Review*, 41.

Aldcroft, D. H. (1989), 'The decline of Europe in the 1920s', *EUI Colloquium Papers*, 136/89, Florence: European University Institute.

Aldcroft, D. H. (1991), 'Destabilising influences in the European economy in the 1920s', in C. Holmes and A. Booth (eds), *Economy and Society: European Industrialisation and its Social Consequences. Essays Presented to Sidney Pollard*, Leicester: Leicester University Press.

Bairoch, P. (1976), 'Europe's gross national product: 1800–1975', *Journal of European Economic History*, 5.

Bandera, V. N. (1964), *Foreign Capital as an Instrument of National Economic Policy: a Study Based on the Experience of East European Countries between the Two World Wars*, The Hague: Nijhoff.

Basch, A. (1944), *The Danube Basin and the German Economic Sphere*, London: Kegan Paul, Trench, Trubner.

Berend, I. T. (1974), 'Investment strategy in East-Central Europe', in H. Daems and H. van der Wee (eds), *The Rise of Managerial Capitalism*, The Hague: Nijhoff.

Berend, I. T. (1985), 'Agriculture', in M. C. Kaser and E. A. Radice (eds), *The Economic History of Eastern Europe 1919–1975*, Vol. I, *Economic Structure and Performance between the Wars*, Oxford: Oxford University Press.

Berend, I. T. and Ranki, G. (1969), 'The economic problems of the Danube region at the break-up of the Austro-Hungarian monarchy', *Journal of Contemporary History*, 4.

Berend, I. T. and Ranki, G. (1974a), *Economic Development in East Central Europe in the 19th and 20th Centuries*, New York: Columbia University Press.

Berend, I. T. and Ranki, G. (1974b), *Hungary: a Century of Economic Development*, Newton Abbot: David and Charles.

Berend, I. T. and Ranki, G. (1985), *The Hungarian Economy in the Twentieth Century*, London: Croom Helm.

Bonnell, A. T. (1940), *German Control over International Economic Relations 1930–1940*, Urbana, IL: University of Illinois Press.

Condliffe, J. B. (1941), *The Reconstruction of World Trade: a Survey of International Economic Relations*, London: Allen and Unwin.

Deldlycke, T., Gelders, H. and Limbor, J. M. (1968), *The Working Population and its Structure: International Historical Statistics*, Vol. I, Brussels: Université Libre de Bruxelles.

Dovring, F. (1965), *Land and Labour in Europe in the Twentieth Century*, The Hague: Martinus Nijhoff.

Ehrlich, E. (1973), 'Infrastructure and an international comparison of relationships with indicators of development in Eastern Europe, 1920–1950', *Oxford Papers in East European Economics*, 33.

Ehrlich, E. (1985), 'Infrastructure', in M. C. Kaser and E. A. Radice (eds), *The Economic History of Eastern Europe, 1919–1975*, Vol. I, *Economic Structure and Performance between the Wars*, Oxford: Oxford University Press.

Einzig, P. (1938), *Bloodless Invasion: German Economic Penetration into the Danubian States and the Balkans*, London: Duckworth.

Ellis, H. S. (1941), *Exchange Control in Central Europe*, Cambridge, MA: Harvard University Press.

Friedman, P. (1974), *Impact of Trade Destruction on National Incomes: A Study of Europe, 1924–1938*, Gainesville, FL: University Presses of Florida.

Friedman, P. (1978), 'An econometric model of national income, commercial policy and the level of international trade: the open economies of Europe, 1924–1938', *Journal of Economic History*, 38.

Gordon, M. S. (1941), *Barriers to World Trade: a Study of Recent Commercial Policy*, New York: Macmillan.

Gorecki, R. (1935), *Poland and her Economic Development*, London: Allen and Unwin.

Harris, S. E. (1936), *Exchange Depreciation: its Theory and its History 1931–35, with some Consideration of Related Domestic Policies*, Cambridge, MA: Harvard University Press.

Hauner, M. (1986), 'Military budgets and the armaments industry', in M. C. Kaser and E. A. Radice (eds), *The Economic History of Eastern Europe 1919–1975*, Vol. II, *Interwar Policy, the War and Reconstruction*, Oxford: Oxford University Press.

Hertz, F. (1947), *The Economic Problem of the Danubian States. A Study in Economic Nationalism*, London: Gollancz.

Heuser, H. (1939), *Control of International Trade*, London: Routledge.

Hiden, J. (1977), *Germany and Europe 1919–1939*, London: Longman.

Hocevar, T. (1965), *The Structure of the Slovenian Economy 1848–1963*, New York: Studia Slovenica.

Hocevar, T. (1987), 'The Albanian economy 1912–1944: a survey', *Journal of European Economic History*, 3.

Jackson, M. R. and Lampe, J. R. (1983), 'The evidence of industrial growth in South Eastern Europe before the Second World War', *East European Quarterly*, 16.

Kaiser, D. E. (1980), *Economic Diplomacy and the Origins of the Second World War: Germany, Britain, France and Eastern Europe, 1930–1939*, Princeton, NJ: Princeton University Press.

Kaser, M. C. and Radice, E. A. (eds), (1985), *The Economic History of Eastern Europe 1919–1975*, Vol. I, *Economic Structure and Performance between the Wars*, Oxford: Oxford University Press.

Kaser, M. C. and Radice, E. A. (eds), (1986), *The Economic History of*

Eastern Europe 1919–1975, Vol. II, *Interwar Policy, the War and Reconstruction*, Oxford: Oxford University Press.

Lampe, J. R. (1986), *The Bulgarian Economy in the Twentieth Century*, London: Croom Helm.

Lampe, J. R. and Jackson M. R. (1982), *Balkan Economic History, 1550–1950*, Bloomington, IN: Indiana University Press.

Landau, Z. and Tomaszewski, J. (1985), *The Polish Economy in the Twentieth Century*, London: Croom Helm.

League of Nations (1932), *Conference for the Restoration of Central and Eastern Europe*, Stresa: League of Nations.

League of Nations (1933), *World Economic Survey, 1932–33*, Geneva: League of Nations.

League of Nations (1935a), *Enquiry into Clearing Agreements*, Geneva: League of Nations.

League of Nations (1935b), *World Economic Survey 1934–35*, Geneva: League of Nations.

League of Nations (1937), *Money and Banking 1936/37*, Vol. I, *Monetary Review 1937*, Geneva: League of Nations.

League of Nations (1938), *Report on Exchange Control*, Geneva: League of Nations.

League of Nations (1939a), *European Conference on Rural Life 1939: the Capital and Income of Farms in Europe as they Appear from Farm Accounts for the Years 1927–28 to 1934–35*, Geneva: League of Nations.

League of Nations (1939b), *European Conference on Rural Life 1939: Population and Agriculture with Special Reference to Agricultural Overpopulation*, Geneva: League of Nations.

League of Nations (1941), *Europe's Trade*, Geneva: League of Nations.

League of Nations (1942), *Commercial Policy in the Inter-War Period*, Geneva: League of Nations.

League of Nations (1943), *Trade Relations between Free Market and Controlled Economies*, Geneva: League of Nations.

League of Nations (1944), *International Currency Experience: Lessons of the Inter-War Period*, Geneva: League of Nations.

Lee, C. H. (1969), 'The effects of the depression on primary producing countries', *Journal of Contemporary History*, 4.

Lethbridge, E. (1985), 'National income and product', in M. C. Kaser and E. A. Radice (eds), *The Economic History of Eastern Europe 1919–1975*, Vol I, *Economic Structure and Performance between the Wars*, Oxford: Oxford University Press.

Macartney, C. A. (1937), *Hungary and her Successors: the Treaty of Trianon and its Consequences 1919–1937*, London: Oxford University Press.

Macartney, C. A. and Palmer, A. W. (1962), *Independent Eastern Europe*, London: Macmillan.

Maddison, A. (1973), *Economic Policy and Performance in Europe, 1913–1970*, London: Collins/Fontana.

Momtchiloff, N. (1944), *Ten Years of Controlled Trade in South-Eastern Europe*, Cambridge: Cambridge University Press.

Moore, W. E. (1945), *Economic Demography in Eastern and Southern Europe*, Geneva: League of Nations.

Morgan, O. S. (ed.) (1933), *Agricultural Systems of Middle Europe*, New York: Macmillan.

Munting, R. and Holderness, B. A. (1991), *Crisis, Recovery and War: an Economic History of Continental Europe, 1918–1945*, London: Philip Allan.

Newman, W. J. (1968), *The Balance of Power in the Interwar Years, 1919–1939*, New York: Random House.

Nötel, R. (1974), 'International capital movements and finance in Eastern Europe, 1919–1949', *Vierteljahrschrift für Sozial-und Wirtschaftsgeschichte,* **61**.

Nötel, R. (1984), 'Money, banking and industry in interwar Austria and Hungary', *Journal of European Economic History,* **13**.

Nötel, R. (1986), 'International credit and finance', in M. C. Kaser and E. A. Radice (eds), *The Economic History of Eastern Europe, 1919–1975*, Vol. II, *Interwar Policy, the War and Reconstruction*, Oxford: Oxford University Press.

Pasvolsky, L. (1928), *Economic Nationalism of the Danubian States*, London: Allen and Unwin

Political and Economic Planning (1945), *Economic Development in South-East Europe*, London: PEP.

Pollard, S. (1981), *Peaceful Conquest: The Industrialization of Europe 1760–1970*, Oxford: Oxford University Press.

Polonsky, A. (1975), *The Little Dictators: the History of Eastern Europe since 1918*, London: Routledge and Kegan Paul.

Pryor, Z. P. (1973), 'Czechoslovak economic development in the interwar period', in V. S. Mamatey and R. Luza (eds), *A History of the Czechoslovak Republic 1918–1948*, Princeton, NJ: Princeton University Press.

Pryor, Z. P. (1979), 'Czechoslovak fiscal policies in the great depression', *Economic History Review,* **32**.

Pryor, Z. P. and Pryor, F. L. (1975), 'Foreign trade and interwar Czechozlovak economic development 1918–1938', *Vierteljahrschrift für Sozial-und Wirtshaftsgeschichte,* **62**.

Ranki, G. (1983), *Economic and Foreign Policy: the Struggle of the Great Powers for the Hegemony of the Danube Valley 1919–1939*, New York: Columbia University Press.

Ranki, G. and Tomaszewski, J. (1986), 'The role of the state in industry, banking and trade', in M. C. Kaser and E. A. Radice (eds), *The Economic History of Eastern Europe, 1919–1975*, Vol. II, *Interwar Policy, the War and Reconstruction*, Oxford: Oxford University Press.

Raupach, H. (1969), 'The impact of the great depression on Eastern Europe', *Journal of Contemporary History*, 4.

Rosenstein-Rodan, P. N. (1943), 'Problems of industrialisation of eastern and south-eastern Europe', *Economic Journal*, 53.

Ross, G. (1983), *The Great Powers and the Decline of the European States System 1914–1945*, London: Longman.

Rothschild, J. (1974), *East Central Europe between the Two World Wars*, Seattle, WA: University of Washington Press.

Royal Institute of International Affairs (1936), *The Balkan States: a Review of the Economic and Financial Development of Albania, Bulgaria, Greece, Roumania and Yugoslavia since 1919*, London: Oxford University Press.

Royal Institute of International Affairs (1937), *The Problem of International Investment*, Oxford: Oxford University Press.

Royal Institute of International Affairs (1939), *South Eastern Europe: a Political and Economic Survey*, London: Oxford University Press.

Royal Institute of International Affairs (1940), *South-Eastern Europe: a Brief Survey*, London: Oxford University Press.

Schönfeld, R. (1975), 'Die Balkanländer in der Weltwirtschaftskrise', *Vierteljahrschrift für Sozial-und Wirtschaftsgeschichte*, 62.

Seton-Watson, H. (1946), *Eastern Europe between the Wars 1918–1941*, Cambridge: Cambridge University Press.

Singleton, F. and Carter, B. (1982), *The Economy of Yugoslavia*, London: Croom Helm.

Smith, L. (1936), 'The zloty, 1924–35', *Journal of Political Economy*, 44.

Spigler, J. (1986), 'Public finance', in M. C. Kaser and E. A. Radice (eds), *The Economic History of Eastern Europe 1919–1975*, Vol. II, *Interwar Policy, the War and Reconstruction*, Oxford: Oxford University Press.

Spulber, N. (1959), 'The role of the state in economic growth in Eastern Europe since 1860' in H. G. Aitken (ed.), *The State and Economic Growth*, New York: Social Science Research Council.

Spulber, N. (1966), *The State and Economic Development in Eastern Europe*, New York: Random House.

Svennilson, I. (1954), *Growth and Stagnation in the European Economy*, Geneva: United Nations.

Taylor, J. (1952), *The Economic Development of Poland 1919–1950*, Ithaca, NY: Cornell University Press.

Teichova, A. (1981), 'Structural changes and industrialisation in interwar Central-East Europe', in P. Bairoch and M. Levy-Leboyer (eds), *Disparities in Economic Development since the Industrial Revolution*, London: Macmillan.

Teichova, A. (1985), 'Industry', in M. C. Kaser and E. A. Radice (eds), *The Economic History of Eastern Europe 1919–1975*, Vol. I, *Economic Structure and Performance between the Wars*, Oxford: Oxford University Press.

Teichova, A. (1988), *The Czechoslovak Economy 1918–1980*, London: Routledge.

Teichova, A. (1989), 'East-Central and South-East Europe 1919–1939', in P. Mathias and S. Pollard (eds), *The Cambridge Economic History of Europe*, Vol. VIII, *The Industrial Economies: the Development of Economic and Social Policies*, Cambridge: Cambridge University Press.

The Economist (1938a), 'The bastion of Europe', 12 March.

The Economist (1938b), 'Germany's trade offensive', 5 November.

The Economist (1939), 'The fight for Romanian trade', 3 June.

Tiltman, H. H. (1934), *Peasant Europe*, London: Jarrolds.

Tomasevich, J. (1949), 'Foreign economic relations', in R. J. Kerner (ed.), *Yugoslavia*, Berkeley, CA: University of California Press.

Tomasevich, J. (1955), *Peasants, Politics and Economic Change in Yugoslavia*, Stanford, CA: Stanford University Press.

Turnock, D. (1986), *The Romanian Economy in the Twentieth Century*, London: Croom Helm.

United Nations (1949a), *Economic Survey of Europe 1948*, Geneva: United Nations.

United Nations (1949b), *International Capital Movements during the Interwar Period*, New York: United Nations.

United Nations (1949c), *Statistical Yearbook 1948*, New York: United Nations.

Warriner, D. (1939), *Economics of Peasant Farming*, Oxford: Oxford University Press.

Warriner, D. (1940), *Eastern Europe after Hitler*, Fabian Research Series 50, London: Gollancz.

Yates, P. L. (1959), *Forty Years of Foreign Trade*, London: Allen and Unwin.

Zaubermann, A. (1976), 'Russia and Eastern Europe, 1920–1970', in C. M. Cipolla (ed.), *The Fontana Economic History of Europe*, Vol. 6, Part 2, *Contemporary Economies*, London: Collins/Fontana.

Zweig, F. (1944), *Poland between the Wars: a Critical Study of Social and Economic Changes*, London: Secker and Warburg.

CHAPTER EIGHT

Europe's Third World? The Peripheral Nations in the Interwar Period

The emergence of Europe's third world

Some historians have tended to regard many of Europe's peripheral countries as also-rans in the process of modern development, dependent for much of the time on the core nations of the West, and therefore unworthy of detailed consideration. Doreen Warriner (1964, p. 75) hinted, for example, that the economic history of Eastern Europe could be relegated to a mere footnote. Chirot (1976, p. 9) in his study of southern Romania regarded the periphery, or at least Eastern Europe, as something akin to a colony of the core before the First World War: 'In a sense, then, Eastern Europe became a colony of Western Europe.' Similarly Herschlag (1968, pp. 31–2), in a somewhat wider context, referred to the semi-colonial status of some nations: 'the richer preferred to keep the less fortunate, retarded areas in a state of underdevelopment and economic dependency as long as international conditions permitted.' (cf. Hinkkanen-Lievonen, 1983, pp. 335–6; Lampe and Jackson, 1982). Ranki (1985, p. 64) expressed a similar view about the Balkans which he claimed were integrated into the world economic system in a way that kept them underdeveloped and structurally backward, not unlike the enclave economies of the Third World (cf. Senghaas, 1985, p. 187). Writing in the 1960s Spulber (1966, pp. 7–8) likened the East European countries to the developing nations of Asia and Africa. Even Spain was seen as an economic colony of the advanced nations by the economic nationalists of the 1920s (Harrison 1985, p. 36).

While superficially attractive, dependency theories probably are of limited relevance to the European scene. There is no conclusive evidence that the emergence of international income inequality was primarily a product of western exploitation, even though the influence of the metropolitan powers was not always in the interests of the European and non-European periphery (Ramirez-Faria, 1991, p. 261; Valério, 1992, p. 131). In any case, both in a political and economic sense it is a somewhat misleading interpretation since some peripheral countries had a more independent existence than others, while the export orientation or dependency of many peripheral nations was lower than the export orientation of the leading western countries (Hanson, 1986, p. 93). Nor can all peripheral nations be classed as impoverished. By the interwar years the Scandinavian countries could in no way be considered impoverished or underdeveloped, nor were they dependent in a Marxian sense on the core colonial powers. There are of course some borderline cases. Spain can no doubt be classsed as a poor and structurally backward country, but there is more of a question mark over Italy, despite the poverty of its southern regions (Arrighi, 1985; Molinas and Prados de la Escosura, 1989).

Clearly there is some definitional problem here which needs to be clarified. As a working concept we might define the impoverished peripherals as those nations with a 50 per cent or more dependency on agriculture and income per capita levels of less than 50 per cent of those in the advanced industrial countries. On these criteria we should then have to include much of Eastern Europe (Poland, Hungary, Romania Yugoslavia and Bulgaria), Greece, Turkey, Spain and Portugal in Southern Europe, along with the three Baltic states of Estonia, Latvia, and Lithuania. As it so happens these are all peripheral nations in a geographic sense and most of them are relatively small countries. However, their experience does vary somewhat during the interwar years.

Marked inequalities in income and wealth among European and non-European countries for that matter, are of relatively recent origin. The relative impoverishment of the peripheral nations is largely a product of modern industrialisation. Inequalities in income and wealth among nations were much less evident at the dawn of modern economic growth than they are today (Bairoch, 1981, 1991; Berend and Ranki, 1982, p. 15). Indeed, countries such as Spain and Portugal were once regarded as part of the European core. Around 1800 only Britain stood well ahead of the pack since the income levels of most of the countries which were to later form the metropolitan core differed little from the European average.

Modern economic growth changed all this. Industrialisation may have taken little heed of national frontiers, as Pollard (1973, p. 467) noted some time ago in his pan-regional analysis of European development, but it certainly left glaring gaps on its way. The north-western sector of the Continent very soon emerged as the core of advanced development and, generally speaking, as one moved south and east the pace of change became noticeably weaker. In 1750 the difference in income per capita between western and eastern Europe was probably no more than 15 per cent and even by 1800 it was little more than 20 per cent (excluding Britain). By 1860 it had leapt to 64 per cent and by the first decade of the twentieth century it was close to 80 per cent

(Bairoch, 1981). Even more marked was the large difference between the richest and poorest nations. The average per capita income of the four wealthiest countries (Britain, Switzerland, Denmark and Belgium) was some three times that of the four poorest (Greece, Poland, Bulgaria and Yugoslavia). Taking eight countries at both extremes tended to narrow the gap somewhat, but the rich core countries were still some two and a half times better off. With the exception of the Baltic states, all the poorest countries were located in southern and eastern Europe and included Spain, Portugal, Greece and Turkey in the South and Hungary, Poland, Romania, Yugoslavia, and Bulgaria in the East (Aldcroft, 1994, p. 11; Good, 1996, p. 71). Moreover, within the poorer countries regional differences in development were very marked. A study by Hocevar (1965, pp. 114–15) found that in the territories which subsequently formed the state of Yugoslavia, the net income per head in Slovenia in 1910 was nearly three times greater than that in the south-eastern corner of the country.

Perhaps an even more striking illustration of the state of backwardness in Europe's lagging nations is provided by the degree of mobility of the inhabitants, a useful proxy for which is the annual number of railway journeys. Berend and Ranki (1982, p. 100) have assembled some very instructive data showing that in the European periphery (southern and eastern Europe) railway journeys per person were a mere 2.5 a year in 1911 as against 21.9 on average in the core countries (Britain, Germany, France, Belgium, Holland and Switzerland). This enormous gap cannot always be attributed to low levels of railway infrastructure in the disadvantaged nations. Spain, for example, had more railway mileage per person than either Britain or Belgium yet her mobility factor was less than 10 per cent of that in the former countries. Taking the periphery as a whole, one finds that railway provision per inhabitant was 66 per cent of that in the core countries whereas mobility was only just over 11 per cent. While by no means a perfect measure, the mobility factor does provide a useful indicator of the state of backwardness in Europe's peripheral nations.

This does not mean that economic growth or industrial development completely bypassed the peripheral countries of Europe. Modern scholarship has shown that economic change of some sort was fairly pervasive throughout the European continent before the First World War (Berend and Ranki, 1982; Good, 1984; Komlos 1983, 1989; Sylla and Toniolo, 1991). This was certainly true in the case of the lands incorporated within the Austro-Hungarian Empire, especially the western half, while even the more outlying areas of the region experienced some awakening in the latter half of the nineteenth century, often as a result of the infiltration of western interests and western capital. According to

Good (1994, p. 5; 1996, p. 69) the Habsburg Empire grew more rapidly in the later nineteenth century than most other European countries, while regional disparities within the Monarchy began to diminish. Quite rapid progress was made in some of the remoter regions: for example, the expansion of large scale industry in Bosnia-Herzegovina was impressive by any standard in the decades before the war, and though the region remained backward in many respects, per capita income levels moved progressively away from Balkan levels and closer to those of Central Europe (Palairet 1993, p. 152). Southern Europe (Spain, Portugal, Greece and Turkey) also experienced phases of expansion during the long nineteenth century (Good, 1996, p. 69; Molinas and Prados de la Escosura, 1989; Nunes, Mata and Valério, 1989).

However, one should not get carried away by the revelations of modern scholarship on the hitherto neglected countries or regions of Europe. While some made a brave effort to slough off their backwardness, modern capitalism in scale and scope could not match that of the West. Often it consisted of no more than an island or two of modernity in a sea of primitive capitalism, heavily concentrated spatially, for example around Budapest in Hungary and Sofia in Bulgaria. Industry proper still accounted for a very small share of national income and employment. Agricultural systems, though by no means completely static, were very primitive and retained many essentially feudal characteristics, especially in the Balkans, so that productive efficiency was very much lower than in the adavanced nations of the western world (Bairoch, 1991)

The focus of this chapter is not the origins of peripheral backwardness but the state of play in the interwar years. Briefly the position can be put as follows: many of the peripheral nations at the start of the period had structural characteristics which relegated them to low-level development, and these characteristics were aggravated by the peculiarly hostile climate of the interwar period.

Characteristics of peripheral nations

The peripheral nations shared several features in common. They all had a high proportion of population dependent on agriculture, ranging from 45 to 50 per cent in the case of Southern Europe (Greece, Spain and Portugal) to between 72 to 81 per cent in the Balkans (Bulgaria, Romania and Yugoslavia), Albania and Turkey. Virtually everywhere agricultural systems were backward and fairly unyielding; productivity levels were very low by western standards, while medieval-type strip farming was quite common in some countries. Surplus agrarian population was prevalent since marginal productivity was low and in some cases negative. It follows therefore that drawing people off the land would have raised average productivity levels. Overpopulation was in turn aggravated by high rates of population growth. Apart from Estonia, most countries had population growth rates well in excess of those in Western Europe. In Albania, Turkey, Portugal, Greece, Poland and the Balkans population was expanding at well over 1 per cent per annum as against 0.5 per cent a year in England and Wales and Norway and 0.7 per cent in Germany and Belgium (Table 8.1). Much of this growth was due to very high birth rates at a time when death rates were

Table 8.1 Population and income levels for selected countries

Country	*% population dependent on agriculture, circa 1930–34*	*Growth rates of population, 1920–39*	*Illiteracy rate: % of 7–10 year olds 1930–34*	*GNP per head in 1929 (US 1960 dollars)*
Turkey	81	2.10[1]	90.0	—
Albania	80	1.50	80.0	—
Yugoslavia	76	1.43	45.2	341
Bulgaria	75	1.30	31.4	306
Romania	72	1.27	42.0	331
Lithuania	70	1.10	37.0[2]	—
Poland	60	1.44	23.1	350
Estonia	56	0.10	4.0	—
Latvia	55	1.00	13.5	—
Hungary	51	0.76	8.8	424
Spain	50	0.90	31.0	455
Portugal	46	1.50	59.0	320
Greece	46	1.93	40.8	390
Sweden	31	0.30	0.1	897
Denmark	30	0.80	—	945
France	29	0.30	8.0	982
Norway	27	0.50	—	1 033
Switzerland	22	0.40	—	1 265
Germany	20	0.70	—	770
Netherlands	18	1.40	—	1 008
Belgium	15	0.70	9.0	1 098
England and Wales	5	0.49	0.0	1 038

Notes:
1. 1927–39.
2. 1923.

Sources: Polonsky (1975), p. 172; Kaser and Radice (1985), pp. 93, 532; Moore (1945), p. 26; Kirk (1946), p. 24; Bairoch (1976), p. 297; Hope (1994), pp. 53–4; Hale (1981), p. 67; private communication from Irena Bakula of Riga, Latvia.

falling rapidly, though in some cases, for example Romania and Greece, there were also large population gains at the beginning of the period due to the territorial changes and population migrations following from the postwar peace settlements. Greece absorbed no less than 1.5 million expatriate Greeks (one-quarter of the country's population) largely from Turkey, as a result of her defeat in Asia Minor, while Turkey in return received some 400 000 Turkish immigrants from Greece (Herschlag, 1968, p. 24; Pentzopoulos, 1962, p. 18). Moreover, compared by western standards, illiteracy rates (*circa* 1930) were very high – 30 to 45 per cent in the Balkans and Lithuania, 59 per cent in Portugal and as high as 80 to 90 per cent in Albania and Turkey (Table 8.1).

High agrarian dependence inevitably meant that modern industry played a relatively small role in the economies of the peripheral countries. At the extreme, Turkey and Albania probably had less than 10 per cent of their labour forces employed in this sector, and even then much of it consisted of small-scale or workshop manufacture. The Balkan countries fared little better in this regard, whereas Poland and Hungary had developed more substantial industrial interests before 1914. Yet however small and insignificant the industrial sector, most countries had experienced some modern development before 1914, even if only through the backwash effects of western development and western capital. True industrial development was often highly concentrated spatially, while the level of efficiency fell well short of western standards (see Berend and Ranki, 1982).

Trade structures of these countries reflected the domestic economic structure. Primary commodities tended to dominate the export trade, sometimes with heavy dependence on one or two products. In the case of Greece, tobacco accounted for some 55 per cent of all exports in 1926–30, while three commodities (tobacco, dried fruit and wine) made up about 80 per cent of total exports (Freris, 1986, p. 87). Romania's dependence was almost as great, since cereals, forest and petroleum products accounted for over 77 per cent of all exports. In Bulgaria cereals, tobacco and eggs and livestock accounted for 73 per cent, while for Yugoslavia cereals, livestock and forest products made up 59 per cent (Lampe and Jackson, 1982, pp. 368–9). Conversely, imports consisted mainly of manufactured or semi-manufactured goods, raw materials and in some cases foodstuffs. The fact that some of these countries were dependent on food imports despite their large agrarian interests is eloquent testimony to the failure of their agrarian systems to respond to the needs of rapidly growing populations.

The final column of Table 8.1 provides some tentative estimates of income per head for the year 1929 based on constant prices. Broadly speaking the peripheral nations had income levels of one-half to one-third of those obtaining in western countries, while in Turkey and Albania they were probably no better than one-fifth to one-quarter. These estimates are somewhat fragile and need to be treated with caution, but circumstantial evidence (for example on productivity levels, capital formation, infrastructure provision) does suggest that they provide a reasonably accurate assessment of comparative levels of income relative to western standards.

The political and social background should also be taken into account when considering Europe's impoverished countries. With the exception of Spain and Portugal, all of them can be classed as new or reconstituted states arising out of the aftermath of the First World War. Large territorial and population shifts occurred as a result of the post-war settlements, including those arising from subsequent conflicts notably that between Turkey and Greece. Parliamentary regimes were installed in most of these states where none had existed before. But consolidating and stabilising the new states proved a difficult task given the weak, often corrupt and unstable administrations and the problem of reconciling divergent interests many of which arose from the ethnic and religious diversity of the populations, especially in Eastern Europe. In time the new democracies were overwhelmed by forces of the right and one by one they succumbed to authoritarian regimes. By the end of the interwar period 16 of the 28 European states had been taken over by some form of dictatorship (Lee, 1987, pp. xi–xv).

The agrarian problem

In the context of the interwar period it was the adverse agrarian structures that were to prove the most vulnerable to the international trends in commodity prices.

The strengthening of nationalistic sentiments after the First World War inevitably meant greater pressure to develop and catch up with the West. For this purpose modern development was equated with industry, not agriculture, and hence policies tended to give priority to the former. Agriculture was relatively neglected, a mistake subsequently perpetrated by many socialist regimes and Third World countries. But given the heavy preponderance of agriculture in the total economy a dynamic primary sector was essential if it was to fulfil the role it had done in western countries in the previous century: that is as a source of capital accumulation, a foreign exchange earner, providing an internal market for non-agrarian products and surplus labour for industry, and of course meeting the needs of a growing population. The first two were perhaps the most important initially since most of the peripheral countries were desperately short of capital and also foreign exchange with which to purchase capital goods.

Unfortunately agrarian systems for one reason or another proved fairly unyielding to the needs of development. That is not to say there was no change at all: indeed some countries, the Baltic States especially, saw a significant shift in their agrarian product mix which proved highly successful in export markets (Zilinskas, 1946, p. 177). But by and large agrarian sectors could not adjust rapidly enough to cope with accelerated development. For one thing it was often as much as they could do to keep pace with the food needs of growing populations, and in some cases even that was not possible. Moreover, greater population pressure and widespread land reform in the postwar years led to more fragmentation of holdings (including the use of strip farming in the east) with detrimental effects initially on efficiency, export promotion and capital accumulation.

But in any case, during the interwar period traditional modes of agriculture were overtaken by events. Weak agricultural prices prevailed for much of the period due to the recovery in European production, increased tariffs and a shift away from cereal products. Even during the 1920s the terms of trade of farm producers were under pressure and they subsequently collapsed in the slump of the early 1930s. By 1929 there had already been a significant deterioration in the terms of trade. In the case of Turkey for example, they had declined by as much as 20 per cent between 1925–29 (Keyder, 1981, pp. 82–3). The overall decline for primary producers in general during this period was about 5 per cent, though longer term, using 1913 as base, the decline works out at about 11 per cent (Drabek, 1985, p. 475). Not all producers were affected to the same extent but there is little doubt that towards the end of the decade commodity prices were coming under pressure and that market prospects were visibly deteriorating. The situation was most acute in the chief food products such as cereals where rising stocks levels reflected the weakness of the market. Stock levels in many commodities had been accumulating since 1925 and the general index of world stocks of staple commodities more than doubled in the period 1925–30. Thus world commodity prices on average were showing distinct signs of weakness in the latter half of the decade (League of Nations, 1933, pp. 92–4). By the third quarter of 1929 world agricultural prices were some 30 per cent lower than the average for 1923–25, while over the same period stock levels had risen by some 75 per cent (Ranki, 1983, pp. 51–2). These price changes and the resulting unfavourable shift in trade terms were important factors in the trade deficits of Hungary and the Balkan countries in 1928–29.

The worst was yet to come, however. On average food and raw material prices fell by one-half and two-thirds between 1929 and 1932, whereas the price of manufactures declined by only just over one-third. Hence the terms of trade of primary producers deteriorated on average by some 27 per cent (Drabeck, 1985, p. 475). For farm producers and peasants the price collapse was devastating (League of Nations, 1931). Eastern Europe probably suffered the worst in this respect. Agrarian incomes declined by up to one-half in Poland and the Balkans and by one-third in Hungary. At times the disparity between agricultural and industrial prices became so wide that farm producers had to give up nearly double the prewar amount of grain and cattle to secure the same amount of manufactured articles (Hertz, 1947, p. 194). As farm incomes declined debt burdens increased as a proportion of income and by 1932/33 many peasants were on the verge of bankruptcy. In Hungary, for example, the interest paid on agricultural loans was more than 25 per cent of total yearly income and some 60 per cent of the land of smallholders was fully mortgaged (Berend and Ranki, 1974, p. 245; Held, 1980, p. 224). Throughout the region indebtedness was a pervasive problem. One contemporary observer who made an extensive tour of the area reckoned that more than 70 per cent of all peasant holdings in Eastern Europe were threatened by debts in the depression and that many peasant households were worse off in terms of purchasing power than before the war (Mazower, 1991b, pp. 248–9; Tiltman, 1934, pp. 118–20, 169, 249).

The collapse of incomes also had serious fiscal implications. At a time when the demand for relief payments and social assistance was increasing, governments were faced with dwindling tax revenues and budget deficits. This meant they were forced to curtail expenditure wherever possible and hence there was little scope for expansive policies to combat depression. As Schönfeld (1975, pp. 197–8) rightly notes, governments had little room for manoevre to tackle the depression with innovative fiscal policies.

Debt burdens and external adjustment

But perhaps the most serious impact of the price collapse was on the international side since this tended to dictate the course of future policy. Export receipts dropped sharply through a combination of price and quantity factors. On average they fell by 40 per cent or more and in the case of Romania by no less than 73 per cent. The enormous shrinkage in export earnings entailed a serious loss of international purchasing power and a rising external debt burden. Since international debts remained fixed in nominal terms the debt servicing power of exports fell by between one-half and two-thirds in the most heavily indebted countries of Hungary and the Balkans (Nötel, 1986, pp. 217–19).

The final blow came with the breakdown of the international financial system in the crisis of 1930–31 which effectively undermined the solvency of debtor countries. Long-term foreign lending from western creditors was already faltering in the later 1920s and by 1931 it had virtually dried up. In the meantime gold and foreign exchange reserves had drained away, while short-term liquidity was hastily withdrawn in the panic flight of capital in the 1931 financial crisis (United Nations, 1949, p. 10). The curtailment of foreign lending not only adversely affected domestic investment and activity, but it also dealt a fatal blow to external equilibrium (League of Nations, 1932). During the later 1920s most of the debtor countries in Eastern Europe and elsewhere had relied heavily on capital imports to plug the gap in their external accounts. Of the total inflow of funds, both long and short term, into Hungary, Poland, Bulgaria and Yugoslavia between 1924 and 1928, one-half went to cover an import surplus of goods and services, while most of the remainder was earmarked for servicing foreign debt. Even by 1929 the writing was on the wall for in that year capital inflows were barely sufficient to cover interest and dividends, and thereafter they dwindled rapidly to insignificant proportions. Through the crisis period as a whole, 1929–33, capital imports covered less than one-half of interest and dividends due on debt, which meant in effect that the former import surplus of goods and services had to be converted into a positive balance (Nötel, 1974, pp. 84–5; 1984, pp. 182–3). The debt servicing burden was heaviest in Eastern Europe, Greece, and to a lesser extent Turkey, which had no war debts but was burdened with former

Table 8.2 Debt servicing as a percentage of export earnings, 1928 and 1931/32

	1928	*1931/32*
Bulgaria	12.3	22.0
Greece	32.0	44.0
Hungary	17.9	48.0
Poland	11.3	27.0
Romania	14.6	36.0
Yugoslavia	18.1	36.0

Sources: Drabeck (1985), p. 425; Nötel, (1986), p. 223; Mazower, (1991b), pp. 112, 202.

Ottoman debts on which there was a moratorium until 1929, whereas it was relatively light in Portugal, Spain and the Baltic States. Debt servicing as a percentage of exports rose rapidly between 1928 and the early 1930s (Table 8.2).

Thus the collapse of export purchasing power, the loss of gold and exchange reserves and the end of foreign credits rendered Eastern Europe virtually insolvent. The financial situation was also exacerbated by the accompanying banking crisis in Central Europe owing to the fact that a substantial proportion of the equity capital of some East European banks was owned by foreigners, including Germans (Cottrell, 1983, p. 309). Nötel (1986, p. 227) has described the sequence as follows:

> The financial crisis of mid-1931, superimposed upon the protracted export crisis in both commodities and manufactures, transformed the haunting spectre of the collapse of national currencies, within a few months or weeks, into an immediately threatening and practically inescapable reality for most east European countries. The sudden shift from continuing, even if irregular, capital imports to fast-spreading capital withdrawal and flight – with the balance-of-payments position already weakened by the sharp and long-lasting fall in export receipts and the rising or at least maintained debt service – in all countries threatened to exhaust, or actually exhausted, the rapidly shrinking proceeds and reserves of foreign exchange.

Policy response

The disintegration of the international economy eventually forced the peripheral nations to turn towards autarkic policies relying on domestic sources of growth. Initially crisis conditions necessitated desperate remedies uninspired by ideological motives (Kofman, 1990, p. 17). These included severe deflationary monetary and fiscal policies together with a battery of restrictions to deal with external imbalances including exchange controls, import quotas and tariffs and limitation or default of debt payments. Though many of these measures reflected a hasty and ill-conceived response to crisis conditions they did have a certain logic about them.

First, there was an almost pathological fear of rekindling the inflationary conditions of the first half of the 1920s which were associated with currency depreciation and budgetary deficits. Hence the emphasis on fiscal prudence and currency stabilisation via exchange control rather than abandoning gold, even though this would be detrimental to the real economy (League of Nations, 1935, p. 6; 1938, para. 8; 1944, p. 167). Most countries therefore instituted exchange control soon after

Table 8.3 Exchange rates and exchange control

Country	*Stabilisation of currency*[1]	*Official suspension of gold standard*	*Introduction of exchange control*	*Depreciation or devaluation in relation to gold*	*Remarks*
Albania	1914	—	—	—	
Bulgaria	1924 (1928)	—	15/10/31	—	
Estonia	1924 (1927)	28/6/33	18/11/31	6/33	Joins sterling bloc 1933
Greece	1928	26/4/32	28/9/31	4/32	Drachma linked to US dollar September 1931
Hungary	1924	—	17/7/31	—	
Latvia	1922	28/9/36	8/10/31	10/36	Linked to sterling September 1936
Lithuania	1922	—	1/10/35	—	Maintains 1922 value
Poland	1926 (1927)	—	26/4/36	—	
Portugal	1929	31/12/31	21/10/32	10/31	
Romania	1927 (1929)	—	18/5/32	7/35	
Spain	Floating	—	18/5/31	1920	Rate stabilised in 1934 to Civil War
Turkey	Floating 1930	—	26/2/30	1915	Pegged to sterling March 1930–Sept. 1931, then to franc till September 1936, then linked to sterling at 1936 parity
Yugoslavia	1925 (1931)	—	7/10/31	7/32	

Note:
1. Dates in brackets in column one refer to *de jure* stabilisation.

Sources: League of Nations (1937a), p. 30, (1937b) p. 16, (1946) p. 93.

Britain left the gold standard, but several maintained their gold parities for some time (Table 8.3). It was only when international conditions began to improve towards the middle of the decade that some relaxation was deemed to be judicious.

Secondly, with a view to restoring international confidence in the hope of encouraging a resumption of foreign lending, debtor nations were reluctant initially to repudiate or default on their foreign obligations. In time, however, default or negotiation of moratoria became unavoidable. For the same reason there was equal reluctance to depreciate currencies since this would weaken international confidence by raising the spectre of inflation, while it would also raise the nominal value of debts and debt service costs in terms of domestic currency (Bandera, 1964, p. 119).

A third and longer-term factor which helped to shape the course of policy was the growing influence of nationalism. This, of course, had been very much in evidence during the previous decade, manifested in the nostrification measures to reduce the incidence of alien property assets (Pasvolsky, 1928, p. 75). It gathered increasing momentum in the 1930s and interacted well with the trend towards greater state intervention, policies encouraging import substitution and self-sufficiency and the rejection of the now discredited liberal capitalism of bourgeois democracy. The emergence of right-wing authoritarian regimes also facilitated the exploitation of nationalist sentiments in both the economic and political spheres.

One final issue which exerted increasing influence on policy in the later 1930s was that of rearmament. Defence expenditure had always been a significant component of the budgets of many of the new states, but the increasing international tension in the latter half of the decade led to an even greater diversion of resources to military purposes. Defence expenditure accounted for between one-quarter to one-third of state budgets in the later 1930s even in the case of small states such as Lithuania (Political and Economic Planning, 1945, pp. 119, 164; Simutis, 1942, p. 108). From the mid-1930s onwards many of the state-sponsored industrial projects in Eastern Europe were geared to strategic considerations (Tomasevich, 1949, p. 179).

Import substitution

Most of the peripheral countries recorded quite impressive gains in industrial production during the 1930s even measuring from peak to peak of the cycle (1929–37/38). The most spectacular occurred in Greece, Portugal, Bulgaria, Turkey and the Baltic States. However, one should bear in mind that they took place from a very low base so that they only had a marginal impact on the economic structures of these countries. Moreover, as Pollard (1981, p. 290) has reminded us, import substitution, rather than relying on comparative advantage, had its drawbacks:

> the result of that choice was inevitably high-cost, inefficient, technically backward industries pushing inferior goods which could survive only by constant protection and official support and therefore generated massive corruption. These symptoms will be recognised as belonging also to Third World industrialisation of post-World War II, to which may be added the high proportion of capital in the major industries owned by the state. Set in the midst of poor, basically agrarian countries, these pampered industries placed an intolerable burden on the peasantry and on the state budget alike, and removed what little chance there had been of success as specialist primary producers.

Much of this criticism is undoubtedly true though in all fairness there were few options left after the débâcle of the 1930s and the increasing international tension in the latter part of the decade. Most policies of induced or forced development tend to lead to relative inefficiency in the course of time, especially if they result in the neglect of the major sector of activity, namely agriculture. Moreover, in many respects none of the countries was fully prepared for rapid industrial development and structural change since so many other factors lagged behind. For example, infrastructure facilities were vastly inferior to those of the West and in some cases, especially in Eastern Europe, they deteriorated further in relative terms in this period (Ehrlich, 1973; Keyder, 1981, pp. 91–2). Investment levels were low and much new investment went into housing, with urban dwellings accounting for some 40–50 per cent of new investment in several East European countries (Political and Economic Planning, 1945, p. 102).

Fiscal systems were not designed for growth. They were highly regressive and all too often they bore the marks of feudal features inherited from a bygone age (Herschlag, 1968, p. 68; Hocevar, 1987, p. 565). Budgetary spending tended to be skewed towards defence and administration. In Turkey, for example, no less than 34 per cent of budget expenditure in 1930 went on civil service salaries (Herschlag, 1968, p. 68). In many countries defence and civil administration along with debt service accounted for 60 per cent or more of budgetary expenditure, leaving barely one-third for economic and social services including infrastructures, whereas in contemporary Sweden these proportions were reversed (Political and Economic Planning, 1945, pp. 118–19, 164). Inevitably, therefore, key support services – transport and communications, utilities, and medical and educational services – were relatively neglected. The last of these was especially important given the low level of educational attainment and training in these countries and the shortage of skilled labour. It is true that all the countries, and especially the Baltic states, made some effort to improve educational provision in the interwar years, but judging by the high rates of illiteracy prevailing in many countries by the early 1930s, investment in human capital probably fell well short of requirements (Nunes, Mata and Valério, 1989, p. 307; Tortella, 1994).

Taxation systems were even more anomalous. Taxes were generally regressive and for the most part they lacked equity and logic. More often than not the administration of the tax system was designed to suit the convenience of officials, as Tomasevich (1955, p. 688) found in the case of Yugoslavia, where indirect taxes accounted for some three-quarters of total revenue. The principles of the State's tax system were those 'of charging its citizens as often as possible and as heavily as possible; taking the money where it could find it, and getting it from those who make the least outcry, rather than according to the principle of the ability to pay'.

Regressive fiscal systems are typical of backward countries and in this respect the European peripherals were no exception. The bulk of public revenue was derived from indirect taxes and much of the burden was borne by the peasantry (Jelavich, 1983, p. 241). In the Balkan countries, for example, some 50 per cent of the total cash incomes of the peasantry disappeared in taxation, and it was probably of a similar order of magnitude in Greece, Turkey and Albania. Given the very low incomes of the peasantry at the time this was a fearful burden and was no doubt the main factor discouraging investment in improvements in agriculture and for the general backwardness of the sector (Political and Economic Planning, 1945, p. 122; Tomasevich, 1955, p. 702). At the same time unfair tax anomalies abounded: while the peasants were squeezed, government officials, rent receivers and businessmen escaped lightly. The structure and administration of fiscal systems was clearly ripe for reform in more ways than one: 'There are few spheres of public policy in which a constructive approach would yield speedier results' (Political and Economic Planning, 1945, p. 124).

More generally, state structures were poorly equipped to pursue effectively policies of modernisation (Aymard, 1985, p. 43; Wallerstein, 1985, p. 36). Many of the defects were part of past heritage, as for example the importance attached to political, military, religious, ethnic and cultural issues which limited the scope for modernisation drives. Weak administrations, political instability, bribery, corruption and overblown bureaucracies were nothing new. Political instability was widespread in the 1920s when many countries were trying to learn the art of parliamentray democracy. Portgual, for example, had no less than 28 governments between January 1919 and May 1926, while revolutions or armed rebellions occurred at least once a year (Oliveira Marques, 1978, p. 95). In Greece political instability 'provided insurmountable obstacles to the development of coherent and consistent economic policies and social legislation' (Psomiades, 1965, p. 198). In some cases, notably Turkey, the State's role was also weakened by external control. Though the allied powers had granted a moratorium on prewar debts until 1929, this concession came at the expense of Turkey's tariff autonomy and it also involved some control of her financial affairs (Rothermund, 1996, p. 75). However, the much vaunted state planning of the Ataturk regime in Turkey was riddled with unethical practices from the old regime such as bribery of officials, nepotism, business trickery, jobs and perks for the favoured families, which led to gross overstaffing in public office (Thornberg, Spry and Soule, 1949, pp. 32–8). Corruption, bribery and graft were as common in the Balkans as they had ever been, especially in Romania where hordes of politicians and officials waxed fat on the Treasury as did the business intimates and friends of the leaders of the Liberal Party (especially the Bratianus brothers), who dispensed largesse liberally to their supporters. Logio (1932, p. 128) claimed that the state administration in Romania was 'annexed by the party bosses and the public budget has been confiscated for the benefit of the clients of these parties'.

Performance

It is difficult to make broad generalisations about the performance of all the peripheral countries during the interwar period since experience was so disparate and much of the aggregate data is fragile and still subject to revision. We know that there was a general move towards industry but for the most part the structural changes to economies were not dramatic. Thus the share of industry in output and employment increased marginally but in most cases the agrarian sector remained the mainstay of activity (Pollard, 1981, p. 290). Agrarian over-population was also still very prevalent.

Some countries made little or no progress: Albania for example was easily the most backward and illiterate country in Europe 'whose economy remained so locked in primitive patterns of agriculture and handicrafts that it barely achieved any economic progress during the interwar years' (Radice, 1985, pp. 63). It had changed little since the turn of the century and by 1939 only about 1.5 per cent of the population was engaged in manufacturing (Crampton, 1994, pp. 22, 144; Hocevar, 1987, p. 565; Radice, 1985, p. 63). Turkey and Bulgaria, despite more signs of industrial life, were also overwhelmingly agrarian and both countries remained basically unchanged by the limited modern developments that occurred. Even Greece's spectacular industrial growth in the 1930s did little to transform the country; it simply 'masked an increasingly backward economic structure' in which small, inefficient firms thrived in a protected market (Mazower, 1991a, pp. 226–8). By the outbreak of the Second World War Greek industry was 'small scale, undiversified, ministering to domestic needs and its structure had hardly changed over almost 20 years' (Freris, 1986, p. 50). Four industries, textiles, food processing, chemicals and tanning, accounted for some three-quarters of manufacturing output throughout the interwar period.

The income per capita changes produced in Table 8.4 provide an overall measure of performance, though with the usual word of warning as to their accuracy. For four countries alternative estimates to those of Bairoch are listed, which only serve to demonstrate the dangers of placing too much credence on them. What they do appear to show is that through the period 1913–38 most countries, excepting Greece and Bulgaria, failed to match the performance of Europe as a whole which implies that the gap between the impoverished nations and the advanced countries of the West did not diminish and may even have widened slightly (Aldcroft and Morewood, 1995, p. 83; Ranki, 1985, p. 71). At least in the case of the Balkans, Berend (1984, p. 272) was certain that the degree of relative backwardness increased during the period. Spain, however, was easily the worst performer being the only country failing to record an advance in per capita income on 1913 (Prados de la Escosura, 1993); this was due largely, though not entirely, to the adverse effects of the Civil War since during the 1920s and early part of the depression Spain had performed relatively strongly, helped by her floating currency. Thereafter the position was one of almost unrelieved depression with only one or two years showing feeble attempts at recovery. The position of Portugal probably requires some modification if we accept the new estimates of Nunes, Mata and Valério (1989) which show a substantial improvement in output per capita between 1913 and 1938, though their estimates have been criticised for being rather on the high side (Lains and Reis, 1991). Some revision may also be appropriate in the case of Turkey, though in this case the estimates are too scrappy to be certain of the precise magnitude. Greece is more of a problem. Bairoch's income estimates appear rather high, though by all accounts industrial growth was very impressive in the 1930s (Mazower, 1985, p. 381; 1991b, p. 311). The data given for the Baltic States may also do less than justice to the transformation of the production and trade structures of Estonia, Latvia and Lithuania in this

Table 8.4 Per capita GNP 1913–38 (1960 US dollars)

	Level				*Percentage change*				
	1913	*1929*	*1933*	*1938*	*1913–29*	*1929–33*	*1933–38*	*1929–38*	*1913–38*
Albania	—	—	—	—	—	—	—	—	—
Baltic countries	—	468	451	501	—	–3.6	11.1	7.1	—
Bulgaria	263	306	270	420	16.3	–11.8	55.6	37.3	59.7
Greece	322	390	506	590	21.1	29.7	16.6	51.3	83.2
Hungary	372	424	396	451	14.0	–6.6	13.9	6.4	21.2
Poland	301	350	332	372	16.3	–5.1	12.0	6.3	23.6
Portugal	292	320	398	351	9.6	24.4	–11.8	9.7	20.2
Romania	320	331	296	343	3.4	–10.6	15.9	3.6	7.2
Spain	367	455	403	337	24.0	–11.4	–16.4	–25.9	–8.2
Yugoslavia	284	341	292	339	20.1	–14.4	16.1	–0.6	19.4
Turkey(a)	—	—	—	—	—	—	—	26.0	—
Europe	534	571	543	671	6.9	–4.9	23.4	17.5	25.7
Greece (b)	—	—	—	—	—	8.9	20.4	31.1	—
Portugal (c)	—	—	—	—	19.1	10.2	4.9	15.5	37.6
Spain (d)	—	—	—	—	31.2	–6.2	–20.9	–25.8	–2.7
Turkey (e)	—	—	—	—	—	8.7	31.6	38.0	—

Sources: Bairoch (1976), p. 297; (a) Herschlag (1954), p. 336; (b) Freris (1986), p. 108, based on GNP estimates of UN; (c) Nunes, Mata and Valério (1989); (d) Prados de la Escosura (1993); (e) Hale (1981), pp. 46, 75–7.

Table 8.5 Changes in industrial/manufacturing production, 1913–38

	1913–29	*1929–32/33*	*1932/33–37/38*	*1929–37/38*	*1913–37/38*
Albania	—	—	—	—	—
Bulgaria	79.0	8.9	25.6	36.9	145.0
Estonia	—	—	—	—	40.5
Greece	—	0.9	60.0	61.5	—
Hungary	13.9	–19.8	64.2	31.7	50.0
Latvia	—	—	—	—	47.8
Lithuania	—	53.7	—	209.4	—
Poland	–14.1	–38.6	99.6	22.5	5.2
Portugal	—	33.0	9.8	46.0	—
Romania	36.9	–18.3	63.4	33.6	82.9
Spain	72.9	–15.7	–19.7[1]	–32.3[2]	17.1[3]
Yugoslavia	40.0	–17.1	63.8	35.7	90.0
World	53.3	–29.3	80.6	27.7	95.8

Notes:
1. 1933–40; 2. 1929–40; 3. 1913–40.

Sources: League of Nations (1945), pp. 134–7; OEEC (1960), p. 9; Berend and Ranki (1974), pp. 298–300; Freris (1986), p. 90; Lains and Reis (1991), p. 450; Lieberman (1995), p. 18; Simutis (1942), pp. 70–71; Royal Institute of International Affairs (1938), p. 151; Mazower (1991b), p. 311; Mitchell (1975), p. 357; Prados de la Escosura (1993).

period as they adapted to the loss of the assured Russian market (Royal Institute of International Affairs, 1938, pp. 103–4; Simutis, 1942, pp. vii, 70–71; von Rauch, 1974).

Though incomplete, the data showing changes in industrial production broadly confirm these conclusions (Table 8.5). Import substitution policies appear to have paid off in the 1930s for some countries since several beat the world industrial index. However, over the longer haul, 1913–38, this was not true since, with the exception of Bulgaria and possibly Greece, all of the peripheral countries lagged behind the world performance. This confirms the view that these countries were unable to reduce their relative backwardness in the interwar years despite their efforts to catch up on the industrial front.

Nevertheless, given the difficult conditions of the period it is remarkable that many of these countries achieved what they did. No doubt much of the industrial development was artificially induced under the highly protective regimes of the 1930s and in this respect it was no match for the competitive international market. Though there was certainly some structural adjustment in favour of industry it was by no means dramatic (Pollard 1981, p. 289). Agriculture still remained the backbone of these countries and in many cases it was very primitive and inefficient. On the other hand, it would be harsh judgement to equate these nations with the Third World countries as some writers have done. Their levels of income and achievements comfortably surpassed those of the majority of Asian and Africa countries in the postwar period, and most of them were able to profit from the sustained growth in the years through to the 1970s.

References

Aldcroft, D. H. (1994), 'The European dimension to the modern world', in D. H. Aldcroft and S. P. Ville (eds), *The European Economy: a Thematic Approach,* Manchester, Manchester University Press.

Aldcroft, D. H. and Morewood, S. (1995), *Economic Change in Eastern Europe since 1918*, Aldershot: Edward Elgar.

Arrighi, G. (ed.) (1985), *Semiperipheral Development: the Politics of Southern Europe in the Twentieth Century'*, Beverly Hills, CA: Sage Publications.

Aymard, M. (1985), 'Nation states and the interregional disparities of development' in G. Arrighi (ed.), *Semiperipheral Development: the Politics of Southern Europe in the Twentieth Century'*, Beverly Hills, CA: Sage Publications.

Bairoch, P. (1976), 'Europe's gross national product: 1800–1975', *Journal of European Economic History,* 5.

Bairoch, P. (1981), 'The main trends in national income disparities since the industrial revolution', in P. Bairoch and M. Lévy-Leboyer (eds), *Disparities in Economic Development since the Industrial Revolution*, London: Macmillan.

Bairoch, P. (1991), 'How and not why: economic inequalities between 1800 and 1913: some background figures', in J. Batou (ed.), *Between Development and Underdevelopment: the Precocious Attempts at Industrialization of the Periphery, 1800–70*, Geneva: Droz.

Bandera, V. N. (1964), *Foreign Capital as an Instrument of National Economic Policy: a Study Based on the Experience of East European Countries Between the Two World Wars*, The Hague: Nijhoff.

Berend, I. T. (1984), 'Balkan economic development', *Economic History Review,* 37.

Berend, I. T. and Ranki, G. (1974), *Economic Development in East Central Europe in the 19th and 20th Centuries*, New York: Columbia University Press.

Berend, I. T. and Ranki, G. (1982), *The European Periphery and Industrialization*, Cambridge: Cambridge University Press.

Chirot, D. (1976), *Social Change in a Peripheral Society: the Creation of a Balkan Economy*, New York: Academic Press.

Cottrell, P. L. (1983), 'Aspects of western equity investment in the banking systems of East Central Europe', in A. Teichova and P. L. Cottrell (eds), *International Business and Central Europe, 1918–1939*, Leicester: Leicester University Press.

Crampton, R. J. (1994), *Eastern Europe in the Twentieth Century*, London: Routledge.

Drabek, Z. (1985), 'Foreign trade performance and policy', in M. C. Kaser and E. A. Radice (eds), *The Economic History of Eastern Europe, 1919–1975*, Vol. I, *Economic Structure and Performance Between the Wars*, Oxford: Oxford University Press.

Ehrlich, E. (1973), 'Infrastructure and an international comparison of relationships with indicators of development in Eastern Europe, 1920–1950', *Oxford Papers in East European Economics,* 33.

Freris, A. F. (1986), *The Greek Economy in the Twentieth Century*, London: Croom Helm.

Good, D. F. (1984), *The Economic Rise of the Habsburg Empire, 1750–1914*, Berkeley, CA: University of California Press.

Good, D. F. (1994), 'The economic transformation of central and eastern Europe in historical perspective: main themes and issues', in D. F. Good (ed.), *Economic Transformations in East and Central Europe: Legacies from the Past and Policies for the Future*, London: Routledge.

Good, D. F. (1996), 'Economic growth in Europe's third world: central and eastern Europe, 1870–1989', in D. H. Aldcroft and R. Catterall (eds), *Rich Nations – Poor Nations: the Long-Run Perspective*, Cheltenham: Edward Elgar.

Hale, W. (1981), *The Political and Economic Development of Modern Turkey*, London: Croom Helm.

Hanson, J. R. II (1986), 'Export shares in the European periphery and the third world before world war I: questionable data, facile analogies', *Explorations in Economic History*, 23.

Harrison, J. (1985), *The Spanish Economy in the Twentieth Century*, London: Croom Helm.

Held, J. (1980), *The Modernization of Agriculture: Rural Transformation in Hungary 1848–1975*, (East European monographs 63), New York: Columbia University Press.

Herschlag, Z. Y. (1954), 'Turkey: achievements and failures in the policy of economic development (during the inter-war period 1919–1939)', *Kyklos*, 7.

Herschlag, Z. Y. (1968), *Turkey: the Challenge of Growth*, Leiden: E. J. Brill.

Hertz, F. (1947), *The Economic Problem of the Danubian States. A Study in Economic Nationalism*, London: Gollancz.

Hinkkanen-Lievonen, M-L (1983), 'Exploited by Britain? The problems of British financial presence in the Baltic States after the first world war', *Journal of Baltic Studies*, 14.

Hjerppe, R. (1996), *Finland's Historical National Accounts 1860–1914: Calculation Methods and Statistical Tables*, Jyväskylä: Kari-Pekka Kivirauma.

Hocevar, T. (1965), *The Structure of the Slovenian Economy 1848–1963*, New York: Studia Slovenica.

Hocevar, T. (1987), 'The Albanian economy 1912–1944: a survey', *Journal of European Economic History*, 3.

Hope, N. (1994), 'Interwar statehood: symbol and reality', in G. Smith (ed.), *The Baltic States*, Basingstoke: Macmillan.

Jelavich, B. (1983), *History of the Balkans. Vol. 2 Twentieth Century*, Cambridge: Cambridge University Press.

Kaser, M. C. and Radice, E. A. (eds) (1985), *The Economic History of Eastern Europe 1919–1975*, Vol. I, *Economic Structure and Performance between the Wars*, Oxford: Oxford University Press.

Kaser, M. C. and Radice, E. A. (eds) (1986), *The Economic History of Eastern Europe 1919–1975*, Vol. II, *Interwar Policy, the War and Reconstruction*, Oxford: Oxford University Press.

Keyder, C. (1981), *The Definition of a Peripheral Economy: Turkey 1923–29*, Cambridge: Cambridge University Press.

Kirk, D. (1946), *Europe's Population in the Interwar Years*, Geneva: League of Nations.
Kofman, J. (1990), 'Economic nationalism in East-Central Europe in the interwar period', in H. Szlajfer (ed.), *Economic Nationalism in East-Central Europe and South America*, Geneva: Droz.
Komlos, J. (1983), *The Habsburg Monarchy as a Customs Union*, Princeton, NJ: Princeton University Press.
Komlos, J. (1989), *Nutrition and Economic Development in the Eighteenth-Century Habsburg Monarchy: an Anthropometric Study*, Princeton, NJ: Princeton University Press.
Lains, P. and Reis, J. (1991), 'Portuguese economic growth, 1833–1985: some doubts', *Journal of European Economic History*, 20.
Lampe, J. R. and Jackson, M. R. (1982), *Balkan Economic History, 1550–1950*, Bloomington, IN: Indiana University Press.
League of Nations (1931), *The Agricultural Crisis*, 2 vols, Geneva: League of Nations.
League of Nations (1932), *World Economic Survey, 1931–32*, Geneva: League of Nations.
League of Nations (1933), *World Economic Survey, 1932–33*, Geneva: League of Nations.
League of Nations (1935), *World Economic Survey, 1934–35*, Geneva: League of Nations
League of Nations (1937a), *Money and Banking, 1936/37*, Geneva: League of Nations
League of Nations (1937b), *World Economic Survey, 1936/37*, Geneva: League of Nations.
League of Nations (1938), *Report on Exchange Control*, Geneva: League of Nations
League of Nations (1944), *International Currency Experience: Lessons of the Interwar Period*, Geneva: League of Nations
League of Nations (1946), *The Course and Control of Inflation: a Review of Monetary Experience in Europe after the World War I*, Geneva: League of Nations.
Lee, S. J. (1987), *The European Dictatorships 1918–1945*, London: Methuen.
Lieberman, S. (1995), *Growth and Crisis in the Spanish Economy, 1940–93*, London: Routledge.
Logio, G. C. (1932), *Rumania: its History, Politics and Economics*, Manchester: Sherratt and Hughes.
Lykogiannis, A. (1994), 'The early post-war Greek economy: from liberation to the Truman doctrine', *Journal of European Economic History*, 23.

Malefakis, E. E. (1992), *Southern Europe in the Nineteenth and Twentieth Centuries: an Historical Overview*, Madrid: Centro de Estudios Avanzados en Ciencias Sociales, Instituto Juan March de Estudios e Investigaciones.

Mazower, M. (1985), L'economia greca durante la grande depressione dei primi anni '30', *Rivista, di Storia Economica, 2.*

Mazower, M. (1991a), 'Banking and economic development in interwar Greece', in H. James, H. Lindgren and A. Teichova (eds), *The Role of Banks in the Interwar Economy*, Cambridge: Cambridge University Press.

Mazower, M. (1991b), *Greece and the Interwar Economic Crisis*, Oxford: Oxford University Press.

Mitchell, B. R. (1975), *European Historical Statistics 1750–1970*, London: Macmillan.

Molinas, C. and Prados de la Escosura, L. (1989), 'Was Spain different? Spanish historical backwardness revisited', *Explorations in Economic History*, 26.

Moore, W. E. (1945), *Economic Demography in Eastern and Southern Europe*, Geneva: League of Nations.

Nötel, R. (1974), 'International capital movements and finance in Eastern Europe, 1919–1949', *Vierteljahrschrift für Sozial-und Wirtschaftsgeschichte*, 61.

Nötel, R. (1984), 'Money, banking and industry in interwar Austria and Hungary', *Journal of European Economic History*, 13.

Nötel, R. (1986), 'International credit and finance', in M. C. Kaser and E. A. Radice (eds), *The Economic History of Eastern Europe 1919–1975*, Vol. II, *Interwar Policy, the War and Reconstruction*, Oxford: Oxford University Press.

Nunes, A. B., Mata, E. and Valério, N. (1989), 'Portuguese economic growth 1833–1985', *Journal of European Economic History*, 18.

Okyar, O. (1987), 'A new look at the problem of economic growth in the Ottoman Empire (1800–1914)', *Journal of European Economic History*, 16.

Oliveira Marques, A. H. de (1978), 'The Portuguese 1920s: a general survey', *Revista de Historica Economica e Social*, 1.

Palairet, M. (1993), 'The Habsburg industrial achievement in Bosnia-Herzogovina, 1878–1914: an economic spurt that succeeded?', *Austrian History Yearbook*, 24.

Pasvolsky, L. (1928), *Economic Nationalism of the Danubian States*, London: Allen and Unwin.

Pentzopoulos, D. (1962), *The Balkan Exchange of Minorities and its Impact on Greece*, Paris: Mouton.

Political and Economic Planning (1945), *Economic Development in South-East Europe*, London: PEP.
Pollard, S. (1973), 'Industrialisation and the European economy', *Economic History Review*, 26.
Pollard, S. (1981), *Peaceful Conquest: the Industrialization of Europe 1760–1970*, Oxford: Oxford University Press.
Polonsky, A. (1975), *The Little Dictators: the History of Eastern Europe since 1918*, London: Routledge and Kegan Paul.
Prados de la Escosura, L. (1993), 'Spain's gross domestic product, 1850–1990', Madrid: Ministerio de Economía y Hacienda.
Psomiades, H. J. (1965), 'The economic and social transformation of Greece', *Journal of International Affairs*, 19.
Radice, E. A. (1985), 'General characteristics of the region between the wars', in M. C. Kaser and E. A. Radice (eds), *The Economic History of Eastern Europe 1919–1975*, Vol. I, *Economic Structure and Performance between the Wars*, Oxford: Oxford University Press.
Ramirez-Faria, C. (1991), *The Origins of Economic Inequality between Nations: a Critique of Western Theories on Development and Underdevelopment*, London: Allen and Unwin.
Ranki, G. (1983), *Economic and Foreign Policy: the Struggle of the Great Powers for the Hegemony of the Danube Valley 1919–1939*, New York: Columbia University Press.
Ranki, G. (1985), 'Problems of southern European economic development (1918–38)', in G. Arrighi (ed.), *Semiperipheral Development: the Politics of Southern Europe in the Twentieth Century*, Beverly Hills, CA: Sage Publications.
Rothermund, D. (1996), *The Global Impact of the Great Depression, 1929–1939*, London: Routledge.
Royal Institute of International Affairs (1938), *The Baltic States*, Oxford: Oxford University Press.
Schönfeld, R. (1975), 'Die Balkanländer in der Weltwirtschaftskrise', *Vierteljahrschrift für Sozial-und Wirtschaftsgeschichte*, 62.
Senghaas, D. (1985), *The European Experience: a Historical Critique of Development Theory*, Leamington Spa: Berg Publishers.
Simutis, A. (1942), *The Economic Reconstruction of Lithuania after 1918*, New York: Columbia University Press.
Spulber, N. (1966), *The State and Economic Development in Eastern Europe*, New York: Random House.
Sylla, R. and Toniolo, G. (eds) (1991), *Patterns of European Industrialization: the Nineteenth Century*, London: Routledge.
Thornburg, M. W., Spry, G. and Soule, G. (1949), *Turkey: an Economic Appraisal*, New York: The Twentieth Century Fund.
Tiltman, H. H. (1934), *Peasant Europe*, London: Jarrolds.

Tomasevich, J. (1949), 'Foreign economic relations', in R. J. Kerner (ed.), *Yugoslavia*, Berkeley, CA: University of California Press.
Tomasevich, J. (1955), *Peasants, Politics and Economic Change in Yugoslavia*, Stanford: Stanford University Press.
Tortella, G. (1994), 'Patterns of economic retardation and recovery in south-western Europe in the nineteenth and twentieth centuries', *Economic History Review,* 47.
United Nations (1949), *International Capital Movements during the Interwar Period*, New York: United Nations.
Valério, N. (1992), 'Some remarks about growth and stagnation in the Mediterranean world in the XIXth and XXth centuries', *Journal of European Economic History,* 21.
von Rauch, G. (1974), *The Baltic States: the Years of Independence 1917–1940*, London: G. Hurst and Company.
Wallerstein, I. (1985), 'The relevance of the concept of semiperiphery to southern Europe' in G. Arrighi (ed.), *Semiperipheral Development: the Politics of Southern Europe in the Twentieth Century*, Beverly Hills, CA: Sage Publications.
Warriner, D. (1964), *Economics of Peasant Farming*, London: Frank Cass.
Zilinkskas, V. L. (1946), 'Independent Lithuania's economic progress', *Baltic Review,* 1.

Index

For Product Safety Concerns and Information please contact our EU representative GPSR@taylorandfrancis.com
Taylor & Francis Verlag GmbH, Kaufingerstraße 24, 80331 München, Germany

www.ingramcontent.com/pod-product-compliance
Ingram Content Group UK Ltd.
Pitfield, Milton Keynes, MK11 3LW, UK
UKHW021833260926
475702UK00049B/534
9781138359666